Microsoft® Office 2000

Small Business

At a Glance

Microsoft® Press

PUBLISHED by **Microsoft Press**
A Division of Microsoft Corporation
One Microsoft Way
Redmond, Washington 98052-6399

Library of Congress Cataloging-in-Publication Data
Microsoft Office 2000 Small Business At a Glance. Perspection, Inc.
     p.   cm.
   Includes index.
   ISBN 0-7356-0546-7
   1. Microsoft Office.   2. Microsoft Word.   3. Microsoft Excel for Windows.   4. Microsoft Outlook.   5. Microsoft Publisher.
6. Small business—Computer programs   7. Word processing.   8. Electronic spreadsheets.   9. Time management—Computer
programs.   10. Personal information management—Computer programs.   11. Desktop publishing   12. Web sites—Design
I. Perspection, Inc.
   HF5548.4.M525M5248   1999
   005.369—dc21
                                98-43584
                                  CIP

Printed and bound in the United States of America.

1 2 3 4 5 6 7 8 9   QEQE   4 3 2 1 0 9

Distributed in Canada by ITP Nelson, a division of Thomson Canada limited.

A CIP catalog record for this book is available from the British Library.

Microsoft Press books are available through booksellers and distributors worldwide. For further information about international editions, contact your local Microsoft Corporation office. Or contact Microsoft Press International directly at fax (425) 936-7329. Visit our Web site at mspress.microsoft.com.

For Perspection, Inc.
Writers: Robin Romer; Marie Swanson
Managing Editor: Steven M. Johnson
Series Editor: Jane E. Pedicini
Production Editor: David W. Beskeen
Developmental Editor: Lisa Ruffolo
Technical Editors: Nicholas Chu; Craig Fernandez

For Microsoft Press
Acquisitions Editors: Kim Fryer; Susanne Forderer
Project Editor: Jenny Moss Benson

Contents

Start an Office program.
See page 6

Get Help with the
Office Assistant.
See page 22

Learn to work with objects.
See page 38

Repairing Office programs.
See page 52

*"How do I work
with multiple
documents?"*

See page 58

Create bulleted lists.
See page 82

Arrange text in columns.
See page 96

Adjust columns and rows.
See page 122

$0.45
$0.45
$0.35
$2.35
$2.20
$2.40
$0.50

=SUM(B4:B10

Create a formula.
See page 124

Create a chart.
See page 140

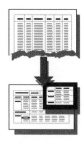

Analyze data using a
PivotTable.
See page 150

Create a contact.
See page 160

Read and post news.
See page 196

Create a new publication.
See page 200

Create a newsletter.
See page 204

A question and an-
swer session is a
good way to quickly
capture the attention
of readers. You can
either compile ques-
tions that you've re-
ceived since the last
edition or you can

Connect text frames.
See page 222

Connect to the Internet.
See page 238

Create Web pages.
See page 258

Hold an online meeting.
See page 270

Create a direct mailing.
See page 296

Produce financial reports.
See page 302

Acknowledgments

The task of creating any book requires the talents of many hardworking people pulling together to meet almost impossible demands. For their effort and commitment, we'd like to thank the outstanding team responsible for making this book possible: the writers, Robin Romer and Marie Swanson; the series editor, Jane Pedicini; the developmental editor, Lisa Ruffolo of the Software Resource; the technical editors, Nicholas Chu and Craig Fernandez; the production team, Gary Bellig and Tracy Teyler; and the indexer, Michael Brackney. We'd also like to thank Elizabeth Reding for her contributions to this book.

At Microsoft Press, we'd like to thank Kim Fryer and Susanne Forderer for the opportunity to undertake this project, and Jenny Benson for project editing and overall help when needed most.

Perspection

Perspection

Perspection, Inc., is a software training company committed to providing information to help people communicate, make decisions, and solve problems. Perspection writes and produces software training books and develops interactive multimedia applications for Windows-based and Macintosh personal computers.

Microsoft Office 2000 Small Business At a Glance incorporates Perspection's training expertise to ensure that you'll receive the maximum return on your time. With this straightforward, easy-to-read reference tool, you'll get the information you need when you need it. You'll focus on the skills that increase productivity while working at your own pace and convenience.

We invite you to visit the Perspection World Wide Web site. You can visit us at:

http://www.perspection.com

You'll find descriptions of all of our books, additional content for our books, information about Perspection, and much more.

About This Book

Microsoft Office 2000 Small Business At a Glance is for anyone who wants to get the most from their software with the least amount of time and effort. We think you'll find this book to be a straightforward, easy-to-read, and easy-to-use reference tool. With the premise that your computer should work for you, not you for it, this book's purpose is to help you get your work done quickly and efficiently so that you take advantage of Microsoft Office while using your computer and its software to the max.

No Computerese!

Let's face it—when there's a task you don't know how to do but you need to get it done in a hurry, or when you're stuck in the middle of a task and can't figure out what to do next, there's nothing more frustrating than having to read page after page of technical background material. You want the information you need—nothing more, nothing less—and you want it now! And the information should be easy to find and understand.

That's what this book is all about. It's written in plain English—no technical jargon and no computerese. There's no single task in the book that takes more than two pages. Just look up the task in the index or the table of contents, turn to the page, and there it is. Each task introduction gives you information that is essential to performing the task, suggesting situations in which you can use the task or providing examples of the benefit you gain from completing the procedure. The task itself is laid out step by step and accompanied by a graphic that adds visual clarity. Just read the introduction, follow the steps, look at the illustrations, and get your work done with a minimum of hassle.

You may want to turn to another task if the one you're working on has a "See Also" in the left column. Because there's a lot of overlap among tasks, we didn't want to keep repeating ourselves; you might find more elementary or more advanced tasks laid out on the pages referenced. We wanted to bring you through the tasks in such a way that they would make sense to you. We've also added some useful tips here and there and offered a "Try This" once in a while to give you a context in which to use the task. But, by and large, we've tried to remain true to the heart and soul of the book, which is that information you need should be available to you *at a glance*.

What's New

If you're looking for what's new in Office 2000, just look for our new icon: **New**2000. We've inserted it throughout this book. You will find the new icon in the table of contents so you can quickly and easily identify new or improved features in Office. You will also find the new icon on the first page of each section. There it will serve as a handy reminder of the latest improvements in Office as you move from one task to another.

Useful Tasks...

Whether you use Office 2000 for work, play, or some of each, we've tried to pack this book with procedures for everything we could think of that you might want to do, from the simplest tasks to some of the more esoteric ones.

...And the Easiest Way to Do Them

Another thing we've tried to do in *Microsoft Office 2000 Small Business At a Glance* is to find and document the easiest way to accomplish a task. Office often provides many ways to accomplish a single result, which can be daunting or delightful, depending on the way you like to work. If you tend to stick with one favorite and familiar approach, we think the methods described in this book are the way to go. If you prefer to try out alternative techniques, go ahead! The intuitiveness of Office invites exploration, and you're likely to discover ways of doing things that you think are easier or that you like better. If you do, that's great! It's exactly what the creators of Office 2000 had in mind when they provided so many alternatives.

A Quick Overview

You don't have to read this book in any particular order. The book is designed so that you can jump in, get the information you need, and then close the book, keeping it near your computer until the next time you need it. But that doesn't mean we scattered the information about with wild abandon. If you were to read the book from front to back, you'd find a logical progression from the simple tasks to the more complex ones. Here's a quick overview.

First, we assume that Office 2000 is already installed on your computer. If it's not, the Setup Wizard makes installation so simple that you won't need our help anyway. So, unlike most computer books, this one doesn't start out with installation instructions and a list of system requirements. You've already got that under control.

Section 2 of the book covers the basics: starting Microsoft Office 2000 programs: working with menus, toolbars, and dialog boxes; displaying the Office Shortcut Bar; getting help; saving documents; and exiting programs.

Section 3 describes tools and features in every Office 2000 program: editing, moving, and copying text; making corrections; drawing and enhancing objects; adding and modifying media clips and WordArt; looking up information; automating your work; and detecting and repairing errors in Office 2000 programs.

Sections 4 through 6 describe tasks for creating documents with Microsoft Word: changing document views; formatting text for emphasis; creating and modifying tables; checking your spelling and grammar; addressing envelopes and labels; and printing documents.

Sections 7 and 8 describe tasks for creating spreadsheets with Microsoft Excel: entering labels and values; creating formulas; formatting worksheets; creating and enhancing charts; creating lists; and analyzing data with PivotTables.

Sections 9 and 10 describe tasks for managing information with Microsoft Outlook: creating and sending e-mail messages; scheduling and changing events and appointments; planning and managing meetings; managing tasks and information; and subscribing to newsgroups and reading newsgroup messages.

Sections 11 and 12 describe tasks for creating publications with Microsoft Publisher: creating and printing newsletters, brochures, Web sites, resumes, and business cards; resizing and moving frames; adding text, pictures,

and objects; and wrapping text around an object.

Section 13 describes tasks for browsing and searching with Internet Explorer 5: connecting to the Internet; browsing the Web and your hard disk; searching for information on the Internet; creating a favorites list; and subscribing to a channel or Web site.

Section 14 describes tasks for creating Web pages with Office 2000 programs: inserting and navigating using hyperlinks; choosing a graphics format; using the Web Page Wizard to create Web pages; saving documents as Web pages; publishing and previewing Web pages; and holding a NetMeeting.

Section 15 describes tasks for integrating information between Office 2000 programs: embedding and linking files between programs; creating Word documents with Excel data; and copying Web tables into Excel workbooks.

Section 16 describes tasks for using the small business programs that come with Office 2000: managing direct mail and customer lists; analyzing financial data; and creating practical and professional-looking business plans.

A Final Word (or Two)

We had three goals in writing this book. We want our book to help you:

◆ Do all the things you want to do with Office 2000.

◆ Discover how to do things you didn't know you wanted to do with Office 2000.

◆ Enjoy doing your work with Office 2000.

Our "thank you" for buying this book is the achievement of those goals. We hope you'll have as much fun using *Microsoft Office 2000 Small Business At a Glance* as we've had writing it. The best way to learn is by doing, and that's what we hope you'll get from this book. Jump right in!

2

Getting Started with Office 2000

As the world hurls toward the new millennium, our expectations are soaring for ourselves and others. We need to accomplish more, faster and better. Microsoft Office 2000 provides the tools to do this. Each of its programs—Word, Excel, Outlook, Publisher, and Internet Explorer—has a special purpose, yet they all work together so you can combine word processing, spreadsheets, scheduling, publications, and Internet communication. The results are professional, dynamic, and effective documents for every occasion.

Working Efficiently with Office

So you can focus on creating the best document rather than recalling how a program works, every Office program uses the same structure of windows, menus, toolbars, and dialog boxes. The Office personalized menus and toolbars display only the commands and toolbar buttons you use most frequently to save space and help efficiency. In addition, you perform your most basic actions the same way in every program. For example, you open, save, and close documents with the same buttons or commands in each Office program. And when you have a question, the identical help feature is available throughout Office.

Starting an Office Program

The two quickest ways to start any Office program are from the Start menu on the taskbar and from the Office Shortcut Bar. Because it saves a few mouse clicks, the Office Shortcut Bar is more convenient. By providing different ways to start a program, Office lets you work the way you like and switch from program to program with a click of a button.

SEE ALSO

See "Displaying the Office Shortcut Bar" on page 24 for information on displaying, adding different toolbars to, and closing the Microsoft Office Shortcut Bar.

TIP

Get Office information on the Web. *Click the Help menu, and then click Office On The Web. Your Web browser opens, displaying the Microsoft Office Update Web site.*

Start an Office Program from the Start Menu

1. Click the Start button on the taskbar.

2. Point to Programs.

3. Click the Office 2000 program you want to open.

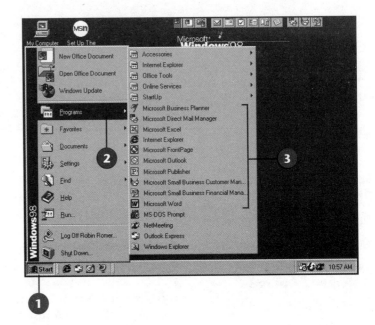

Start an Office Program from the Office Shortcut Bar

◆ Click the button on the Office Shortcut Bar for the Office program you want to start.

Word
Excel   Outlook   Publisher

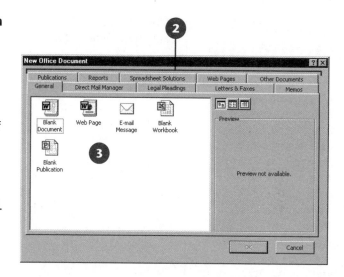

Start any Office program and open a document from Windows Explorer. *Double-clicking any Office document icon in Windows Explorer opens that file and its associated program.*

Start any Office program and a new document from the desktop. *Right-click the desktop, point to New on the shortcut menu, and then click the type of Office document you want to create. The program starts and a new document opens.*

See "Choosing Templates and Wizards" on page 18 for information on using templates and wizards to create Office documents.

Start Microsoft Small Business Tools. *Office 2000 includes a package of small business tools, which include the Small Business Customer Manager, Business Planner, Direct Mail Manager, and Small Business Financial Manager. You start the Small Business Tools as you would any other Office 2000 program.*

Start an Office Program and Open a New Office Document

1 Click the Start button on the taskbar, and then click New Office Document.

2 Click the tab for the type of document you want to create.

3 Double-click a document icon to start the program and open a new document.

NEW OFFICE DOCUMENT ICONS	
Icon	Description
	Creates a document with Microsoft Word
	Creates an e-mail message with Microsoft Outlook
	Creates a spreadsheet with Microsoft Excel
	Creates a publication with Microsoft Publisher

Opening an Existing File

Before you can begin working, you need to open a document. You can open the file and its program at one time, or you can open the file from within its Office program. If you can't recall a file's name or location, use the Find feature in the Open dialog box to locate the file based on the information (or *criteria*) you can recall, such as its creation date, content, author, styles, and so forth.

TIP

Open a recent file quickly.
You can open a file on which you recently worked in any Office program by clicking the appropriate filename at the bottom of the File menu.

TIP

Open a copy of a file quickly. *When opening a file from the Open dialog box, click the Open button drop-down arrow, and click Open As Copy. This creates a new copy of the file in the same folder with the filename Copy of [Filename].*

Open an Existing File from the Start Menu

1. Click the Start button on the taskbar, and then click Open Office Document.

2. Click an icon on the Places bar to open a frequently used folder.

3. If necessary, click the Look In drop-down arrow, and then click the drive where the file is located.

4. Double-click the folder in which the file is stored.

5. Double-click a filename to start the program and open that file.

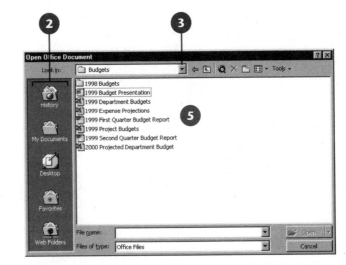

Open an Existing File from Within an Office Program

1. Click the Open button on the Standard toolbar.

2. Click an icon on the Places bar to open a frequently used folder.

3. If necessary, click the Look In drop-down arrow, and then click the drive where the file is located.

4. Double-click the folder in which the file is stored.

5. Double-click the file you want to open.

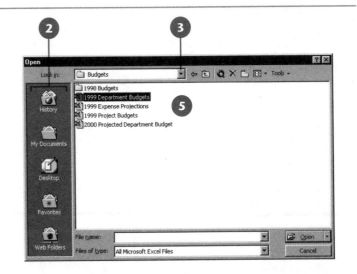

Use wildcards to search for filenames. *When you recall only part of the name of the file you want to open, type a question mark (?) for any one unknown character or an asterisk (*) for two or more unknown characters.*

What are criteria? *Each criterion contains a property, such as* **filename**, *condition, such as* **includes**, *and value, such as* **Letter***.*

Move or copy a file quickly. *You can cut and paste files directly in the Open or Save As dialog box. Right-click the file you want to move or copy, click Cut or Copy on the shortcut menu, open the folder where you want to paste the file, right-click again, and then click Paste.*

Delete or rename a file. *You can delete or rename any closed file from the Open or Save As dialog box. Click the file, click the Tools drop-down arrow, and then click Delete or Rename.*

Find a File Quickly Using the Open Dialog Box

1 Click the Open button on the Standard toolbar.

2 Click the Tools drop-down arrow, and then click Find.

3 Click the Look In drop-down arrow, and then click the drive you want to search.

4 Click to select the Search Subfolders check box.

5 Enter as much identifying information as you recall about the file you want to find, such as filename, creation date, author, keywords, and so on.

6 Click Find Now.

7 Double-click the file you want to open in the Open dialog box.

Identifies information about the file to be found

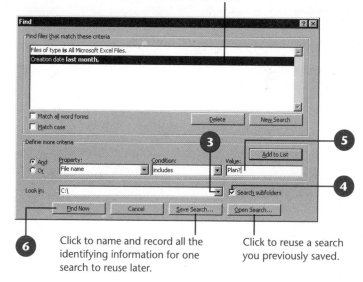

Click to name and record all the identifying information for one search to reuse later.

Click to reuse a search you previously saved.

Saving a File

Saving your files frequently ensures that you don't lose work during an unexpected power loss. The first time you save, specify a filename and folder in the Save As dialog box. The next time you save, Office saves the file with the same name in the same folder. If you want to change a file's name or location, you can use the Save As dialog box again to create a copy of the original file.

TIP

What's the difference between the Save and Save As commands? *The Save command saves a copy of your current document to a previously specified name and location. The Save As command creates a copy of your current document with a new name, location, or type.*

TIP

Don't worry about file-name extensions. *When you name a file, you do not have to type the filename extension. The Office program adds the correct filename extension to the name you give your file.*

Save a File for the First Time

1. Click the Save button on the Standard toolbar.

2. Click an icon on the Places bar to open a frequently used folder.

3. If necessary, click the Save In drop-down arrow, and then click the drive where you want to save the file.

4. Double-click the folder in which you want to save the file.

5. Type a name for the file, or use the suggested name.

6. Click Save.

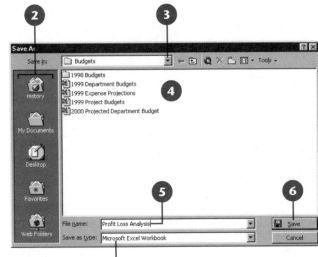

Shows in which file format the file will be saved.

Save a File with Another Name

1. Click the File menu, and then click Save As.

2. Click an icon on the Places bar or click the Save In drop-down arrow, and then click the drive or folder where you want to save the file.

3. Type a new filename.

4. Click Save.

Click to change the Save In location.

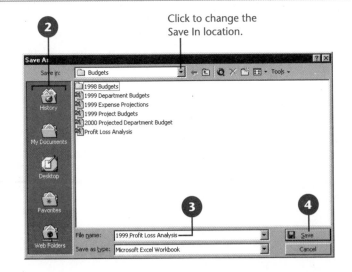

Save a File in a New Folder

1. Click the File menu, and then click Save As.

2. Locate and select the drive and folder where you want to create the new folder.

3. Click the Create New Folder button.

4. Type the new folder name, and then click OK.

5. Click Save.

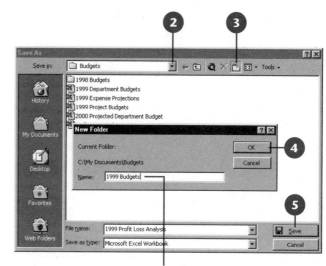

Type a folder name here.

Save a File as a Different Type

1. Click the File menu, and then click Save As.

2. Click the Save As Type drop-down arrow.

3. Click the file type you want.

   You can select file types for previous versions of Office programs.

4. Click Save.

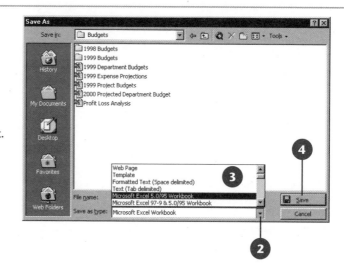

Choosing Menu and Dialog Box Options

A *menu* is a list of related commands. For example, the Edit menu contains commands for editing a document, such as Delete and Cut. A *shortcut menu* opens right where you're working and contains commands related to a specific object. Clicking a menu command followed by an ellipsis (...) opens a *dialog box*, where you choose various options and provide information for completing the command. As you switch between programs, you'll find that all Office menus and dialog boxes look similar and work in the same way.

TIP

Personalized menus. *When you first open a menu, the commands you used most recently appear first. Point to the More Commands drop-down arrow to display the full menu.*

Choose Menu Commands

1 Click a menu name on the menu bar, or right-click an object (such as a toolbar, spreadsheet cell, picture, or selected text).

2 If necessary, click the double arrow to expand the menu and display more commands.

3 Click a menu command you want, or point to the arrow to the right of the menu command to display a submenu of related commands, and then click the command you want.

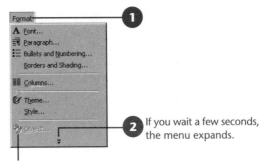

If you wait a few seconds, the menu expands.

Menu options displayed in light gray type are currently unavailable.

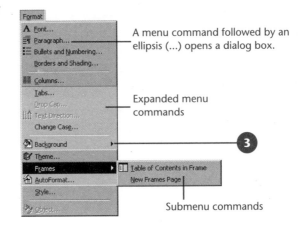

A menu command followed by an ellipsis (...) opens a dialog box.

Expanded menu commands

Submenu commands

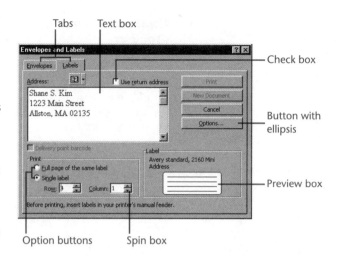

2

TIP

Toolbar buttons and keyboard shortcuts are faster than menu commands. *You can learn the toolbar button equivalents of menu commands by looking at the toolbar button icon to the left of a menu command. Keyboard shortcuts (such as Ctrl+V) appear to the right of their menu commands. To use a keyboard shortcut, press and hold the first key (such as Ctrl), press the second key (such as V), and then release both keys.*

TIP

The OK and Cancel buttons. *The most common dialog box buttons are the OK button, which confirms your selections and closes the dialog box, and the Cancel button, which closes the dialog box without accepting your selections.*

TRY THIS

Use the Tab key to navigate a dialog box. *Rather than clicking to move around a dialog box, you can press Tab to move from one box or button to the next.*

Choose Dialog Box Options

All Office dialog boxes contain the same types of options, including:

◆ Tabs. Click a tab to display its options. Each tab groups a related set of options.

◆ Option buttons. Click an option button to select it. You can usually select only one.

◆ Spin box. Click the up or down arrow to increase or decrease the number, or type a number in the box.

◆ Check box. Click the box to turn on or off the option. A checked box means the option is selected; a cleared box means it's not.

◆ List box. Click the drop-down arrow to display a list of options, and then click the option you want.

◆ Text box. Click in the box and type the requested information.

◆ Button. Click a button to perform a specific action or command. A button name followed by an ellipsis (...) opens another dialog box.

◆ Preview box. Many dialog boxes show an image that reflects the options you select.

Tabs   Text box

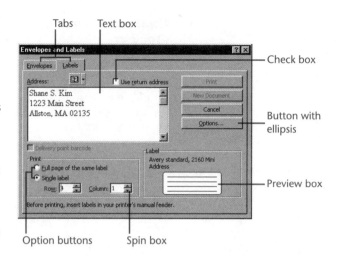

Check box

Button with ellipsis

Preview box

Option buttons   Spin box

Confirms your selections and closes the dialog box

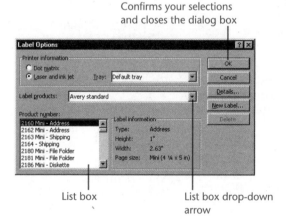

List box   List box drop-down arrow

Working with Toolbars

Each Office *toolbar* contains a collection of buttons you click to select frequently used menu commands. Most programs open with a Standard toolbar (with commands such as Save and Print) and a Formatting toolbar (with commands for selecting fonts and sizes) side by side. You can also display toolbars designed for specific tasks, such as drawing pictures, importing data, or creating charts. The toolbars are personalized as you work, showing only the buttons you use most often. Additional toolbar buttons are available by clicking the More Buttons drop-down arrow at the end of the toolbar.

SEE ALSO

See "Displaying the Office Shortcut Bar" on page 24 for information on working with the Microsoft Office Shortcut Bar.

Display and Hide a Toolbar

1 Right-click any visible toolbar.

2 Click the name of the toolbar you want to display or hide.

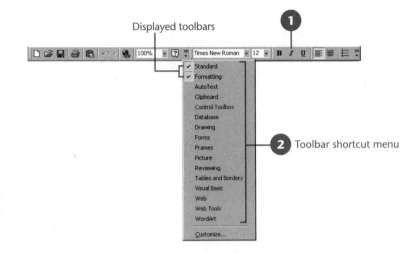

Displayed toolbars

Toolbar shortcut menu

Move and Reshape a Toolbar

◆ To move a toolbar that is *docked* (attached to one edge of the window) or *floating* (unattached) over the window, click the gray bar on the left edge of the toolbar and drag it to a new location.

◆ To return a floating toolbar to its previous docked location, double-click its title bar.

◆ To change the shape of a floating toolbar, drag any border until the toolbar is the shape you want.

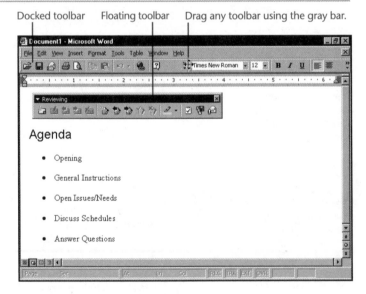

Docked toolbar   Floating toolbar   Drag any toolbar using the gray bar.

Personalized toolbars.
When you first open a toolbar, the buttons you used most recently are visible. Click the More Buttons drop-down arrow to display any other toolbar buttons. To display the full toolbar, double-click the gray bar on the left edge of the toolbar.

Display a toolbar button's name. *To find out the name of a toolbar button, position the pointer over the button on the toolbar. The name of the button, or the ScreenTip, appears below the button.*

Hide ScreenTips. *To hide ScreenTips, click the Tools menu, click Customize, click the Options tab, click to clear the Show ScreenTips On Toolbars check box, and then click OK.*

Customize your Excel Chart toolbar. *Display the Chart toolbar in Excel. Customize it by adding the Spelling toolbar button and several other toolbar buttons.*

Display More Buttons on a Toolbar

◆ To display more buttons on a toolbar, click the More Buttons drop-down arrow at the right end of that toolbar.

Click to display any hidden buttons.

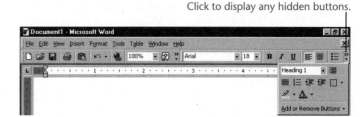

Customize a Toolbar

1. Click the More Buttons drop-down arrow on the toolbar you want to change.

2. Click Add Or Remove Buttons.

3. To add or remove a toolbar button, click the button name in the list. A check mark means the button appears on the toolbar; no check mark means it doesn't.

4. When you're done, click in the document window to update the toolbar.

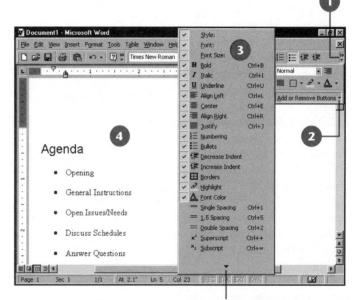

Click to see more button options.

Arranging Windows

Every Office program and document open inside a *window*, which contains all the program commands and is where you create and edit your documents. Most often, you'll probably fill the entire screen with one window. But when you want to move or copy information between programs or documents, it's easier to display several windows at once. You can arrange two or more windows from one program or from different programs on the screen at once. However, you must make the window active to work in it. You can also click the document buttons on the taskbar to switch between open Office documents.

Resize and Move a Window

All windows contain the same sizing buttons:

◆ Maximize button

Click to make a window fill the entire screen.

◆ Restore button

Click to reduce a maximized window to about half its full size.

◆ Minimize button

Click to shrink a window to a taskbar button. To restore the window to its previous size, click the appropriate taskbar button.

You can move a window to any location on the screen by clicking its title bar and dragging the window. Release the mouse button when the window is where you want it.

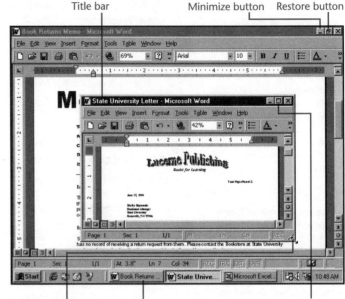

Title bar

Minimize button   Restore button

Use this pointer to drag any window border to increase or decrease the size of the window.

Click to place that document on top of any other open documents.

Maximize button

SEE ALSO

See "Working with Multiple Documents" on page 58 for information on arranging multiple windows within a program.

TIP

Use shortcut keys to work with windows. *Open and close windows, and switch between windows quickly with keyboard shortcuts. To close the active window, press Ctrl+W. To switch to the next window, press Ctrl+F6, and to switch to the previous window, press Ctrl+Shift+F6.*

TIP

Make a window active. *Only one window can be active at a time. You can tell whether a window is active by its title bar. An active window's title bar is colored and dark rather than light gray. To make an inactive window active, click it.*

TRY THIS

Tile two documents. *Open a Word document and an Excel worksheet. Tile the windows vertically. Click in the Word window to make it active, and then press Ctrl+F6 to make the Excel worksheet active.*

Arrange Multiple Windows

1. Right-click the taskbar anywhere except on a program button.

2. Click Tile Horizontally, Tile Vertically, or Cascade Windows.

   The example shows two tiled windows.

3. Right-click the taskbar, and then click Undo Tile or Undo Cascade to return to a single window.

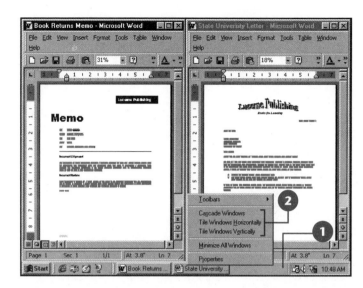

Switch Between Document Windows

◆ Each open Office document displays its own button on the Windows taskbar. You can click the buttons on the taskbar to switch between the open Office documents.

Active document window   Click to open the document window.

Choosing Templates and Wizards

Office makes it easy to create many common documents based on a template or using a wizard. A *template* opens a document (such as a letter) with predefined formatting and placeholder text that specifies what information you should enter (such as your address). A *wizard* walks you through the steps to create a finished document tailored to your preferences. First the wizard asks you for information, and then, when you click Finish, the wizard creates a completely formatted document based on the options and content you entered. Use a template to add information to a designed document, and use a wizard to add a design to information you supply.

Choose a Template

1 Click the New Office Document button on the Start menu, or click the File menu and then click New.

2 Click the tab for the type of document you want to create.

3 Click the template you want to use.

4 Check the Preview box to verify the template will create the right style of document.

5 Click OK.

6 Type text for placeholders such as *[Click here and type your letter text]*.

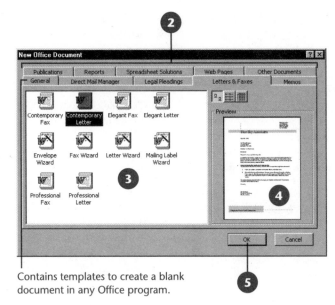

Contains templates to create a blank document in any Office program.

Select any text you want to replace or delete.

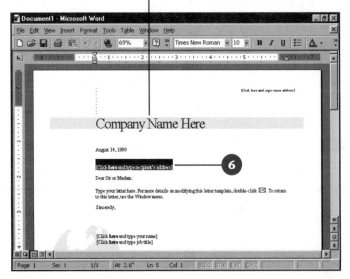

How does Word create a document using a wizard?
If you create a Word document using a wizard, Word bases the document on the Normal document template. However, the styles used in the document reflect the formatting that you select when responding to the wizard.

Use a wizard to create and send a fax. *Click the Start button, click Open New Office Document, and then double-click the Fax Wizard icon on the Letters & Memos tab. Enter all the requested information, and then click Finish to send the fax. (You need a fax modem in order to send your fax.)*

Create your own letterhead. *Try using the Memo Wizard to create a professional-style interoffice memo or personal letterhead.*

See "Applying a Style" on page 79 for information about styles used in templates.

Choose and Navigate a Wizard

1 Click the New Office Document button on the Start menu, or click the File menu and then click New.

2 Click the tab for the type of document you want to create.

3 Double-click the icon for the wizard you want to use.

4 Read and select options (if necessary) in the first wizard dialog box.

5 Click Next to move to the next wizard dialog box.

Each wizard dialog box asks for different information.

6 Continue to select options, and then click Next.

7 When you reach the last wizard dialog box, click Finish.

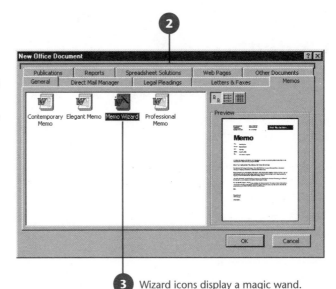

3 Wizard icons display a magic wand.

Fill in the requested information.

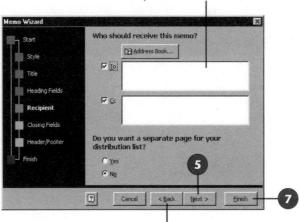

Click to return to a previous dialog box.

Getting Help in an Office Program

At some point, everyone has a question or two about the program they are using. The Office online Help system provides the answers you need. *ScreenTips* show toolbar names and short descriptions about anything you see on the screen or in a dialog box. You can also search an extensive catalog of Help topics by an index or a table of contents to locate specific information.

TIP

Use the mouse pointer to view toolbar ScreenTips.
You can hold the mouse pointer over any toolbar button to see its name.

SEE ALSO

See "Getting Help from the Office Assistant" on page 22 for information about turning off the Assistant and learning how to accomplish a task.

Get a ScreenTip

1. Click the Help menu, and then click What's This, or click the Help button on a dialog box's title bar to display the Help pointer.

2. Click any item or command to display a definition box.

3. Click anywhere to close the definition box.

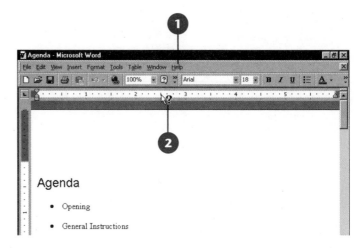

A definition box contains a description of the selected item.

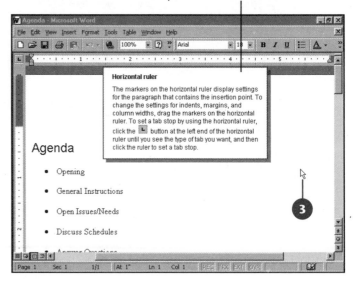

The Help button opens the Assistant or Help window. *Click the Help button. You see the Assistant if it is turned on. If the Assistant is turned off, the Help pane appears.*

Get the latest information from the Web. *If you have Internet access, you can get additional help, access technical resources, download free product enhancements, and even provide your feedback for every Office program. Click the Help menu, click Office On The Web, and then click the topic you want to read.*

Read the Help window as you work. *Get help on a topic, and then click the Hide button to reduce the size of the Help window. Work on your document as you read, and follow the directions in the Help window.*

Get Help Without the Office Assistant

1. Turn off the Office Assistant.

2. Click the Help button on the Standard toolbar.

3. Click the Show button.

4. Click the Index tab to search for a particular topic.

   ◆ Use the Contents tab to find a topic in the Help table of contents.

   ◆ Use the Answer Wizard tab to get help to specific questions. Enter your question in everyday language.

5. Type a keyword about which you want more information. As you type each letter, the keywords list scrolls to match the letters you type.

6. Double-click a keyword that reflects the information you want.

7. Double-click a topic.

   The topic you want appears in the right pane. Read the topic, and click any hyperlink to get information on related topics or definitions.

8. When you are done, click Close.

Click to hide the tabs and to view more of your document.

Click a hyperlink to get related Help information.

Getting Help from the Office Assistant

Often the easiest way to learn how to accomplish a task is to ask someone who knows. Now, with Office, that knowledgeable friend is always available in the form of the Office Assistant. Tell the Office Assistant what you want to do in the same everyday language you use to ask a colleague or friend, and the Office Assistant walks you through the process step by step. If the personality of the default Office Assistant—Clippit—doesn't appeal to you, choose from a variety of other Office Assistants.

TIP

Hide the Office Assistant.
When the Office Assistant is turned on, you can hide the Office Assistant. To hide the Office Assistant, right-click the Assistant, and then click Hide.

Ask the Office Assistant for Help

1. Click the Help button on the Standard toolbar, or click the Office Assistant.

2. Type your question about a task you want help with.

3. Click Search.

4. Click the topic you want help with.

5. Read and follow the directions. After you're done, click the Close button on the Help window.

6. Click the Help button on the Standard toolbar to hide the Office Assistant.

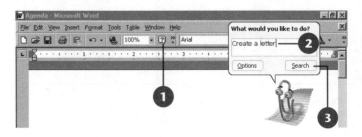

You can work on document while the Help window is open.

Click to display Contents, Answer Wizard, and Index tabs.

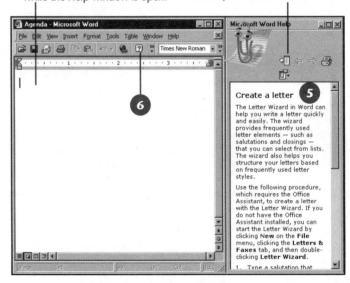

Use the Office Assistant to get help at any time. *When you begin to create a common type of document (such as a letter), the Office Assistant appears and offers you help. You can have the Office Assistant walk you through the process or complete the task alone.*

Get useful tips from the Office Assistant. *When a light bulb appears above the Office Assistant, click the Office Assistant to see a tip for a simpler or more efficient way to accomplish a task.*

Turn on or show the Office Assistant. *You can turn on the Assistant after turning it off or show the Assistant after hiding it. Click the Help menu, and then click Show The Office Assistant.*

Choose an Office Assistant

1 Right-click the Assistant and click Options, or click the Options button in the Assistant window.

2 Click the Gallery tab.

3 Click Next and Back to preview different Assistants.

4 Leave the Assistant you want to use visible.

5 Click OK.

If you are prompted, insert the Office 2000 CD-ROM in your drive, and then click OK.

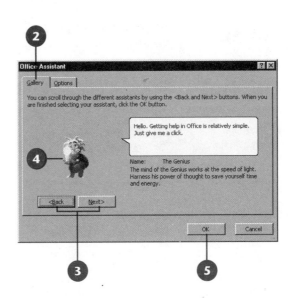

Turn Off the Office Assistant

1 Right-click the Office Assistant and click Options, or click the Options button in the Assistant window.

2 Click the Options tab.

3 Click to clear the Use Office Assistant check box.

4 Click OK.

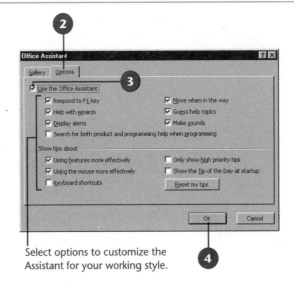

Select options to customize the Assistant for your working style.

Displaying the Office Shortcut Bar

The Office Shortcut Bar provides access to all the Office programs on your computer with one or two clicks of a button. You can display one or more toolbars and customize buttons on the Office Shortcut Bar. The Office Shortcut Bar itself can be *floating*, not attached to any part of your screen, or *docked*, attached to the left, right, or top edge of your screen.

TIP

Display the Office Shortcut Bar. *Click the Start button, point to Programs, point to Microsoft Office Tools, click Microsoft Office Shortcut Bar, install the component if necessary, and then click Yes or No to start the Office Shortcut Bar automatically whenever Windows is started.*

SEE ALSO

See "Working with Toolbars" on page 14 for more information about resizing toolbars.

Display Different Toolbars on the Office Shortcut Bar

1. Right-click anywhere on the Office Shortcut Bar except the title bar.

2. Click the name of the toolbar you want to display.

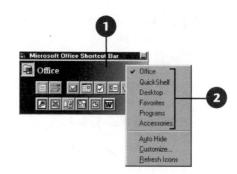

Customize the Office Shortcut Bar

1. Right-click anywhere on the Office Shortcut Bar except the title bar, and then click Customize.

2. Click the Buttons tab.

3. Click to select or clear the buttons you want to show or hide on the toolbar.

4. Click OK.

Click to move the selected button up or down on the toolbar.

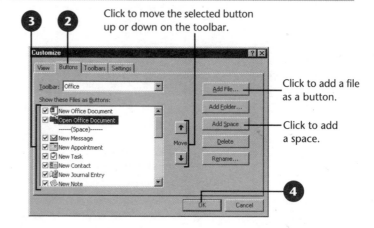

Click to add a file as a button.

Click to add a space.

Close the Office Shortcut Bar

1. Click the Office icon on the title bar.

2. Click Exit.

Closing a File

To conserve your computer's resources, close any files you are not working on. You can close open documents one at a time, or you can use one command to close all open files without closing the program. Either way, if you try to close a document without saving your final changes, a dialog box appears, prompting you to do so.

TIP

Microsoft Word document Close button. *When two or more documents are open in Word, the window contains one Close button. The Close button closes the document without exiting the program. You might need to click a Word document button on the taskbar to make it active before you click the Close button.*

SEE ALSO

See "Saving a File" on page 10 for information on saving changes to your documents.

Close One File

1. Click the Close button.
2. If necessary, click Yes to save your changes.

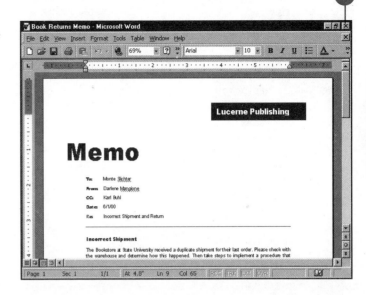

Close All Open Files

1. Press and hold Shift.
2. Click the File menu, and then click Close All.
3. If necessary, click Yes to save your changes.

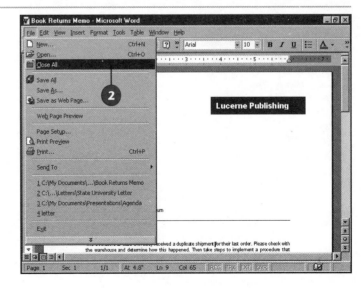

Quitting an Office Program

When you decide to stop working for the day, the last thing you must do is quit any running programs. All open documents close when you quit. If you haven't saved your final changes, a dialog box appears, prompting you to do so.

Close button

TRY THIS

Quit a program and close any open files. *Click the Close button on the title bar without closing any files first. All saved files close and the program ends. Click Yes to save the changes.*

Quit an Office Program

1 Click the Close button, or click the File menu and then click Exit.

2 If necessary, click Yes to save any changes you made to your open documents before the program quits.

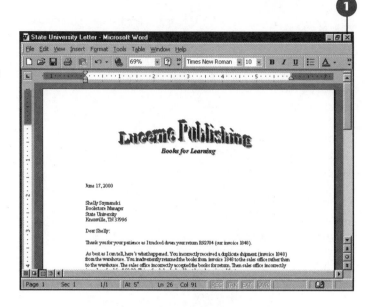

Click to close the document and program without saving your final changes.

Click to return to the program and document without saving your latest changes.

3

Using Shared Office 2000 Tools

The Microsoft Office 2000 programs are designed to work together so you can focus on *what* you need to do, rather than *how* to do it. In fact, the Office programs share tools and features for your most common tasks so you can work uninterrupted and move seamlessly from one program to another.

Many Common Features

All the Office programs work with text and objects in the same way. This means that once you know how to move, find, correct, and comment on text in one program, you know how to do these tasks in every program. The same is also true of drawing objects, creating WordArt, inserting clip art, adding charts, and compiling organization charts. If you know how to perform a task in Word, you probably already know how to perform the task in Excel and Publisher. To ensure that your work is uninterrupted, each program can detect and fix problems in the program itself.

In addition, you can create documents with any language in all the Office programs. And once you set up the programs to work with another language, special features appear in each program that you can use to format and manipulate text in that language.

Editing Text

Before you can edit text, you need to highlight, or *select*, the text you want to modify. Then you can delete, replace, move (*cut*), or *copy* text within one document or between documents even if they're from different programs. In either case, the steps are the same. Unlike the Windows Clipboard, which only stores a single piece of information at a time, the *Office Clipboard*, a temporary storage area, collects and stores up to 12 selections, any or all of which you can paste to a new location. You can also move or copy selected text without storing it on the Clipboard by using *drag-and-drop editing*.

TIP

Cut or copy one selection quickly. *Press Ctrl+X to cut or Ctrl+C to copy your highlighted selection. Then press Ctrl+V to paste it in the new location.*

Select and Edit Text

1. Move the pointer to the left or right of the text you want to select.

2. Drag the pointer to highlight the text you want to select.

3. Type to replace the selected text, or press Delete or Backspace to erase the selected text.

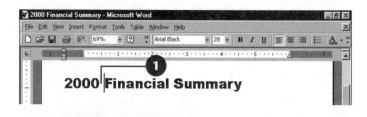

Move or Copy Text

1. Select the text you want to move or copy.

2. Click the Cut or Copy button on the Standard toolbar.

3. If you want to collect multiple selections, repeat steps 1 and 2.

4. Click where you want to insert the text.

5. Click any icon on the Clipboard toolbar to paste that selection, or click the Paste All button on the Clipboard toolbar to paste all the selections at once.

6. When you're done, click the Close button.

Pastes only your most recent cut or copied selection.

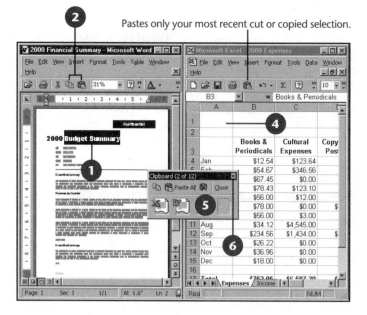

SEE ALSO

See "Selecting Text" on page 63 for more information on ways to select text easily and quickly.

SEE ALSO

See "Arranging Windows" on page 16 for information on how to open and display multiple windows.

TIP

Erase the Office Clipboard. *You can remove all the cut and copied selections stored on the Office Clipboard. Click the Clear Clipboard button on the Clipboard toolbar.*

TIP

Distinguish Office Clipboard selections easily. *Point to an icon on the Clipboard toolbar to read a ScreenTip of the contents.*

TIP

Paste information in a different format. *Select the object or text, click the Copy button on the Standard toolbar, click to indicate where you want to paste the object, click the Edit menu, click Paste Special, click the object type you want, and then click OK.*

Move or Copy Text Using Drag and Drop

1 If you want to drag text between programs or documents, display both windows.

2 Select the text you want to move or copy.

3 Point to the selected text, and then click and hold the mouse button.

If you want to copy the text to a new location, also press and hold Ctrl. A plus sign (+) appears in the pointer box, indicating that you are dragging a copy of the selected text.

4 Drag the selected text to the new location, and then release the mouse button (and Ctrl, if necessary).

5 Click anywhere in the document to deselect the text.

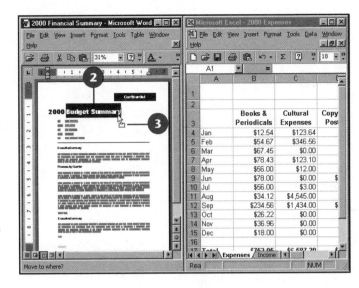

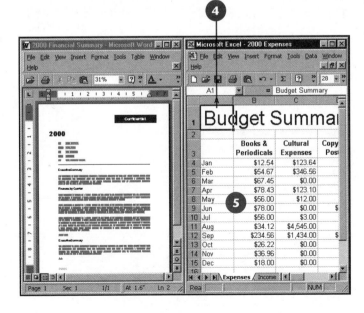

Finding and Replacing Text

The Find and Replace commands make it easy to locate or replace specific text or formulas in a document. For example, you might want to find each figure reference in a long report to verify that the proper graphic appears. Or you might want to replace all references to cell A3 in your Excel formulas with cell G3. The Find And Replace dialog boxes vary slightly from one Office program to the next, but the commands work essentially in the same way.

Find Text

1. Click at the beginning of the document.

2. Click the Edit menu, and then click Find.

3. Type the text you want to locate.

4. Select other options as appropriate.

5. Click Find Next until the text you want to locate is highlighted.

   You can click Find Next repeatedly to locate each instance of the text.

6. If a message box opens when you reach the end of the document, click OK.

7. When you're done, click Close or Cancel.

You might need to drag the dialog box out of the way to see the selected text.

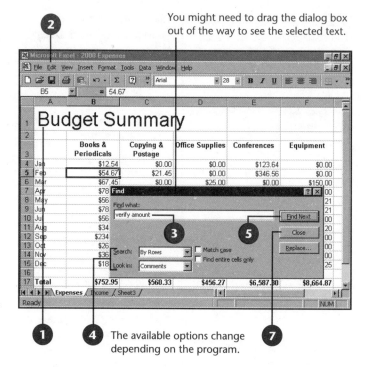

The available options change depending on the program.

Find and replace special characters and document elements. *In a Word document, you can search for and replace special characters (for example, an em dash) and document elements (for example, a tab character). Click the More button in the Find And Replace dialog box, click Special, and then click the item you want from the menu.*

Format text you find and replace. *In a Word document, you can search for and replace text with specific formatting features, such as a font and font size. Click the More button in the Find And Replace dialog box, click Format, click the formatting option you want, and then complete the corresponding dialog box.*

**Replace straight quotes (")
with typeset curly quotes
(").** *Find all quotation marks in your Word document and replace them with quotation marks. AutoCorrect changes any straight marks to curly.*

Replace Text

1. Click at the beginning of the document.

2. Click the Edit menu, and then click Replace.

3. Type the text you want to search for.

4. Type the text you want to substitute.

5. Select other options as appropriate. In Word, click the More button to display the additional options.

6. Click Find Next to begin the search and select the next instance of the search text.

7. Click Replace to substitute the replacement text, or click Replace All to substitute text through out the entire document.

   You can click Find Next to locate the next instance of the search text without making a replacement.

8. If a message box appears when you reach the end of the document, click OK.

9. When you're done, click Close or Cancel.

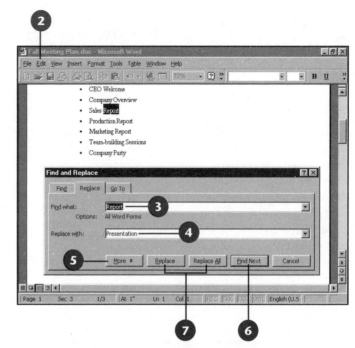

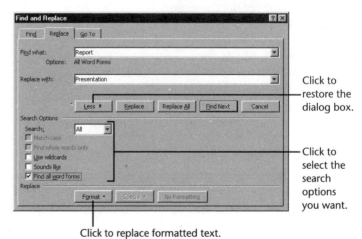

Click to restore the dialog box.

Click to select the search options you want.

Click to replace formatted text.

Using Multiple Languages

International Microsoft Office users can change the language that appears on their screens by changing the default language settings. Users around the world can enter, display, and edit text in all supported languages, including European languages, Japanese, Chinese, Korean, Hebrew, and Arabic, to name a few. You'll probably be able to use Office programs in your native language. If the text in your document is written in more than one language, you can automatically detect languages or designate the language of selected text so the spelling checker uses the right dictionary.

Add a Language to Office Programs

1 Click Start on the taskbar, point to Programs, point to Microsoft Office Tools, and then click Microsoft Office Language Settings.

2 Click to select the language check boxes for the languages you want to use.

3 Click OK.

4 Click Yes to quit and restart Office.

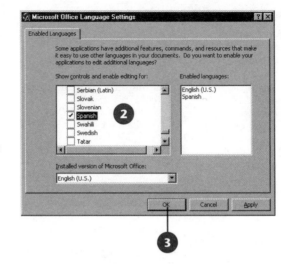

Detect Languages Automatically in Word

1. Start Word.

2. Click the Tools menu, point to Language, and then click Set Language.

3. Click to select the Detect Language Automatically check box.

4. If you want, click to select the Do Not Check Spelling Or Grammar check box to skip other language words while checking spelling and grammar.

5. Click OK.

Mark Text as a Language in Word

1. Start Word.

2. Select the text you want to mark.

3. In Word, Click the Tools menu, point to Language, and then click Set Language.

4. Click the language you want to assign to the selected text.

5. Click OK.

Spanish words won't be marked as misspellings.

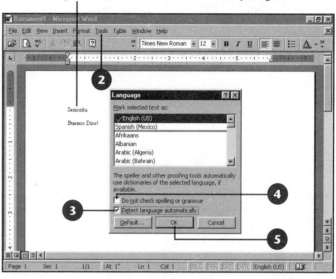

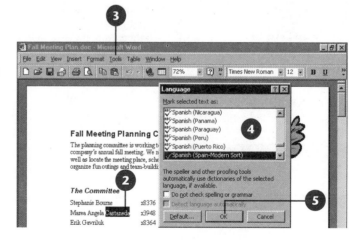

Correcting Text Automatically

Since the dawn of typing, people have consistently mistyped certain words or letter combinations. How many times do you misspell *and* or press and hold Shift too long? *AutoCorrect* fixes common misspellings and incorrect capitalization as you type. It also replaces typed characters, such as -- (two hyphens), with typographical symbols, such as — (an em dash). What's more, you can add your personal problem words to the AutoCorrect list. In most cases, AutoCorrect corrects errors after you press Enter or the Spacebar.

Replace Text as You Type

◆ To correct capitalization or spelling errors automatically, continue typing until AutoCorrect makes the required correction.

◆ To replace two hyphens with an em dash, turn ordinals into superscripts (for example, *1st* to *1st*), or stack a fraction (for example, $^{1}/_{2}$), continue typing until AutoCorrect makes the appropriate change.

◆ To create a bulleted or numbered list, type **1.** or ***** (for a bullet), press Tab or Spacebar, type any text, and then press Enter. AutoCorrect inserts the next number or bullet. To end the list, press Backspace to erase the unneeded number or bullet.

EXAMPLES OF AUTOCORRECT CHANGES		
Type of Correction	If You Type	AutoCorrect Inserts
Capitalization	cAP LOCK	Cap Lock
Capitalization	TWo INitial CAps	Two Initial Caps
Capitalization	ann Marie	Ann Marie
Capitalization	microsoft	Microsoft
Capitalization	thursday	Thursday
Common typos	accomodate	accommodate
Common typos	can;t	can't
Common typos	windoes	windows
Superscript ordinals	2nd	2nd
Stacked fractions	1/2	$^{1}/_{2}$
Smart quotes	" "	" "
Em dashes	Madison--a small city in southern Wisconsin--is a nice place to live.	Madison—a small city in southern Wisconsin—is a nice place to live.
Symbols	(c)	©
Symbols	(r)	®
Hyperlinks	www.microsoft.com	www.microsoft.com

Create exceptions to AutoCorrect. *You can specify abbreviations and terms that you don't want AutoCorrect to correct. Click the Exceptions button and add these items to the list of exceptions.*

Delete an AutoCorrect entry. *Click the Tools menu, click AutoCorrect, select the AutoCorrect entry you want to delete, and then click Delete.*

Prevent automatic corrections. *Click the Tools menu, click AutoCorrect, click to clear the Replace Text As You Type check box, and then click OK.*

AutoComplete finishes your words. *As you enter common text, such as your name, months, today's date, and common salutations and closings, Word provides the rest of the text in a ScreenTip. Press Enter to have Word complete your words.*

Add or Edit AutoCorrect Entries

1. Click the Tools menu, and then click AutoCorrect.

2. Click the AutoCorrect tab.

   To edit an AutoCorrect entry, select the entry you want to change.

3. Type the incorrect text you want AutoCorrect to correct.

4. Type the text or symbols you want AutoCorrect to use as a replacement.

5. Click Add or Replace.

6. When you're done, click OK.

In Word, click these tabs to display AutoCorrect formatting settings.

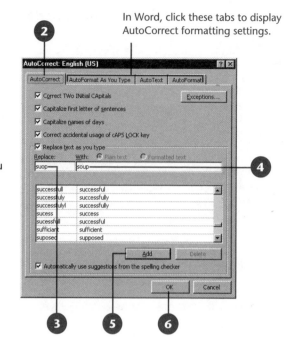

Making Corrections

Everyone makes mistakes and changes their mind at some point, especially when creating or revising a document. With Office you can instantly correct typing errors by pressing a key. You can also reverse more complicated actions, such as typing an entire word, formatting a paragraph, or creating a chart, with the Undo button. If you change your mind, you can just as easily click the Redo button to restore the action you reversed.

TIP

Use the keyboard to quickly undo your last action. *To undo, press Ctrl+Z. To redo your undo, press Ctrl+Y.*

TRY THIS

Use Undo or Redo to reverse or restore multiple actions. *To undo or redo a series of actions, continue clicking either the Undo or Redo button until you've reversed or restored all the actions in the series.*

Undo or Redo an Action

◆ Click the Undo button to reverse your most recent action, such as typing a word, formatting a paragraph, or creating a chart.

◆ Click the Redo button to restore the last action you reversed.

◆ Click the Undo drop-down arrow, and then select the consecutive actions you want to reverse.

◆ Click the Redo drop-down arrow, and then select the consecutive actions you want to restore.

Undo button   Undo drop-down arrow

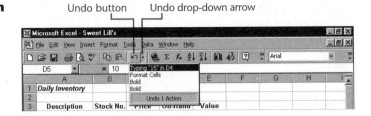

Redo button   Redo drop-down arrow

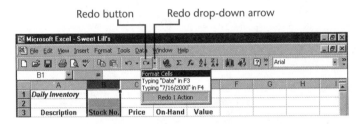

CORRECT TYPING ERRORS USING THE KEYBOARD	
To Delete	**Press**
One character at a time to the left of the insertion point	Backspace
One word at a time to the left of the insertion point	Ctrl+Backspace
One character at a time to the right of the insertion point	Delete
One word at a time to the right of the insertion point	Ctrl+Delete
Selected text	Backspace or Delete

Inserting Comments

When you review an Office document, you can insert comments to the author or other reviewers. *Comments* are like electronic adhesive notes tagged with your name. They appear as red triangles in Excel or as selected text in Word. You can use comments to get feedback from others or to remind yourself of revisions you plan to make.

Insert a Comment

1. Right-click any toolbar, and then click Reviewing.

2. Click where you want to insert a comment.

3. Click the Insert Comment or New Comment button on the Reviewing toolbar.

4. Type your comment in the comment box or pane.

5. Click outside the comment box. In Word, click the Close button to close the pane.

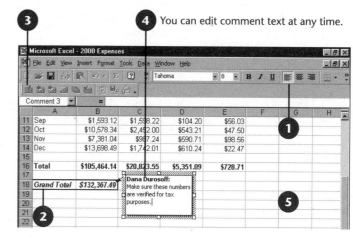

You can edit comment text at any time.

Read a Comment

1. Point to a red triangle in Excel or selected text in Word.

2. Read the comment.

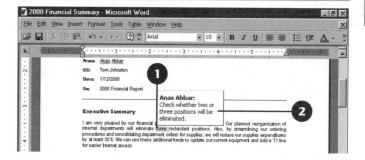

Delete a Comment

1. Click the selected word or the cell with a red triangle.

2. Click the Delete Comment button on the Reviewing toolbar.

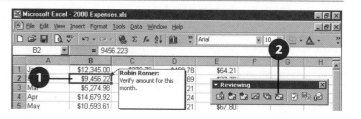

Selecting, Moving, and Resizing Objects

As you learn more about and use each Office program, you'll want to enhance your documents with more than just text or formulas. To do so, you can insert an object. An *object* is a picture or graphic image you create with a drawing program or insert from an existing file of another program. For example, you can insert a company logo that you have drawn yourself, or you can insert *clip art*—copyright-free pictures that come with Office. To work with an object, you need to select it first. Then you can resize or move it with its selection *handles,* the little squares that appear on the edges of the selected object.

Select and Deselect an Object

◆ Click an object to display its handles.

   To select more than one object at a time, hold down Shift as you click each object.

◆ Click elsewhere within the document window to deselect a selected object.

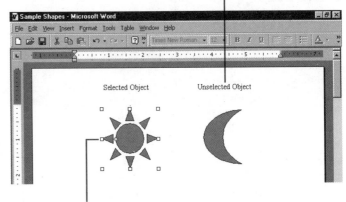

No handles appear around an unselected object.

Square white handles appear around a selected object.

Move an Object

1. Click an object to select it.

2. Drag the object to a new location indicated by the dotted outline of the object.

3. Release the mouse button to drop the object in the new location.

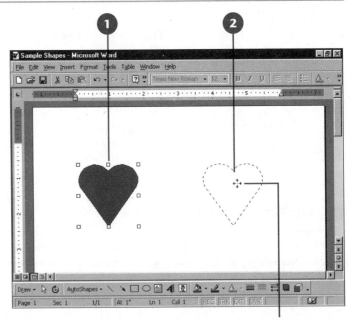

This pointer might look different or not appear at all.

Resize an Object

① Click the object you want to resize.

② To resize the object:

- ◆ Vertically or horizontally: drag a top, bottom, left, or right sizing handle.

- ◆ Proportionally in both the vertical and horizontal directions: drag a corner sizing handle.

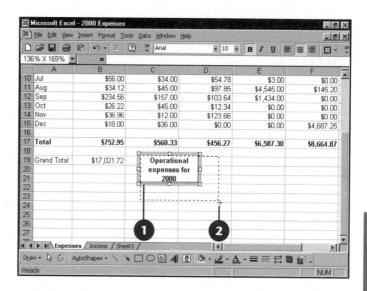

Resize an Object Precisely

① Right-click the object you want to resize, and then click Format Object, Picture, AutoShape, or Text Box (depending on the program and object).

② Click the Size tab.

③ Click to select the Lock Aspect Ratio check box to keep the object in its original proportion.

④ Click the Scale Height and Width up and down arrows to resize the object.

⑤ Click OK.

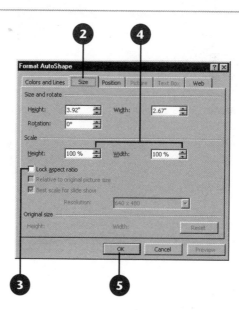

Drawing and Enhancing Objects

Drawn objects, like curved lines or lightning bolts, can enliven your document or help make your point. You can use the options on the Drawing toolbar to draw numerous objects without leaving your current program. After you add an object to your document, you can enhance it with a host of colors and special effects that reflect you, your company, or your organization. Select the object you want to enhance, and then select the effect you prefer. To make your documents easy to read, take care not to add too many lines, shapes, or other objects to the same spreadsheet or page.

> **TIP**
>
> **Draw perfect squares or circles.** *Click the Rectangle or Oval button on the Drawing toolbar, and then press and hold Shift while you draw.*

Draw Lines and Shapes

1. Display the Drawing toolbar, if necessary.

2. Click the AutoShapes button on the Drawing toolbar, point to Lines or Basic Shapes or any other option, and then select the line or shape you want.

3. Click in the document window, drag the pointer until the line or shape is the size you want, and then release the mouse button.

    When you draw some curvy lines, you need to click the mouse button once for every curve you want, and then double-click to end the line.

4. If you make a mistake, press Delete while the line or shape is still selected, and try again.

Click to draw a box.

Click to draw a circle.

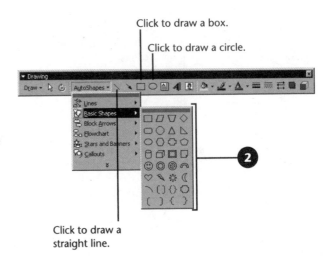

Click to draw a straight line.

Sample lines and shapes you can draw

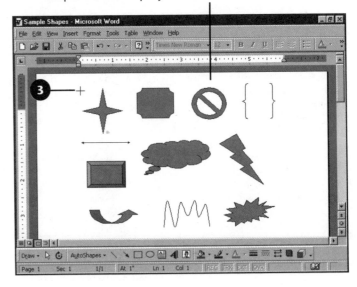

TIP

Display the Drawing toolbar. *Right-click any toolbar, and then click Drawing on the shortcut menu. A check mark next to the toolbar name indicates the toolbar is already displayed.*

TIP

Use the Drawing toolbar to align, group, or rotate objects. *Click the Draw button on the Drawing toolbar to use commands to group, reorder, align or distribute, and rotate or flip objects.*

TRY THIS

Draw lines, arrows, rectangles, and ovals. *Use the Line, Arrow, Rectangle, or Oval button on the Drawing toolbar to draw these lines and shapes. Then enhance the object by changing the line or fill color, the line or arrow style, and the shadow or 3-D effects.*

SEE ALSO

See "Selecting, Moving, and Resizing Objects" on page 38 for information on working with objects.

Add Color, Shadows, Line Styles, and 3-D Effects

1. Display the Drawing toolbar, if necessary.

2. Select the object in which you want to add an effect, and then select an option.

   ◆ To fill a shape with color, click the Fill Color drop-down arrow, and then select the color you want.

   ◆ To change the line color, click the Line Color drop-down arrow, and then select the color you want.

   ◆ To change the line style, click the Line Style button or the Dash Style button, and then select the style you want.

   ◆ To change the line arrow style, click the Arrow Style button, and then select the style you want.

   ◆ To add a shadow, click the Shadow button, and then select the shadow you want.

   ◆ To change an object to 3-D, click the 3-D button, and then select the 3-D effect you want.

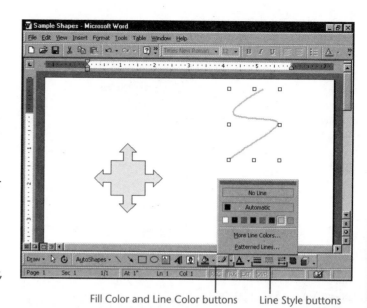

Fill Color and Line Color buttons   Line Style buttons

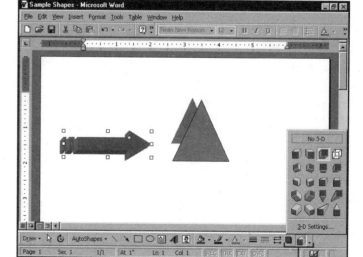

Shadow and 3-D buttons

Adding WordArt

To add life to your documents, you can add a WordArt object to your document. *WordArt* is a Microsoft Office program that allows you to add visual enhancements to your text that go beyond changing a font or font size. You can select a WordArt style that stretches your text horizontally, vertically, or diagonally. You can also change the character spacing and reshape the text. Like many enhancements you can add to a document, WordArt is an object that you can move, resize, and even rotate. WordArt is a great way to enhance a newsletter or resume, jazz up an invitation or flyer, or produce a creative report cover or eye-catching envelope.

Insert WordArt button

Create WordArt

1. Right-click any toolbar and then click Drawing.

2. Click the Insert WordArt button on the Drawing toolbar.

3. Double-click the style of text you want to insert.

4. Type the text you want in the Edit WordArt Text dialog box.

5. Click the Font drop-down arrow, and then select the font you want.

6. Click the Size drop-down arrow, and then select the font size you want, measured in points.

7. If you want, click the Bold button, the Italic button, or both.

8. Click OK.

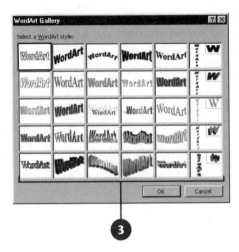

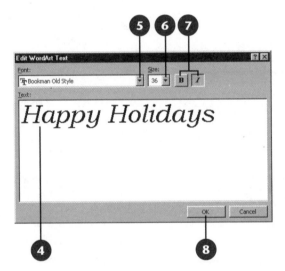

9 With the WordArt object selected, drag any handle to reshape the object until the text is the size you want.

10 Use the WordArt toolbar buttons to format or edit the WordArt.

Refer to the table for more information on the WordArt toolbar buttons.

11 Drag the WordArt object to the location you want.

12 Click outside the WordArt text to deselect the object and close the toolbar.

USING WORDART TOOLBAR BUTTONS		
Icon	**Button Name**	**Purpose**
	Insert WordArt	Create new WordArt
	Edit Text	Edit the existing text in a WordArt object
	WordArt Gallery	Choose a new style for existing WordArt
	Format WordArt	Change the attributes of existing WordArt
	WordArt Shape	Modify the shape of an existing WordArt object
	Free Rotate	Rotate an existing object
	WordArt Same Letter Heights	Make uppercase and lowercase letters the same height
	WordArt Vertical	Change horizontal letters into a vertical formation
	WordArt Alignment	Modify the alignment of an existing object
	WordArt Character Spacing	Change the spacing between characters

3

Adding Media Clips

You can insert clips from Microsoft's Clip Gallery or your own files. *Clips*—copyright-free images or pictures, sounds, and motion clips—enhance any Office document. A *motion clip* is an animated picture—also known as an animated GIF—frequently used in Web pages or videos. You can also insert your own files you scanned or created in a drawing program.

TIP

Connect to the Web for access to additional clip art. *Click the Clips Online button to open your Web browser and connect to a clip art Web site to download files.*

TIP

Search for clips by keyword. *Find the exact clip you want by typing a keyword in the Search For Clips box and pressing Enter. All related clips in any category appear.*

Insert a Clip

1. Click where you want to insert a clip.
2. Click the Insert menu, point to Picture, and then click Clip Art.
3. Click the tab (Pictures, Sounds, or Motion Clips) for the type of clip you want.
4. Click a category button.
5. Click any clip art image.
6. Click Insert Clip.
7. Repeat steps 3 through 6 to insert additional clips.
8. Click the Close button.

Click to view all available clip categories.

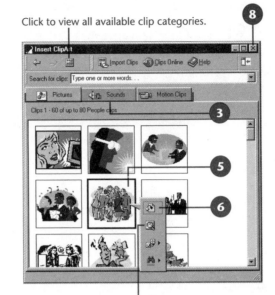

Click to preview a larger version of the image.

Find Similar Clips

1. Click the Insert menu, point to Picture, and then click Clip Art.
2. Click a clip similar to the ones you want to find.
3. Click the Find Similar Clips button on the shortcut menu.
4. Click Artistic Style, Color & Shape, or one of the keywords to narrow your search.
5. Click the Close button.

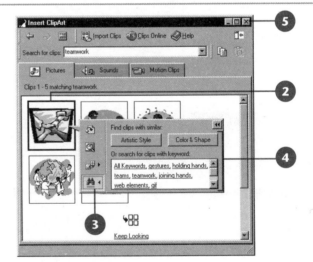

TIP

Display the Picture toolbar. *If the Picture toolbar doesn't appear when you select a clip or picture, right-click any toolbar, and then click Picture.*

TIP

Add a border to a picture. *Select the image, click the Line Style button on the Picture toolbar, and then click the line style you want.*

TIP

Preview a motion clip. *To see how a motion clip will appear on the Web, click the File menu, and then click Web Page Preview.*

TIP

Collect your favorites. *Right-click a clip, click the Add Clip To Favorites button on the shortcut menu, select a category, and then click OK.*

SEE ALSO

See "Modifying Media Clips" on page 46 for information on modifying clip art and pictures.

Insert a Picture

1. Click where you want to insert a picture.

2. Click the Insert menu, point to Picture, and then click From File.

3. Open the folder where your picture is stored.

4. Double-click the image you want to use.

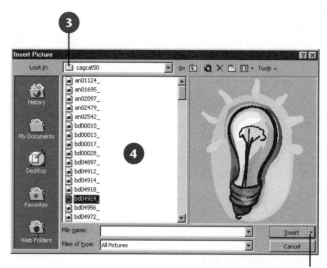

Click the drop-down arrow and then click Link To File to have the inserted image reflect any changes made to the original file.

Insert a Picture from a Scanner or Camera

1. Click the Insert menu, point to Picture, and then click From Scanner Or Camera.

2. Click the Device drop-down arrow, and select the device connected to your computer.

3. Select the resolution (the visual quality of the image).

4. Click Insert or Custom Insert.

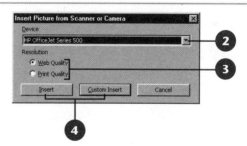

3

Modifying Media Clips

After you insert clip art or a picture, you can *crop*, or cut out, a section of the image. You can also change the clip's default colors to grayscale, black and white, or *watermark* (text or graphics that appear over or behind existing text).

TIP

Change an image's brightness and contrast. *Select the image, and then click the More Brightness or Less Brightness button on the Picture toolbar, or click the More Contrast or Less Contrast button on the Picture toolbar to the desired effect.*

TIP

Set an image color to transparent. *Select the image, and then click the Set Transparent Color button on the Picture toolbar.*

Crop a Picture

1. Click the picture or clip art image.

2. Click the Crop button on the Picture toolbar.

3. Drag the sizing handles until the borders surround the area you want to crop.

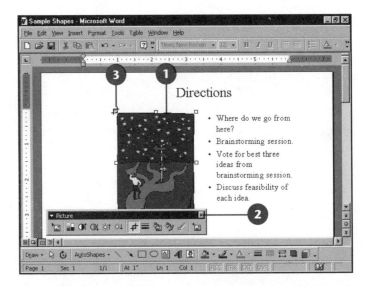

Choose a Color Type

1. Click the object whose color type you want to change.

2. Click the Image Control button on the Picture toolbar.

3. Click one of the Image Control options.

   ◆ Automatic (default coloring)

   ◆ Grayscale (whites, blacks, and grays)

   ◆ Black & White (white and black)

   ◆ Watermark (whites and very light colors)

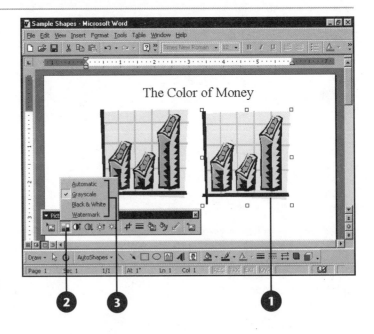

Creating an Organization Chart

An *organization chart* shows the personnel structure in a company or organization. You can create an organization chart, also known as an *org chart*, in any Office document with Microsoft Organization Chart. When you insert an org chart, *chart boxes* appear into which you enter the names and titles of company personnel. Each box is identified by its position in the chart. For example, Managers are at the top, Subordinates are below, Co-workers are to the sides, and so on.

TIP

Edit an org chart. *Double-click the organization chart, and then click the chart title or chart box you want to edit.*

TIP

Change an org chart style. *Click the Edit menu, point to Select, click All, click the Styles menu, and then click a chart style.*

Create a New Org Chart

1. Click the Insert menu, point to Picture, and then click Organization Chart.

   ◆ Or click the Insert menu, click Object, click the Create New tab, and double-click MS Organization Chart 2.0.

2. Type a name in the open chart box.

3. Click a chart box type button on the toolbar, and then click the chart box to which you want to attach the new chart box.

4. Select the placeholder text, and then type a name or other text.

5. Click the File menu, and then click Exit And Return To Document1.

Open and Format an Org Chart

1. Double-click the org chart.

2. Click the Edit menu, point to Select, and select the items you want to format.

3. Click the Boxes or Lines menu, point to an item, and then click a format option.

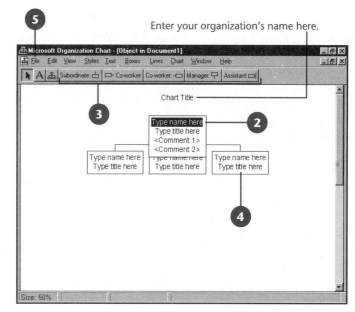

Enter your organization's name here.

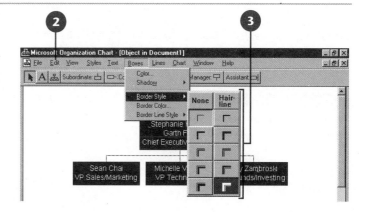

Creating a Graph Chart

A chart often makes numerical data more visual and easier to grasp. With Microsoft Graph, you can create a chart in Office programs. Just enter your numbers and labels in the *datasheet*, a spreadsheet-like grid of rows and columns that holds your data in *cells* (intersections of rows and columns), and watch Graph create the *chart*, a graphical representation of the data. Each *data series*, all the data from a row or column, has a unique color or pattern on the chart. You can format *chart objects*, individual elements that make up a chart, such as an axis, legend, or data series, to suit your needs.

Create a Graph Chart

1. Click where you want to insert the chart.

2. Start Microsoft Graph.
   - ◆ Click the Insert menu, click Object, double-click Microsoft Graph 2000 Chart.
   - ◆ In Word, click the Insert menu, point to Picture, and then click Chart.

3. Click the datasheet's upper-left button to select all the cells, and then press Delete to erase the sample data.

4. Enter new data in each cell, or click the Import Data button on the Standard toolbar to insert data from another source, such as Excel.

5. Edit and format the data in the datasheet as you like.

6. Click the Close button on the datasheet to close it.

7. Click outside the chart to quit Microsoft Graph and return to your document.

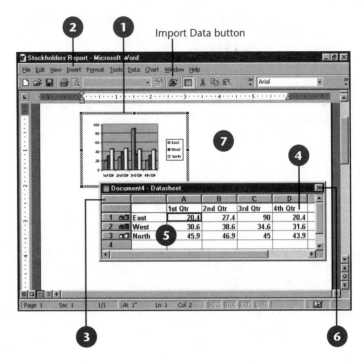

Import Data button

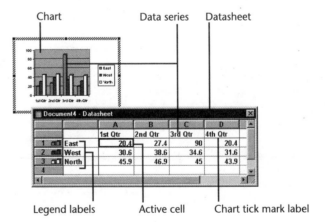

Chart   Data series   Datasheet

Legend labels   Active cell   Chart tick mark label

SEE ALSO

See "Viewing the Excel Window" on page 112 for information on active cells, moving among cells, and entering data in cells.

TIP

Edit a Graph chart. *Double-click the Graph chart, and then click the datasheet or chart you want to edit.*

TIP

Change the chart type. *Select the chart, click the Chart Type drop-down arrow, and click a chart type. You can also click the Chart menu, click Chart Type, click the Standard or Custom tab, select a 2-D or 3-D chart type, and then select a chart sub-type if necessary.*

TIP

Select a chart object. *Click the Chart Objects drop-down arrow on the Standard toolbar, and then click the chart object you want to select. You can also click a chart object to select it.*

Format a Chart Object

1. Double-click the chart object you want to format, such as an axis, legend, or data series.

2. Click the tab (Patterns, Scale, Font, Number, or Alignment) corresponding to the options you want to change.

3. Select the options to apply.

4. Click OK.

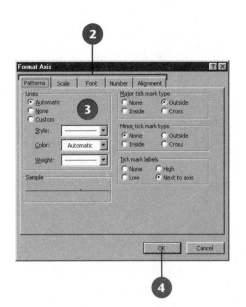

Customize a Chart

1. Select the chart.

2. Click the Chart menu, and then click Chart Options.

3. Click the tab (Titles, Axis, Gridlines, Legend, Data Labels, or Data Table) corresponding to the chart object you want to customize.

4. Make your changes.

5. Click OK.

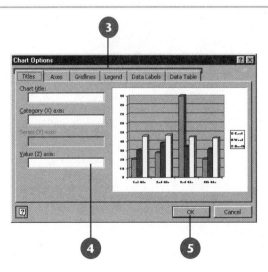

Automating Your Work

Do you often redo many tasks that require the same, sometimes lengthy, series of steps? Rather than repeat the same actions, work faster by recording the entire series of keystrokes and commands in a custom command, or *macro*. Macros are a perfect way to speed up routine formatting, combine multiple commands, and automate complex tasks. The macro recorder archives every mouse click and keystroke you make until you stop the recorder. Any time you want to repeat that series of actions, "play," or *run*, the macro. If a macro doesn't work exactly the way you want it to, you can fix the problem without re-creating the macro. Instead of recording the macro over again, Office allows you to *debug*, or repair, an existing macro so that you change only the actions that aren't working correctly.

Record a Macro

1. Click the Tools menu, point to Macro, and then click Record New Macro.

2. Enter a one-word macro name.

3. Assign a toolbar button or keyboard shortcut to the macro.

4. Select where you want to store the macro.

5. Enter a detailed description of the macro.

6. Click OK.

7. Perform each command or action to complete the task.

   The macro recorder doesn't record mouse movements within a document. For example, you cannot use the mouse to select, copy, or move objects. Instead, you must use keystrokes.

8. Click the Stop Recording button on the Stop Recording toolbar.

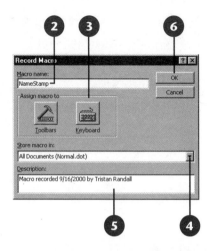

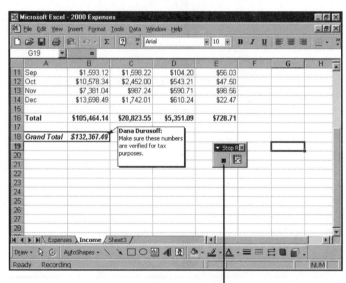

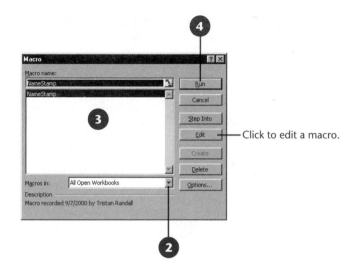

TIP

Valid macro names. *Macro names must start with a letter and can be as many as 80 letters and numbers. Macro names cannot contain spaces, periods, or other punctuation.*

TIP

Re-record a macro. *If you make a mistake as you record a macro, click the Stop Recording button on the Stop Recording toolbar. Then record the macro again using the same name. Click Yes in the dialog box to confirm that you want to replace the existing macro with the same name.*

TIP

Delete a macro. *You can delete a macro from the Macros dialog box. Click the Tools menu, point to Macro, click Macros, click the name of the macro you want to delete, and then click Delete.*

TIP

Store macros in the appropriate location. *If you want a macro to be available in all your Word documents, store it in the Normal template. If you want a macro available in all your worksheets, store it in the Personal Workbook.*

Run a Macro

① Click the Tools menu, point to Macro, and then click Macros.

② If necessary, click the Macros In drop-down arrow, and then click the document that contains the macro you want to run.

③ Click the name of the macro you want to run.

④ Click Run.

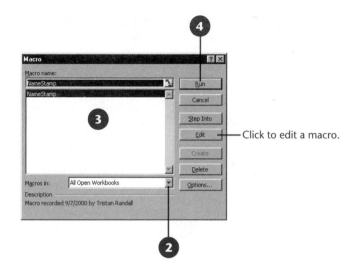

Click to edit a macro.

Debug a Macro Using Step Mode

① Click the Tools menu, point to Macro, and then click Macros.

② Click the name of the macro you want to debug.

③ Click Step Into.

④ Click the Debug menu, and then click Step Into to proceed through each action.

⑤ When you're done, click the File menu, and then click Close And Return To [Program name].

Module sheet

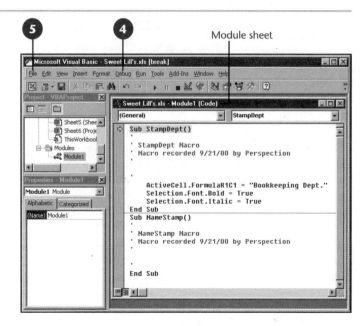

3

Repairing Office Programs

Never again do you need to worry when Office stops working for no apparent reason. All the Office programs are now self-repairing, which means that Office checks if essential files are missing or corrupt as a program opens and fixes the files as needed. You may never even realize there was a problem. Other times, Office starts fine but might have another problem, such as a corrupted font file or a missing template. These kinds of problems used to take hours to identify and fix. Now Office does the work for you with the *Detect And Repair* feature, which locates, diagnoses, and fixes any errors in the program itself. If you need to add or remove features or remove Office entirely, you can use Office Setup's maintenance feature.

Detect and Repair Problems

1 Click the Help menu, and then click Detect And Repair.

2 Click Start.

Insert the Office CD in your CD-ROM drive.

3 If necessary, click Repair Office, and then click the Reinstall Office or Repair Errors In Your Office Installation option button.

4 Click Finish.

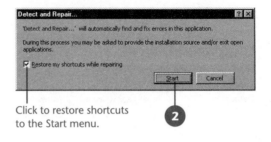

Click to restore shortcuts to the Start menu.

Perform Maintenance on Office Programs

1 In Windows Explorer, double-click the Setup icon on the Office CD.

2 Click one of the following maintenance buttons.

◆ Repair Office to repair or reinstall Office.

◆ Add Or Remove Features to determine which and when features are installed or removed.

◆ Remove Office to uninstall Office.

3 Follow the wizard instructions to complete the maintenance.

Creating a Document with Word 2000

Whether you're typing a carefully worded letter, creating that knock-your-socks-off resume, or producing a can't-miss promotional newsletter for your business or neighborhood group, Microsoft Word 2000 is the program for you. Word contains all the tools and features you need to produce snazzy documents that say exactly what you mean and that have the look to match.

Introducing Word

Microsoft Word, a *word processing program*, is designed especially for working with text, so it's a snap to create and edit letters, reports, mailing lists, tables, or any other word-based communication. The files you create and save in Word are called *documents*. What makes Word perfect for your documents is its editing capabilities combined with its variety of views. For example, you can jot down your ideas in Outline view. Then switch to Normal view to expand your thoughts into complete sentences and revise them without retyping the entire page. Tools such as the Spelling and Grammar Checker and Thesaurus help you present your thoughts accurately, clearly, and effectively. Finally, in Print Layout view you can quickly add formatting elements such as bold type and special fonts to make your documents look professional.

Viewing the Word Window

Menu bar
The nine menus provide access to all Word options. Click a menu to display a list of related commands, and then click the command you want.

Title bar
The document name and Microsoft Word appear in the title bar. *Document1* is a temporary name Word uses until you assign a new one.

Standard and Formatting toolbars
These and other toolbars contain buttons that provide quick access to a variety of Word commands and features. If you're not sure what a specific button does, move the mouse pointer over it to display its name.

Insertion point
The blinking insertion point (also called a cursor) shows you where the next character you type will appear.

Mouse pointer
In the document, the mouse pointer appears as an I-beam. The pointer changes shape depending on where you point in the window.

Document
You enter text and graphics here.

Status bar
The status bar tells you the location of the insertion point in a document and provides information about current settings and commands.

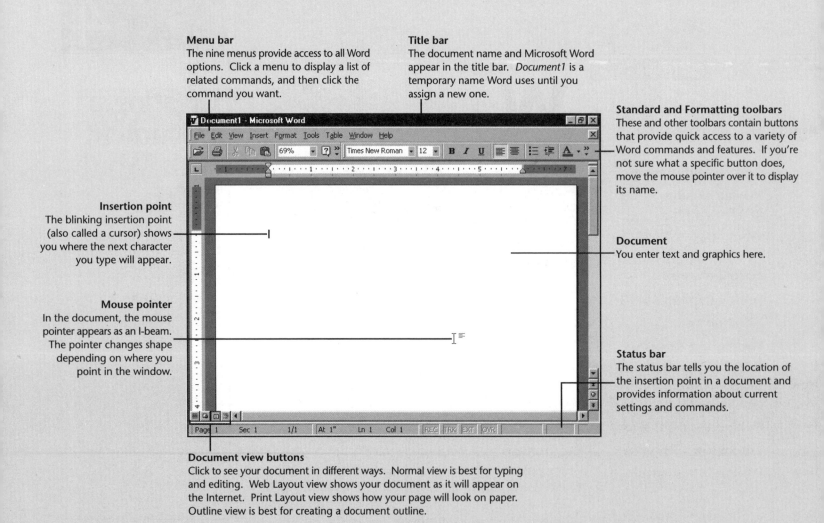

Document view buttons
Click to see your document in different ways. Normal view is best for typing and editing. Web Layout view shows your document as it will appear on the Internet. Print Layout view shows how your page will look on paper. Outline view is best for creating a document outline.

Changing Document Views

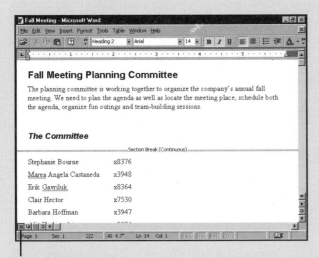

Normal View button

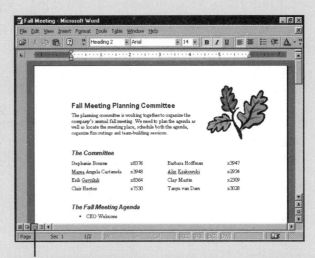

Print Layout View button

Web Layout View button

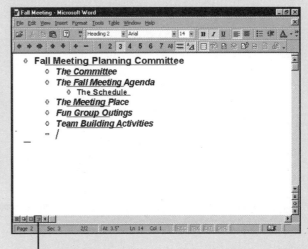

Outline View button

4

Creating a Document

When you open a new Word document, it's blank, ready for you to enter text. You can open and work on as many new documents as you'd like. As you type, text moves, or *wraps*, to a new line when the previous one is full. You can move the insertion point anywhere within the document so that you can insert new text and *edit* (or insert, revise, or delete) existing text. You can enter or edit text in any view.

SEE ALSO

See "Selecting Text" on page 63 for information on different ways to select text.

TIP

Turn off features not viewable in older versions.
Click the Tools menu, click Options, click the Compatibility tab, click the Recommended Options For drop-down arrow, and click the version you want. Click to select the option check boxes you don't want, and then click OK.

Open a New Document

1. Click the New Blank Document button on the Standard toolbar.

Enter Text in a Document

1. Click where you want to insert text.

2. Begin typing.

3. Press Enter when you want to begin a new paragraph or insert a blank line.

Words wrap to the next line within a paragraph.

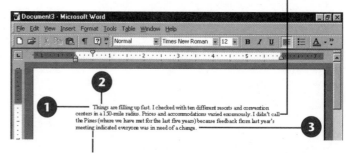

The characters you type appear at the insertion point.

Edit Text in a Document

1. Click where you want to insert text, or select the text you want to edit.

2. Make the change you want.

   ◆ Type to insert new text.

   ◆ Press Enter to begin a new paragraph or insert a blank line.

   ◆ Press Backspace or Delete to erase text to the left or right of the insertion point.

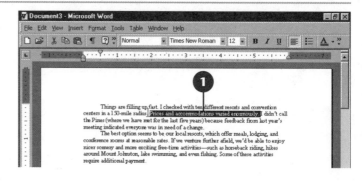

Moving Around in a Document

As your document gets longer, some of your work shifts out of sight. You can easily move any part of a document back into view. *Scrolling* moves the document line by line. *Paging* moves the document page by page. *Browsing* moves you through your document by the item you specify, such as to the next word, comment, picture, table, or heading. The tools described here move you around a document no matter which document view you are in.

TIP

Change view options. *Click the Tools menu, click Options, click the View tab, select the show, view, and format options you want, and then click OK.*

SEE ALSO

See "Finding and Replacing Text" on page 30 for information on locating specific text.

Scroll, Page, and Browse Through a Document

◆ To scroll through a document one line at a time, click the up or down scroll arrow on the vertical scroll bar.

◆ To scroll quickly through a document, click and hold the up or down scroll arrow on the vertical scroll bar.

◆ To scroll to a specific page or heading in a document, drag the scroll box on the vertical scroll bar until the page number or heading you want appears in the yellow box.

◆ To page through the document one screen at a time, press Page Up or Page Down on the keyboard.

◆ To browse a document by page, edits, headings, or other items, click the Browse button and then click that item. If a dialog box opens, enter the name or number of the item you want to find, and then click the Previous or Next button to move from one item to the next.

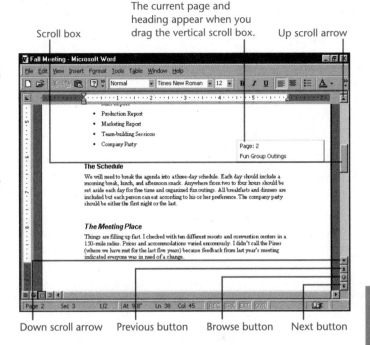

Scroll box — The current page and heading appear when you drag the vertical scroll box. — Up scroll arrow

Down scroll arrow   Previous button   Browse button   Next button

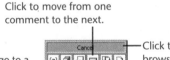

Click to move from one comment to the next.

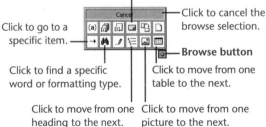

Click to go to a specific item. — Click to find a specific word or formatting type. — Click to move from one heading to the next. — Click to cancel the browse selection. — Browse button — Click to move from one table to the next. — Click to move from one picture to the next.

4

Working with Multiple Documents

The number of documents you can open at one time depends on your computer's resources. Multiple open documents are handy if you want to refer to an old report or copy parts of one letter into another, for example. You can view each document in its own window or all open documents in horizontally tiled windows. To view different parts of a document (convenient for summarizing a long report), you can split it into two windows that you view simultaneously but edit and scroll independently. No matter how you display documents, Word's commands and buttons work the same as usual.

SEE ALSO

See "Arranging Windows" on page 16 for information on tiling windows and switching between open documents.

Switch Between Open Documents

1. Click the Window menu.

2. Click the document on which you want to work.

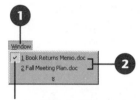

A check mark appears before the active document.

View All Open Documents Simultaneously

1. Click the Window menu, and then click Arrange All.

   Each document appears in its own window.

2. Click the window of the document you want to work on (it becomes the active document), and then edit the document as usual.

3. Click the Maximize button in the active window to display only one document.

Inactive document

The title bar of the inactive document is grayed out.

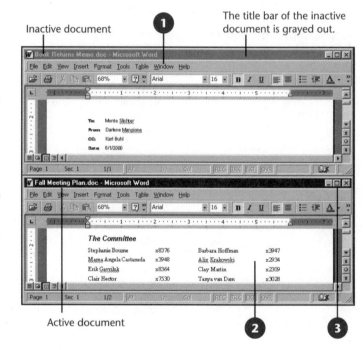

Active document

Work on Two Parts of the Same Document

1. Click the Window menu, and then click Split.

2. Drag the split bar until the two window panes are the sizes you want.

3. Click to set the split and display scroll bars and rulers for each pane.

4. Click to place the insertion point in each pane and scroll to the parts of the document you want to work on. Each pane scrolls independently. Edit the text as usual.

5. To return to a single pane, click the Window menu, and then click Remove Split.

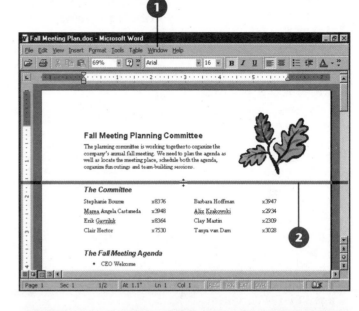

Setting Margins

Margins are the blank space between the edge of a page and the text. The default setting for Word documents is 1.25 inches on the left and right, and 1 inch on the top and bottom. You can set new margins for an entire document or a specific section. To set new margins, you drag the margin boundaries on the rulers. To set precise measurements for the new margins or to set new margins for the document from the insertion point forward, use the Page Setup dialog box.

TRY THIS

Reset margins from each view. *Adjust the left and right margins from Normal or Web Layout view, and then switch to Print Layout view or Print Preview to adjust the top and bottom margins.*

SEE ALSO

See "Displaying Rulers" on page 76 for information about displaying and hiding the horizontal and vertical rulers.

Set Margins for the Entire Document

1 Click the Print Layout View button or click the Print Preview button on the Standard toolbar.

2 Position the pointer over a margin boundary on the horizontal or vertical ruler.

3 Press and hold Alt to display the measurements of the text and margin areas as you adjust the margin.

4 Drag the left, right, top, or bottom margin boundary to a new position.

Set Margins for a Part of the Document

1 Select the text for which you want to change the margins. Or click in the paragraph where you want the new margins to begin. (When changing margins for the entire document, it doesn't matter where the insertion point is located.)

2 Click the File menu, click Page Setup, and then click the Margins tab.

3 Type new margin measurements (in inches) in the Top, Bottom, Left or Right boxes.

4 Check your changes in the Preview box.

5 Click the Apply To drop-down arrow, and then click Selected Text, This Point Forward, or Whole Document.

6 To make the new margin settings the default for all new Word documents, click Default, and then click Yes.

7 Click OK.

You don't need to type the inch symbol (").

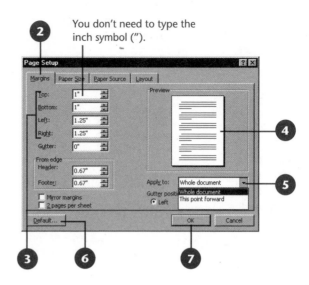

Setting Up the Page

Every document you produce and print might need a different page setup. You can achieve the look you want by printing on a standard paper size (such as letter, legal, or envelope), international standard paper sizes, or any custom size that your printer accepts. You can also print several pages on one sheet. Choose the page orientation that best fits the entire document or any section. *Portrait* orients the page vertically (taller than it is wide) and *Landscape* orients the page horizontally (wider than it is tall).

TIP

Use Page Setup to set advanced print options. *The Layout tab in the Page Setup dialog box contains advanced word processing options, such as dividing a document into sections and printing headers and footers.*

Set the Paper Size and Page Orientation

1 Click the File menu, and then click Page Setup.

2 Click the Paper Size tab.

3 If necessary, specify the size of the paper in your printer.

4 If necessary, change the page orientation.

5 Click the Apply To drop-down arrow, and then select This Section, This Point Forward, or Whole Document.

6 Verify your selections in the Preview box.

7 To make your changes the default settings for all new documents, click Default and then click Yes.

8 Click OK.

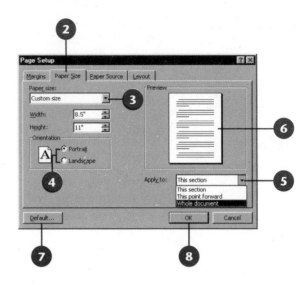

Selecting Text

The first step in working with text is to highlight, or *select*, the text you want. Once you've selected it, you can copy, move, format, and delete words, sentences, and paragraphs. When you finish with or decide not to use a selection, you can click anywhere in the document to *deselect* the text.

TRY THIS

Select your entire document quickly. *Press Ctrl+A to select the document.*

SEE ALSO

See "Editing Text" on page 28 and "Formatting Text for Emphasis" on page 72 for more information on the various tasks you can perform with selected text.

Select Text

① Position the pointer in the word, paragraph, line, or part of the document you want to select.

② Choose the method that accomplishes the task you want to complete in the easiest way.

Refer to the table for methods to select text.

SELECTING TEXT	
To select	**Do this**
A single word	Double-click the word.
A single paragraph	Triple-click a word within the paragraph.
A single line	Click in the left margin next to the line.
Any part of a document	Click at the beginning of the text you want to highlight, and then drag to the end of the section you want to highlight.
A large selection	Click at the beginning of the text you want to highlight, and then press and hold Shift while you click at the end of the text you want to highlight.
The entire document	Triple-click in the left margin.

Highlighting indicates that this text is selected.

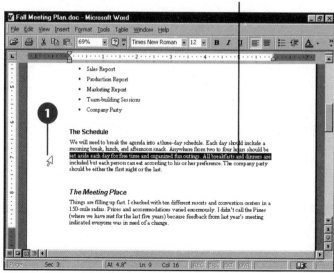

4

Finding and Replacing Formatting

Suddenly you realize all the bold text in your report would be easier to read as italics. Do you spend hours making these changes one by one? No. The Find and Replace feature locates the formatting and instantly substitutes new formatting. The Go To tab quickly moves you to a place or item in your document.

TIP

Replace text and formatting. *You can use the Find And Replace dialog box to locate formatted words, and then change the text, the formatting, or both. The Match Case option specifies exact capitalization.*

SEE ALSO

See "Finding and Replacing Text" on page 30 for information on locating and substituting text.

Find Formatting

1. Click the Edit menu, and then click Find.

2. If you want to locate formatted text, type the word or words.

3. Click the More button, click Format, and then click the formatting you want to find.

4. Click Find Next to select the next instance of the formatted text.

5. Click OK to confirm Word finished the search.

6. Click Cancel.

Find an Item or Location

1. Press F5.

2. Click an item in the Go To What box.

3. Enter the item number or name in the Enter box.

4. Click Next, Previous, or Go To to locate the item.

5. When you're done, click Close.

Unless you search All, you may be asked whether to continue searching from the beginning of the document.

Click to reduce the size of the dialog box and to change the button to More.

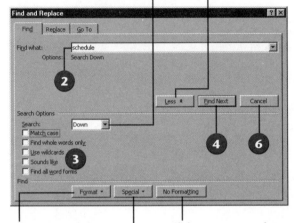

Click to open dialog boxes in which you can specify formatting you want to locate.

Click to remove any formatting settings from the search text.

Click to select special characters and symbols you want to locate, such as paragraph marks, page breaks, and em dashes.

This setting tells Word to go to the third page break.

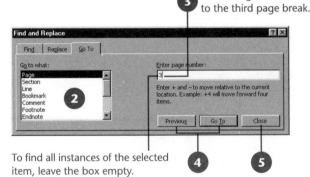

To find all instances of the selected item, leave the box empty.

Replace Formatting

1. Click the Edit menu, and then click Replace.

2. If you want to locate formatted text, type the word or words.

3. Click the More button, click Format, and then click the formatting you want to find. When you're done, click OK

4. Press Tab, and then type any text you want to substitute.

5. Click Format, and then click the formatting you want to substitute. When you're done, click OK

6. To substitute every instance of the formatting at once, click Replace All.

   To substitute the formatting one instance at time, click Find Next, and then click Replace.

7. If necessary, click Yes to search from the beginning of the document.

   If you want to cancel the replace, click Cancel.

8. Click OK to confirm Word finished searching.

9. Click Close.

Click to substitute every instance of the search text and formatting with the replacement text and formatting.

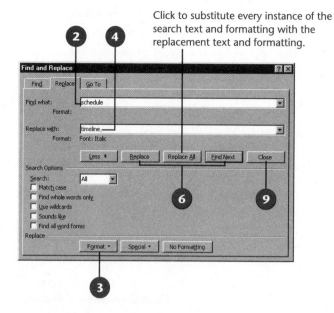

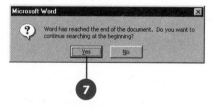

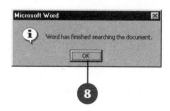

4

Checking Spelling and Grammar

As you type, a red wavy line appears under words not listed in Word's dictionary (such as misspellings or names) or duplicated words (such as *the the*). A green wavy underline appears under words or phrases with grammatical errors. You can correct these errors as they arise or after you finish the entire document. Before you print your final document, use the Spelling and Grammar Checker to ensure that your document is error-free.

SEE ALSO

See "Using Multiple Languages" on page 32 for information on automatically detecting languages and marking selected words in any language to eliminate false misspellings.

TIP

Hyphenate words. *Click the Tools menu, point to Language, click Hyphenation, click to select Automatically Hyphenate Document check box, and then click OK.*

Correct Spelling and Grammar as You Type

1. Right-click a word with a red or green wavy underline.

2. Click a substitution, or click Ignore All (or Ignore Grammar) to skip any other instances of the word.

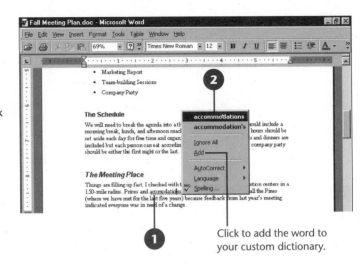

Click to add the word to your custom dictionary.

Change Spelling and Grammar Options

1. Click the Tools menu, and then click Options.

2. Click the Spelling & Grammar tab.

3. Click to select or clear the spelling option check boxes you want.

4. Click to select or clear the grammar option check boxes you want.

5. If you want, click Settings, click to select or clear the grammar and style advanced option check boxes, and then click OK.

6. Click OK.

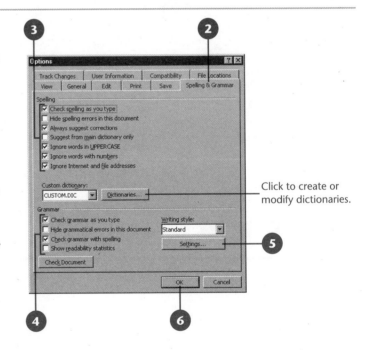

Click to create or modify dictionaries.

TIP

Select text to check part of a document. *You can check spelling and grammar in only part of a document by first selecting the text you want to check and then following the steps for checking the entire document.*

TIP

Check only spelling. *If you want to check only your spelling, click to clear the Check Grammar check box in the Spelling And Grammar dialog box.*

TIP

Rely on AutoCorrect. *AutoCorrect fixes common misspellings and other mistakes (such as the accidental usage of the Caps Lock key) as you type.*

SEE ALSO

See "Correcting Text Automatically" on page 34 for information on correcting errors as you type.

Correct Spelling and Grammar

1. Click at the beginning of the document, and then click the Spelling And Grammar button on the Standard toolbar.

2. As it checks each sentence in the document, Word selects misspelled words or problematic sentences and provides appropriate alternatives in the Suggestions box.

3. Choose an option.

   ◆ Click a suggestion, and then click Change to make a substitution.

   ◆ Click Ignore to skip the word or rule, or click Ignore All or Ignore Rule to skip every instance of the word or rule.

   ◆ If no suggestion is appropriate, click in the document and edit the text yourself. Click Resume to continue.

4. Click OK to return to the document.

Click to add a word to your custom dictionary.

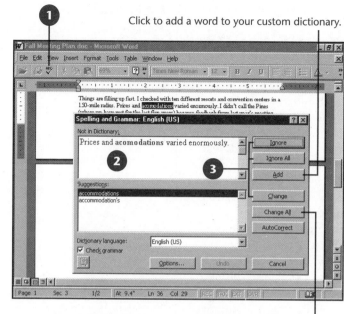

Click to change every instance of the word in the document.

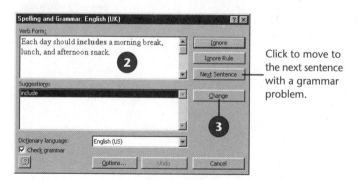

Click to move to the next sentence with a grammar problem.

Finding the Right Words

Repeating the same word in a document can reduce a message's effectiveness. Instead, replace some words with *synonyms*, words with similar meanings. Or find *antonyms*, words with opposite meanings. If you need help finding exactly the right word, use the shortcut menu to look up synonyms quickly or search Word's Thesaurus for more options. This feature can save you time and improve the quality and readability of your document. You can also install a thesaurus for another language.

SEE ALSO

See "Checking Spelling and Grammar" on page 66 for information on checking spelling and multilanguage recognition.

TRY THIS

Find a synonym for *invite*. *Use both the shortcut menu and the Thesaurus to see how your choices vary.*

Find a Synonym

1. Right-click the word for which you want a synonym.

2. Point to Synonyms.

3. Click the synonym you want to substitute.

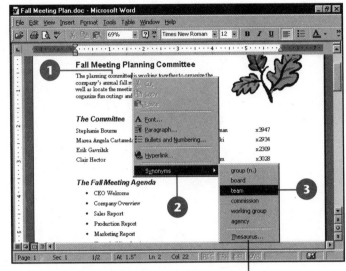

Click to open the Thesaurus and find other synonyms.

Use the Thesaurus

1. Select the word you want to look up.

2. Click the Tools menu, point to Language, and then click Thesaurus.

3. Click a word to display its synonyms and antonyms.

4. Click the word you want to use.

5. Click Replace.

6. If necessary, click Cancel to close the dialog box.

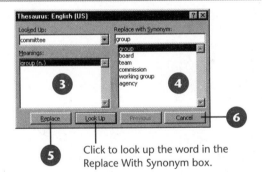

Click to look up the word in the Replace With Synonym box.

Previewing a Document

Before printing, you should verify that the page looks the way you want. You save time, money, and paper by avoiding duplicate printing. *Print Preview* shows you exactly how your text will be placed on each printed page. This is especially helpful when you have a multipage document divided into sections with different headers and footers. The Print Preview toolbar provides the tools you need to proof the presentation of each page.

TIP

Edit in Print Preview. *Zoom the document to a closer view. Click the Magnifier button on the Print Preview toolbar, click the document, and then edit as usual.*

SEE ALSO

See "Setting Margins" on page 60 for information on adjusting the space between the edge of a page and the text in a header or footer.

Preview a Document

1. Click the Print Preview button on the Standard toolbar.

2. Preview your document.

   ◆ To view one page at a time, click the One Page button.

   ◆ To view multiple pages, click the Multiple Pages button and select the number of pages to view at a time.

   ◆ To change the view size, click the Zoom drop-down arrow to select a magnification percentage.

   ◆ To shrink to fit a page, click the Shrink To Fit button to reduce the document to one page.

   ◆ To display the full screen, click the Full Screen button to hide everything but the toolbar.

3. When you're done, click the Close button on the Print Preview toolbar.

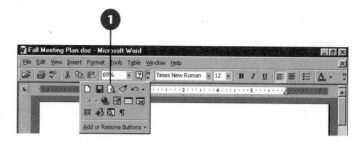

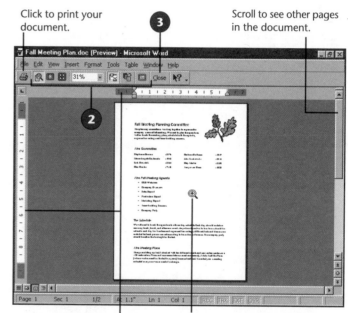

Click to print your document.

Scroll to see other pages in the document.

You can adjust the document's margins from these rulers.

Click the Magnifer pointer to get a closer look.

Printing a Document

Printing a paper copy is the most common way to share your documents. Print one copy of your document using the current settings or open the Print dialog box to print your document and set how many copies to print, specify a series of pages to print, and choose what to print. Besides a document, you can print comments, a list of styles used in the document, and AutoText entries, for example. To review a long document on fewer pages, print multiple pages on one sheet with *print zoom*. Word also allows you to scale pages to fit different paper sizes, such as A4.

TIP

Change other print options. *Click the Tools menu, click Options, click the Print tab, select the options you want, and then click OK.*

Print a Document Quickly

1. Click the Print button on either the Standard toolbar or the Print Preview toolbar.

Print All and Part of Documents

1. Click the File menu, and then click Print.

2. If necessary, click the Name drop-down arrow, and then click the printer you want.

3. Type the number of copies you want to print.

4. Specify the pages to print.

   ◆ All prints the entire document.

   ◆ Current Page prints the page with the insertion point.

   ◆ Selection prints the selected text.

   ◆ Pages prints the specified pages.

5. Specify what you want to print.

6. Specify how many pages to print per sheet of paper, and select the paper size to which to scale pages.

7. Click OK.

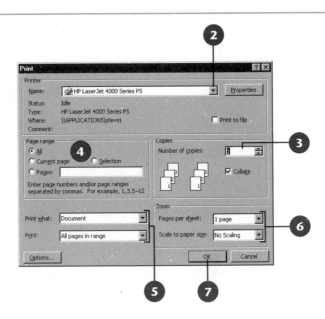

Formatting a Document with Word 2000

5

The text of your document is perfect, but now how do you get others to notice your resume, read your newsletter, or think your document is fun, professional, interesting, dynamic, or extraordinary? Try Microsoft Word's extensive formatting features to lay out the information in your documents and create the exact look and mood you want.

Templates and Styles

Word documents are based on *templates*, which are predesigned and preformatted files that serve as the documents' foundation. Each template is made up of styles that have common design elements, such as coordinated fonts and sizes, colors, and page layout designs. Start with a Word template for memos, reports, fax cover pages, Web pages, and so on. Apply the existing styles for headings, titles, body text, and so forth. Then modify the template's styles or create your own to better suit your needs. Make sure you get the look you want by adding emphasis with italics, boldface, and underline; changing text alignment; adjusting line and paragraph spacing; setting tabs and indents; and creating bulleted and numbered lists. When you're done, your document is sure to demand attention and convey your message's tone in its appearance.

Formatting Text for Emphasis

You'll often want to *format*, or change the style, of certain words or phrases to add emphasis to parts of a document. **Boldface**, *italics*, underlines, highlights, and other text effects are *toggle switches*, which means you simply click to turn them on and off. For special emphasis you can combine formats, such as bold and italics. Using one *font*, or letter design, for headings and another for main text adds a professional look to your document.

Format Existing Text Quickly

1 Select the text you want to emphasize.

2 Click the Bold, Italic, Underline, or Highlight button on the Formatting toolbar.

You can add more than one formatting option at a time. For example, *this text uses both boldface and italics*.

3 Click anywhere in the document to deselect the formatted text.

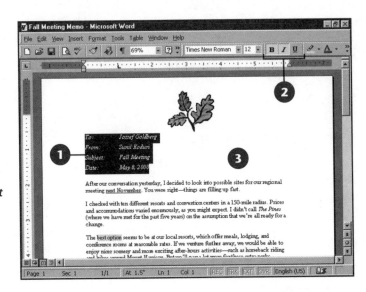

Change the Font or Size of Existing Text Quickly

1 Select the text you want to format.

2 Click the Font drop-down arrow on the Formatting toolbar, and then click a new font.

3 Click the Font Size drop-down arrow on the Formatting toolbar, and then click a new point size.

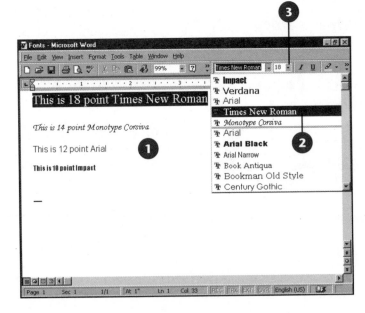

Format text as you type.
You can add most formatting options to text as you type. First select the formatting options you want, and then type the text. If necessary, turn off the formatting options when you're done.

Have Word automatically format your document.
Click the Format menu, and then click AutoFormat. Select a document type (General Document, Letter, Email) and indicate if you want to review each change.

Highlight key points in a memo. *Open an existing memo, and then use the Highlight button on the Formatting toolbar to highlight key points in bright yellow.*

See "Creating and Modifying a Style" on page 80 for information on using Word styles to format text consistently throughout a document.

Apply Formatting Effects to Text

1. Select the text you want to format.

2. Click the Format menu, and then click Font.

3. Click the Font tab.

4. Click the formatting you want.

5. Click to select the effects you want.

6. To change character spacing settings, click the Character Spacing tab.

7. Change the spacing as you want.

8. To add animation effects, click the Text Effects tab, and click an animation.

9. Check the results in the Preview box.

10. To make the new formatting options the default for all new Word documents, click Default, and then click Yes.

11. Click OK.

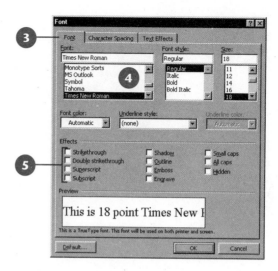

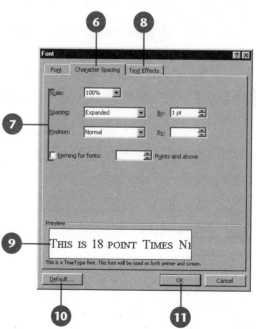

Setting Text Alignment

Text starts out positioned evenly along the left margin, and uneven, or *ragged*, at the right margin. Left-aligned text works well for body paragraphs in most cases, but other alignments vary the look of a document and help lead the reader through the text. *Right-aligned text,* which is even along the right margin and ragged at the left margin, is good for adding a date to a letter. *Justified text* spreads text evenly between the margins, creating a clean, professional look, often used in newspapers and magazines. *Centered text* is best for titles and headings.

TIP

Click-And-Type anywhere in a document to type.
When you double-click the text alignment pointer, Word adds extra lines and tabs, and sets the alignment and text wrapping as needed. Use Click-And-Type to quickly center titles or set different text alignment on the same line.

Align New Text with Click-And-Type

◆ Place the I-beam at the left, right, or center of the line where you want to insert new text.

When the I-beam shows the appropriate alignment, double-click to place the insertion point, and then type your text.

Align Existing Text

1 Place the I-beam or select at least one line in each paragraph to align.

2 Click the appropriate button on the Formatting toolbar.

◆ Align Left button

◆ Center button

◆ Align Right button

◆ Justify button

TEXT POINTERS	
Pointer	**Purpose**
I	Left-aligns text
I	Right-aligns text
I	Centers text
I	Creates a new line in the same paragraph

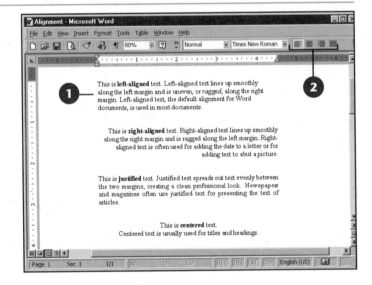

Changing Line Spacing

The lines in all Word documents are single-spaced by default, which is appropriate for letters and most documents. But you can easily change your document line spacing to double or 1.5 lines to allow extra space between every line. This is useful when you want to make notes on a printed document. Sometimes, you'll want to add space above and below certain paragraphs, such as for headlines or indented quotations to help set off the text.

Adjust Line Spacing

1. Select one or more paragraphs you want to change.

2. Click the Format menu, click Paragraph, and then click the Indents And Spacing tab.

3. Click the Line Spacing drop-down arrow, and then click the spacing you want.

4. If necessary, type the precise line spacing you want.

5. Click OK.

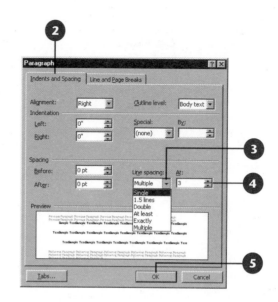

Set Paragraph Spacing

1. Select one or more paragraphs you want to change.

2. Click the Format menu, click Paragraph, and then click the Indents And Spacing tab.

3. Type the space you want to add above each selected paragraph (in points).

4. Type the space you want to add below each selected paragraph (in points).

5. Click OK.

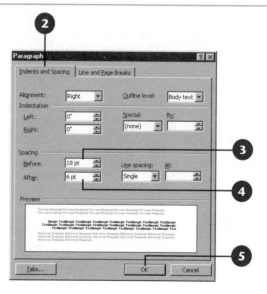

Displaying Rulers

Word rulers do more than measure. The *horizontal ruler* above the document shows the length of the typing line, and lets you quickly adjust left and right margins and indents, set tabs, and change column widths. The *vertical ruler* along the left edge of the document lets you adjust top and bottom margins and change table row heights. Hide the rulers to get more room for your document. As you work with long documents, use the document map to jump to any heading in your document. Headings are in the left pane and documents in the right.

Show and Hide the Rulers

1. Click the View menu, and then click Ruler.

   ◆ To view the horizontal ruler, click the Normal View button.

   ◆ To view the horizontal and vertical rulers, click the Print Layout View button.

Vertical ruler   Horizontal ruler

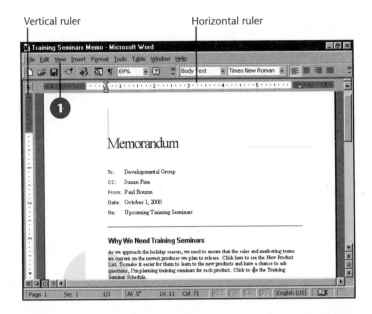

Display a Document Map

1. Click the Document Map button on the Standard toolbar.

2. Switch to any document view you want.

3. Click a heading in the left pane to scroll the document in the right pane.

4. Edit and format your document as usual.

5. Click the Document Map button on the Standard toolbar when you're done.

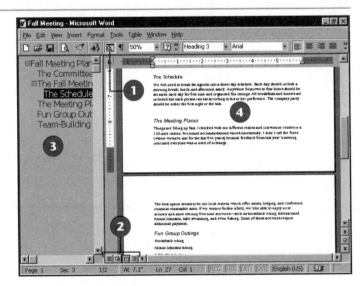

Setting Paragraph Tabs

In your document, *tabs* set how text or numerical data aligns in relation to the document margins. A *tab stop* is a predefined stopping point along the document's typing line. Default tab stops are set every half-inch, but you can set multiple tabs per paragraph at any location. Choose from four text tab stops: left, right, center, and decimal (for numerical data). The bar tab inserts a vertical bar at the tab stop.

TIP

Display tab characters. *If you don't see a tab character, which looks like →, when you press Tab, click the Show/Hide ¶ button on the Standard toolbar.*

TRY THIS

Move a tab stop. *Type "Tab Stop Fun" after a tab mark on a blank line, set a center tab stop at 1.25", and then drag the tab marker to the 3" mark. Watch the text move positions in the document.*

Create and Clear a Tab Stop

1. Select one or more paragraphs in which you want to set a tab stop.

2. Click the Tab button on the horizontal ruler until it shows the type of tab stop you want.

3. Click the ruler where you want to set the tab stop.

4. If necessary, drag the tab stop to position it where you want.

   To display a numerical measurement in the ruler where the tab is placed, press and hold Alt as you drag.

5. To clear a tab stop, drag it off the ruler.

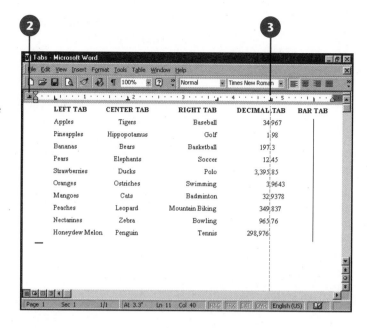

TAB STOPS	
Tab Stop	**Purpose**
L	Aligns text to the left of the tab stop
⌐	Aligns text to the right of the tab stop
⊥	Centers text on the tab stop
⊥·	Aligns numbers on the decimal point
I	Inserts a vertical bar at the tab stop

5

Setting Paragraph Indents

Quickly indent lines of text to precise locations from the left or right margin with the horizontal ruler. Indent the first line of a paragraph (called a *first-line indent*) as books do to distinguish paragraphs. Indent the second and subsequent lines of a paragraph from the left margin (called a *hanging indent*) to create a properly formatted bibliography. Indent the entire paragraph any amount from the left and right margin (called *left indents* and *right indents*) to separate quoted passages.

Indent Paragraph Lines Precisely

Click the paragraph or select multiple paragraphs to indent.

◆ To change the left indent of the first line, drag the First Line Indent marker.

◆ To change the indent of the second and subsequent lines, drag the Hanging Indent marker.

◆ To change the left indent for all lines, drag the Left Indent marker.

◆ To change the right indent for all lines, drag the Right Indent marker.

As you drag a marker, the dotted guideline helps you position the indent accurately. Or press and hold Alt to see a numerical measurement in the ruler.

First Line Indent marker

Hanging Indent marker

Left Indent marker

Right Indent marker

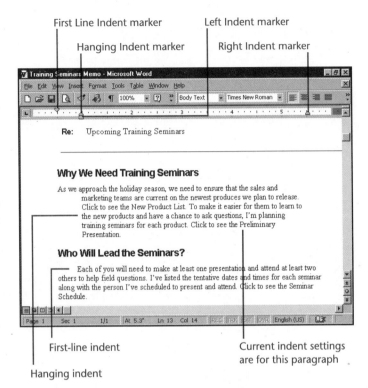

First-line indent

Hanging indent

Current indent settings are for this paragraph

Indent a Paragraph

1 Click the paragraph or select multiple paragraphs to indent.

2 Click the Increase Indent button or Decrease Indent on the Formatting toolbar to move the paragraph right or left one half inch.

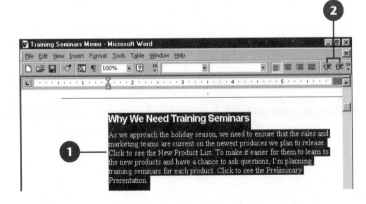

Applying a Style

The *Format Painter* copies and pastes formatting from one batch of selected text to another without copying the text. When you want to apply multiple groupings of formatting, save each as a style. A *style* is a collection of formatting settings saved with a name in a document or template that you can apply to text at any time. If you modify a style, you make the change once, but all text tagged with that style changes to reflect the new format.

TIP

Paint a format multiple times. *Select the formatting you want to copy. Double-click the Format Painter button, and then select the text to format in each location. Click the Format Painter button when you finish.*

SEE ALSO

See "Enhancing Web Pages" on page 264 for information on applying themes (documents with predefined styles).

Copy a Style with the Format Painter

1. Select the text with the formatting you want to copy.

2. Click the Format Painter button on the Standard toolbar.

3. Select the text you want to format with the Format Painter pointer.

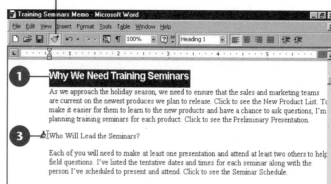

Apply a Style Using the Style List Box

1. Select the text to which you want to apply a style.

2. Click the Style drop-down arrow on the Formatting toolbar.

   Each style name shows its formatting and a summary.

3. Click the style you want to apply.

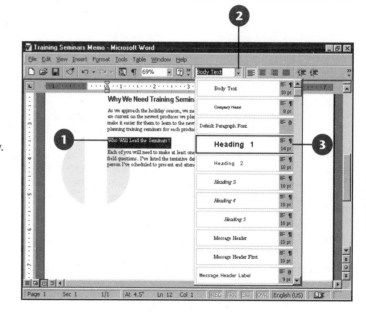

Creating and Modifying a Style

Word provides a variety of styles you can choose from. But sometimes you need to create a new style or modify an existing one to get the exact look you want. When you create a new style, specify if it applies to paragraphs or characters. Also, give the style a short, descriptive name that describes its purpose so you and others recall when to use that style. To modify a style, adjust the formatting settings of an existing style.

TIP

View different Style lists.
When looking at the list of styles in the Style dialog box you can select what types of styles to view: Styles In Use, All Styles, and User-Defined Styles. The styles that appear in the Styles list box are based on the option you choose.

Create a New Style

1 Select the text whose formatting you want to save as a style.

2 Click the Format menu, click Style, and then click New.

3 Type a short, descriptive name.

4 Click the Style Type drop-down arrow, and then click Paragraph to include the selected text's line spacing and margins in the style, or click Character to include only formatting, such as font, size, and bold, in the style.

5 Click the Style For Following Paragraph drop-down arrow, and then click the name of style you want to be applied after a paragraph with the new style.

6 Click the Add To Template check box to save the new style in the current template.

7 Click OK.

8 Click Apply or click Close.

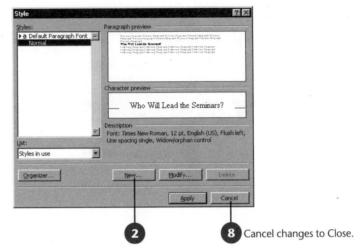

8 Cancel changes to Close.

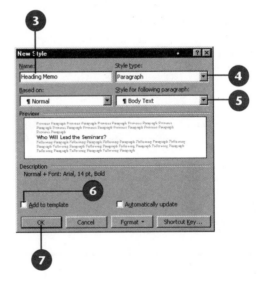

SEE ALSO

See "Working with Templates and Add-ins" on page 84 for information on applying predefined template styles to a document.

Modify a Style

1. Click the Format menu, and then click Style.

2. Click the style you want to modify.

3. Click Modify.

4. Click Format, and then click the type of formatting you want to modify.

   ◆ To change character formatting, such as font type and boldface, click Font.

   ◆ To change line spacing and indents, click Paragraph.

5. Select the formatting options you want, and then click OK.

6. Check the Preview box and review the style description. Make any formatting changes necessary.

7. Click OK.

8. Click Apply or click Close.

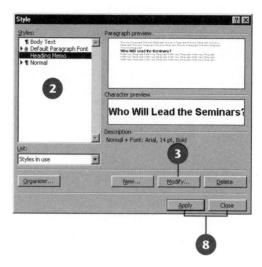

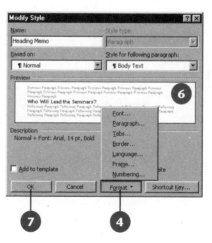

Creating Bulleted and Numbered Lists

The best way to draw attention to a list is to format the items with bullets or numbers. You can even create multilevel lists. For different emphasis, change any bullet or number style to one of Word's many pre-defined formats. For example, switch round bullets to check boxes or Roman numerals to lowercase letters. You can also customize the list style or insert a picture as a bullet. If you move, insert, or delete items in a numbered list, Word sequentially renumbers the list for you.

Create a Bulleted List

1. Click where you want to create a bulleted list.

2. Click the Bullets button on the Formatting toolbar.

3. Type the first item in your list, and then press Enter to insert a new bullet.

4. Type the next item in your list, and then press Enter.

5. Click the Bullets button on the Formatting toolbar or press Enter again to end the list.

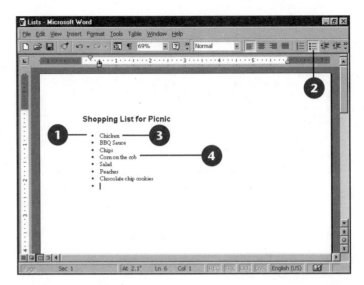

Create a Numbered List

1. Click where you want to create a numbered list.

2. Click the Numbering button on the Formatting toolbar.

3. Type the first item in your list, and then press Enter to insert the next number.

4. Type the next item in your list, and then press Enter.

5. Click the Numbering button on the Formatting toolbar or press Enter again to end the list.

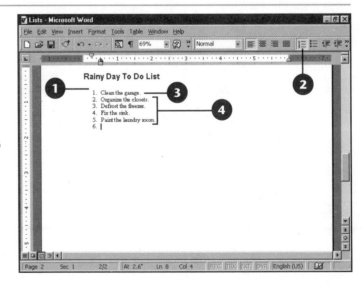

Change spacing between bullets or numbers and text. *Click Customize in the Bullets And Numbering dialog box, and then change the Bullet (or Number) Position and Text Position options to specify where you want the bullet (or number) to appear and how much to indent the text.*

Reorder a numbered list. *Create a numbered list with five items. Select item 5 and drag it before item 2 (release the mouse button when the vertical insertion point is before item 2). The reordered list remains numbered consecutively.*

Switch between bulleted and numbered lists. *If you decide a bulleted list should be numbered or vice versa, just click the Bullets or Numbering button on the Formatting toolbar.*

Create picture bullets. *Graphics make effective and interesting bullets in documents and on Web pages. Change the bullet style to any picture, and Word repeats it in subsequent bullets. Word mixes picture bullets with themes so they change with the themes.*

Create a Multilevel Bulleted or Numbered List

1 Start the list as usual.

2 Press Tab to indent a line to the next level bullet or number, type the item, and then press Enter to insert the next bullet or number.

3 Press Shift+Tab to return to the previous level bullet or number.

4 End the list as usual.

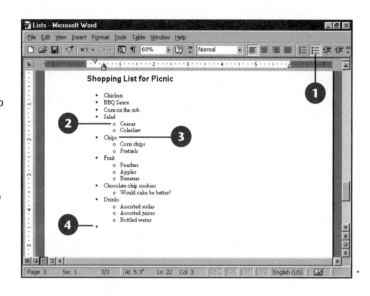

Change Bullet or Number Styles

1 Select the list, click the Format menu, and then click Bullets And Numbering.

2 Click the Bulleted tab or the Numbered tab.

3 Click a predefined format.

4 To add a graphic bullet, click Picture, and then select the picture you want.

5 Click Customize to change the format style.

6 Click OK.

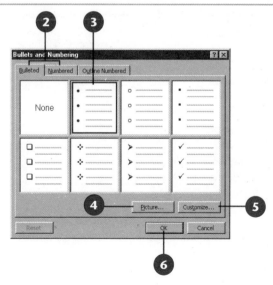

Working with Templates and Add-ins

A *template* is a special document that stores text, styles, formatting, macros, and page information for use in other documents. Start with a predefined Word template or use one you created. Quickly try a new look by attaching a different template to your current document. The attached template's styles replace the styles in your document. To extend Word's functions, load a*dd-ins,* supplemental programs that add custom commands and features to Word. You must reload an add-in each time you start Word unless you put it in the Startup folder located in the Microsoft Office folder on your hard disk drive.

SEE ALSO

See "Choosing Templates and Wizards" on page 18 for information about choosing a template to create a document.

Save a Document as a Template

1 Open a new or existing document.

2 Add any text, graphics, and formatting you want to appear in all documents based on this template. Adjust margin settings and page size, and create new styles as necessary.

3 Click the File menu, and then click Save As.

4 Click the Save As Type drop-down arrow, and then click Document Template.

5 Make sure the Templates folder (usually located in the Microsoft Office folder in the Programs folder) or one of its subfolders appears in the Save In box.

6 Type a name for the new template.

7 Click Save.

You can open the template and make and save other changes just as you would any other document.

Use the folders to organize your templates.

Attach a Template to an Existing Document

1. Open the document to which you want to apply a new template.

2. Click the Format menu, click Theme, and then click Style Gallery.

3. Click a template name to preview it.

4. Click OK to add the template styles to the document.

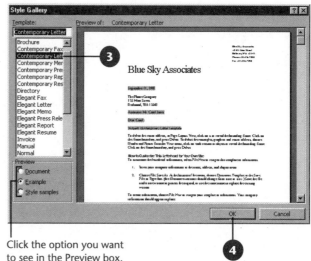

Click the option you want to see in the Preview box.

Load an Add-in

1. Click the Tools menu, and then click Templates And Add-Ins.

2. Click the add-in you want to load.

3. To add one to the list, click Add, switch to the folder that contains the add-in, click the Files Of Type drop-down arrow, select Word Add-ins, click the add-in, and then click OK.

4. Click OK.

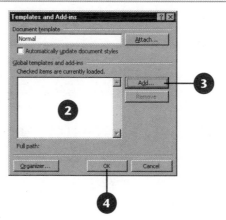

Inserting New Pages and Sections

When you fill a page, Word inserts a page break and starts a new page. As you add or delete text, this *soft page break* moves. To start a new page before the current one is filled, insert a *hard page break* that doesn't shift as you edit text. A *section* is a mini-document within a document that stores margin settings, page orientation, page numbering, and so on.

Insert and Delete a Hard Page Break

1. Click where you want to insert a hard page break.

2. Click the Insert menu, and then click Break.

3. Click the Page Break option button.

4. Click OK.

5. To delete a page break, click the page break in Normal view, and then press Backspace or Delete.

Insert and Delete a Section Break

1. Click where you want to insert a section break.

2. Click the Insert menu, and then click Break.

3. Click the type of section break you want.

4. Click OK.

5. To delete a section break, click the section break in Normal view, and then press Backspace or Delete.

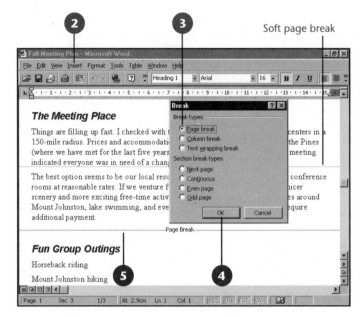

Soft page break

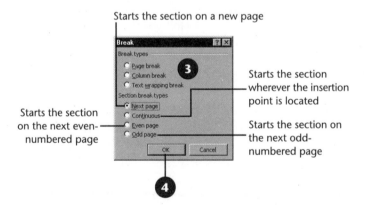

Starts the section on a new page

Starts the section on the next even-numbered page

Starts the section wherever the insertion point is located

Starts the section on the next odd-numbered page

Addressing Envelopes and Labels

A formatted document needs a matching envelope or mailing label. Addresses can contain text, graphics, and bar codes. The POSTNET bar code is a machine-readable depiction of a U.S. zip code and delivery address; the FIM-A code identifies the front of a courtesy reply envelope. You can print a single label or multiple labels.

TIP

Format address text. *Select the text, right-click the selected text, click Font, and then format as usual.*

SEE ALSO

See "Creating a Form Letter" on page 106 for information on printing multiple envelopes or labels with different addresses.

Address and Print Envelopes

1. Click the Tools menu, click Envelopes And Labels, and then click the Envelopes tab.

2. Type the recipient's name and address, or click the Address button to search for it.

3. Type your name and address.

4. Click Options, select a size, placement, bar code, and font, and then click OK.

5. Insert an envelope in your printer, and then click Print.

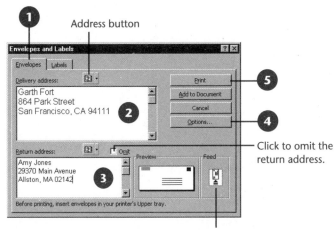

Address button

Click to omit the return address.

Shows direction to insert envelope in printer

Address and Print Mailing Labels

1. Click the Tools menu, click Envelopes And Labels, and then click the Labels tab.

2. Type the recipient's name and address.

3. Select which labels to print.

4. Click Options, select a type or size, and then click OK.

5. Insert labels in your printer, and then click Print.

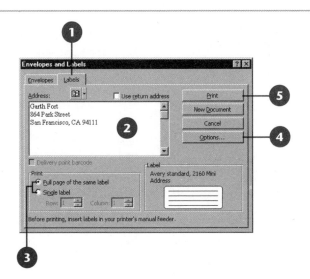

5

Creating Bookmarks

A *bookmark* is a location, text, table, or graphic that you select and name. Word places an electronic marker with the name you specify at your selection. Add a bookmark to items or paragraphs in a long document that you want to return to often and quickly. Bookmarks are more than placeholders; for example, you use them to create hyperlinks and cross-references.

SEE ALSO

See "Moving Around in a Document" on page 57 for information on using Go To as a way to move quickly to elements or items in your document.

Tag a Location with a Bookmark

1. Click where you want to insert a bookmark.

2. Click the Insert menu, and then click Bookmark.

3. Type a descriptive name (fewer than 40 characters).

4. Click Add.

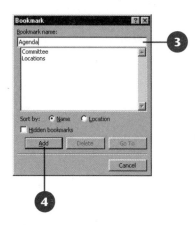

Go to a Bookmark Location

1. Click the Edit menu, and then click Go To.

2. Click Bookmark.

3. Click the Enter Bookmark Name drop-down arrow, and then click the bookmark you want to move to.

4. Click Go To.

5. If you want, choose another bookmark.

6. Click Close.

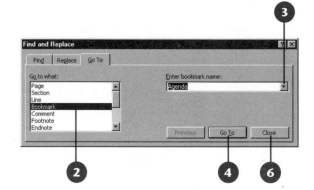

6

Enhancing a Document with Word 2000

Once you've mastered the basics, Microsoft Word 2000 has plenty of advanced features to enhance your documents. Whether it's a single-page flyer or a twenty-page report, you can arrange the text and add enhancements that make your document appealing and easy to read.

Enhancing Your Document

After you create your basic document, consider how you can improve its appearance and communicate its message more effectively. For example, if your document is a brochure or newsletter, arrange the text in columns and add an enlarged capital letter to the first word to convey expertise and quality. Or organize information in a table to draw attention to important data or clarify the details of a complicated paragraph.

Another way to impress clients, business associates, social groups, or even family members is to create personalized form letters for any occasion—an upcoming meeting, a holiday greeting, or a family announcement. Create a formatted document and enter the text that doesn't change. Any data that changes from person to person (such as names) goes into another file, which you merge with the form letter. In a snap, you've got personalized letters that show you care.

Creating Headers and Footers

Most books, including this one, use headers and footers to help you keep track of where you are. A *header* is text printed in the top margin of every page. *Footer* text is printed in the bottom margin. Commonly headers and footers contain your name, the document title, the filename, the print date, and page numbers. If you divide your document into sections, you can create different headers and footers for each section.

Create and Edit Headers and Footers

1 Click the View menu, and then click Header And Footer.

2 If necessary, click the Switch Between Header And Footer button on the Header And Footer toolbar to display the footer text area.

3 Click the header or footer box, and then type the text you want.

4 To insert common phrases, click the Insert AutoText button on the Header And Footer toolbar, and then click the text you want.

AutoText inserts the text you see along with the field that provides that information.

5 Edit and format header or footer text as usual.

6 When you're finished, click the Close button on the Header And Footer toolbar.

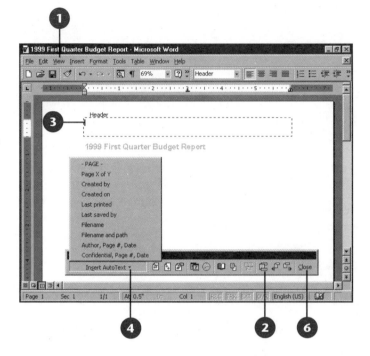

This header text is printed on every page.

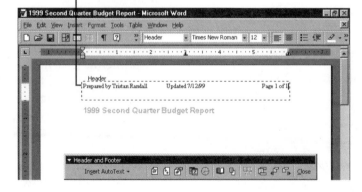

TIP

Use default tab stops to align header and footer text. *Headers and footers have two default tab stops. The first, in the middle, centers text. The second, on the far right, aligns text on the right margin. To left align text, don't press Tab. You can add and move the tab stops as needed.*

TIP

What are odd and even pages? *As in books, odd pages appear on the right and even pages appear on the left.*

TRY THIS

Add the filename to the footer. *If you include the filename in the footer of all your printouts, you can quickly locate their files. Click in the footer box, click the Insert AutoText button, and then click Filename And Path to insert that filename and location.*

SEE ALSO

See "Setting Margins" on page 60 for information about setting margins for headers and footers.

Create Different Headers and Footers for Different Pages

1. Click the View menu, and then click Header And Footer.

2. Click the Page Setup button on the Header And Footer toolbar.

3. Click the Layout tab.

4. To create different headers or footers for odd and even pages, click to select the Different Odd And Even check box.

   To create a unique header or footer for the document's first page, click to select the Different First Page check box.

5. Click OK.

6. Click the Show Previous and Show Next buttons to move from one header to the next; enter and format the text in the remaining headers and footers.

   To move between the header and footer, click the Switch Between Header And Footer button.

7. Click the Close button on the Header And Footer toolbar.

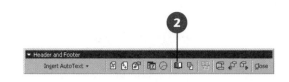

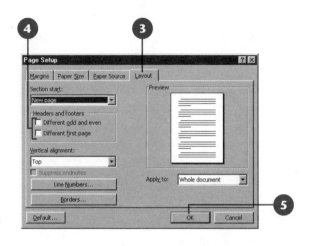

Click to insert the correct page number on each page.

Click to insert the current date from your computer's calendar.

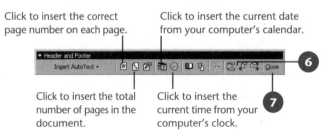

Click to insert the total number of pages in the document.

Click to insert the current time from your computer's clock.

Inserting Page Numbers and the Date and Time

Page numbers help you keep your document in order or find a topic from the table of contents. Number the entire document consecutively or each section independently; pick a numbering scheme, such as roman numerals or letters. The date and time field ensures you know which printout is the latest. Word uses your computer's internal calendar and clock as its source. You can insert the date and time for any installed language. Add page numbers and the date in a footer to conveniently keep track of your work.

SEE ALSO

See "Creating Headers and Footers" on page 90 for information on inserting headers and footers.

Insert Page Numbers

1. Click the Insert menu, and then click Page Numbers.

2. Click the Position drop-down arrow, and select a location.

3. Click the Alignment drop-down arrow, and then select the horizontal placement.

4. Click Format.

5. Click the Number Format drop-down arrow, and then select a numbering scheme.

6. Select the starting number.

7. Click OK.

8. Click OK.

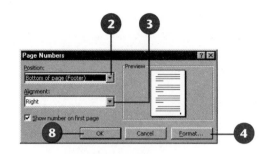

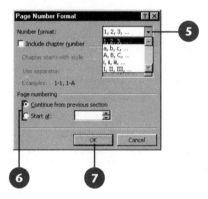

Insert the Date or Time

1. Click the Insert menu, and then click Date And Time.

2. If necessary, click the Language drop-down arrow, and then select a language.

3. Click to select the Update Automatically check box.

4. Double-click the date and time format you want.

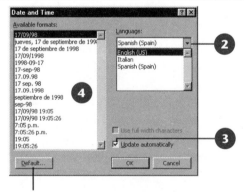

Sets the selected date as the default

Inserting Symbols and AutoText

Word comes with a host of symbols and special characters for every need. Insert just the right one to keep from compromising a document's professional appearance with a hand-drawn arrow («) or missing mathematical symbol (å). *AutoText* stores text and graphics you want to reuse, such as a company logo, boilerplate text, or formatted table. Use the AutoText entries that come with Word, or create your own.

TIP

Assign a shortcut key to insert a symbol. *Click the Insert menu, click Symbol, select a symbol, click Shortcut Key, and then enter the shortcut key information requested.*

TIP

Create your own AutoText. *Select the text or object for your AutoText entry, click the Insert menu, point to AutoText, click New, enter a name for the entry, and then click OK.*

Insert Symbols and Special Characters

1. Click the document where you want to insert a symbol or character.

2. Click the Insert menu, and then click Symbol.

3. Click the Symbols tab or the Special Characters tab.

4. To see other symbols, click the Font drop-down arrow, and then click a new font.

5. Click a symbol or character.

6. Click Insert.

7. Click Close.

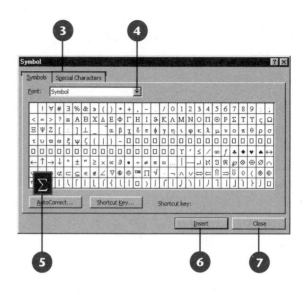

Insert AutoText

1. Click the document where you want to insert AutoText.

2. Click the Insert menu, and then point to AutoText.

3. Point to an AutoText category.

4. Click the AutoText entry you want.

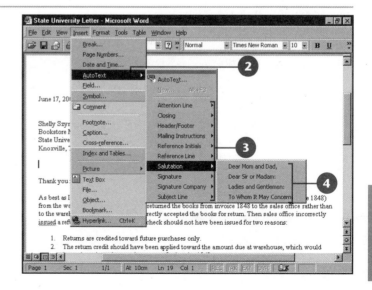

6

Adding Desktop Publishing Effects

A few simple elements—drop caps, borders, and shading—make your newsletters and brochures look like a design whiz produced them. A *drop cap* is the enlarged first letter of a paragraph. *Borders* are lines or graphics that appear around a page, paragraph, selected text, or table cells. *Shading* is a color that fills the background of selected text, paragraphs, or table cells. For more attractive pages, add clips or columns.

SEE ALSO

See "Arranging Text in Columns" on page 96 for information on changing text to columns.

Add a Dropped Capital Letter

1. Click the Print Layout View button.

2. Click the paragraph where you want the drop cap.

3. Click the Format menu, and then click Drop Cap.

4. Click a drop cap position.

5. Change the drop cap font.

6. Change the drop cap height.

7. Enter the distance between the drop cap and paragraph.

8. Click OK.

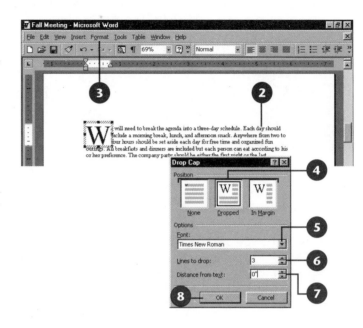

Add a Page Border

1. Click the Format menu, click Borders And Shading, and click the Page Border tab.

2. Click a box setting.

3. Click the Art drop-down arrow, and then select a line or art style.

4. Enter a border width.

5. Select the pages you want to have borders.

6. Click OK.

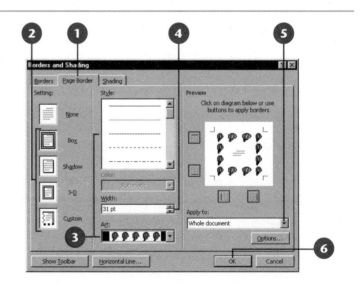

Insert a text box. *A text box is a graphic you can type in, as well as resize, move, and format. Click the Insert menu, click Text Box, drag to create the box, and then type and format text as usual.*

Add borders and shading to table cells. *You can add borders and shading to table cells the same way you add them to paragraphs. Select one or more cells you want to border and shade, and then click the appropriate buttons on the Tables And Borders toolbar.*

Change case. *You can quickly change any text you type into first-letter or first-word uppercase, all lowercase, all uppercase, or uppercase for the first letter of each word. Select the text, click the Format menu, click Change Case, select an option, and then click OK.*

Apply individual borders. *Use the Preview box to add a border to specific sides of your page, text box, or cell.*

Add Paragraph Borders and Shading

1 Select the text you want to shade or border.

2 Click the Tables And Borders button on the Standard toolbar.

3 If necessary, click the Draw Table button to deselect it.

4 Click the Line Style drop-down arrow, and then select a line pattern.

5 Click the Line Weight drop-down arrow, and then select a border thickness.

6 Click the Border Color drop-down arrow, and then select a color.

7 Click the Border drop-down arrow, and then select the border you want to add.

8 Click the Shading Color drop-down arrow, and then select the back-ground shading you want, if any.

9 When you're done, click the Close button on the Tables And Borders toolbar.

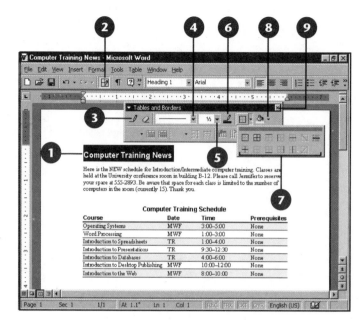

Arranging Text in Columns

Newspaper-style columns can give newsletters and brochures a more polished look. You can format an entire document, selected text, or individual sections into columns. If necessary, Word inserts a section break, and then balances the columns. To view the columns side-by-side, switch to print layout view.

Create Columns

1. Click the Print Layout View button.

2. Select the text you want to arrange in columns.

3. Click the Columns button on the Standard toolbar.

4. Drag to select the number of columns you want.

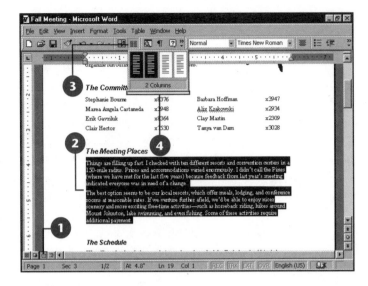

Modify Columns

1. Click the Print Layout View button, and then click in the columns you want to modify.

2. Click the Format menu, and then click Columns.

3. Click a column format.

4. If necessary, enter the number of columns you want.

5. Enter the width and spacing you want for each column.

6. Click OK.

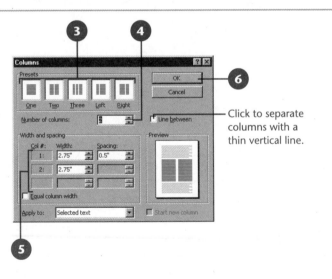

Click to separate columns with a thin vertical line.

Inserting a Table of Contents

A *table of contents* provides an outline of main topics and page locations. Word builds a table of contents based on the styles in a document that you choose. By default, Heading 1 is the first-level entry, Heading 2 the second level, and so on. In a printed table of contents, a *leader,* a line whose style you select, connects an entry to its page number. In Web documents, entries become hyperlinks. Hide nonprinting characters before creating a table of contents so text doesn't shift to other pages as you print.

TIP

Hyphenate your text.
Hyphenation prevents ugly gaps and short lines in text. Click the Tools menu, point to Language, click Hyphenation, click to select the Automatically Hyphenate Document check box, set the hyphenation zone and limit the number of consecutive hyphens (usually two), and then click OK.

Insert a Table of Contents

1. Click the Insert menu, and then click Index And Tables.

2. Click the Table Of Contents tab.

3. Select the Show Page Numbers and the Right Align Page Numbers check boxes.

4. Click the Tab Leader drop-down arrow, and select a leader style.

5. Click the Formats drop-down arrow and select a table of contents style.

6. Enter the number of heading levels you want.

7. Click Options.

8. Delete any numbers, and then type 1 next to the first-level style, 2 next to the second-level style, and so on.

9. Click OK.

10. Click OK.

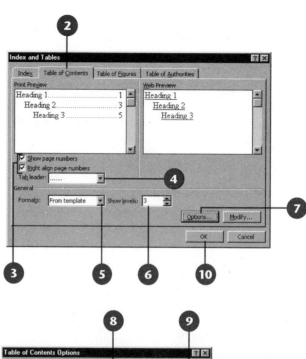

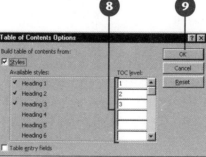

6

Creating a Table

A *table* organizes information neatly into rows and columns. The intersection of a row and column is called a *cell*. You can draw a custom table with various sized cells and then enter text, or you can create a table from existing text separated by paragraphs, tabs, or commas. In addition, now you can create *nested tables* (a table created within a table cell), *floating tables* (tables with text wrapped around them), or *side-by-side tables* (separate but adjacent tables). If you decide not to use a table, you can convert it to text.

Draw a Custom Table

1. Click the Tables And Borders button on the Standard toolbar.

2. Click the Draw Table button on the Tables And Borders toolbar to select it.

3. Draw the table.
   - ◆ A rectangle creates individual cells or the table boundaries.
   - ◆ Horizontal lines create rows.
   - ◆ Vertical lines create columns.
   - ◆ Diagonal lines split cells.

4. Press and hold Shift and click one or more lines to erase them.

Create a Table from Existing Text

1. Select the text for the table.

2. Click the Table menu, point to Convert, and then click Text To Table.

3. Enter the number of columns.

4. Select a column width.

5. Click a symbol to separate text into cells.

6. Click OK.

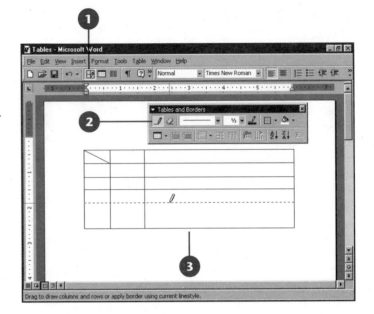

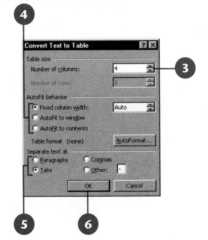

Entering Text in a Table

Once you create your table you enter text into cells just as you would in a paragraph, except pressing Tab moves you from cell to cell. The first row in the table is good for column headings, whereas the leftmost column is good for row labels. To enter text in cells, you must move around the table. Knowing how to select the rows and columns of a table is also essential to working with the table itself.

Enter Text and Move Around a Table

The insertion point shows where text you type will appear in a table. After you type text in a cell.

◆ Press Enter to start a new paragraph within that cell.

◆ Press Tab to move the insertion point to the next cell to the right (or to the first cell in the next row).

◆ Press the arrow keys or click in a cell to move the insertion point to a new location.

Press Tab to move to the first cell in the next row.

Press Tab to move to the next cell.

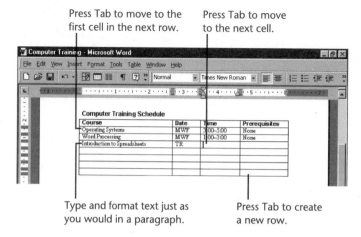

Type and format text just as you would in a paragraph.

Press Tab to create a new row.

Select Table Elements

Refer to this table for methods of selecting table elements, including:

◆ The entire table

◆ One or more rows and columns

◆ One or more cells

SELECTING TABLE ELEMENTS

To Select	Do This
The entire table	Click ⊞ next to the table or click anywhere in the table, click the Table menu, point to Select, and then click Table.
One or more rows	Click in the left margin next to the first row you want to select, and then drag to select the rows you want.
One or more columns	Click just above the first column you want to select, and then drag with ↓ to select the columns you want.
The column or row with the insertion point	Click the Table menu, point to Select, and then click Column or Row.
A single cell	Drag a cell or click the cell with ➚.
More than one cell	Drag with ➚ to select a group of cells.

6

Modifying a Table

As you begin to work on a table, you might need to modify its structure by adding more rows, columns, or cells to accommodate new text, graphics, or other tables. The table realigns as needed to accommodate the new structure. When you insert rows, columns, or cells, the existing rows shift down, the existing columns shift right, and you choose in what direction the existing cells shift. Similarly, when you delete unneeded rows, columns, or cells from a table, the table realigns itself.

Insert Additional Rows

1. Select the row above which you want the new rows to appear.

2. Drag to select the number of rows you want to insert.

3. Click the Insert Rows button on the Standard toolbar.

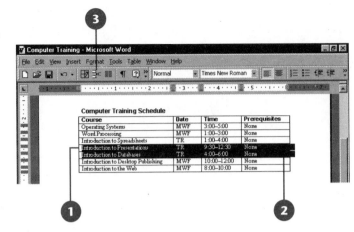

Insert Additional Columns

1. Select the column to the left of which you want the new columns to appear.

2. Drag to select the number of columns you want to insert.

3. Click the Insert Columns button on the Standard toolbar.

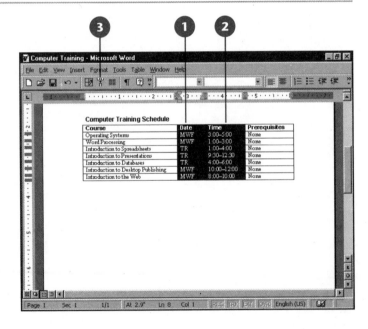

Move rows and columns.
You can reorder rows and columns as needed. Select the rows or columns you want to move, and then position the pointer over them until the pointer changes to a move pointer. Then drag the selected rows or columns to a new table position.

Distribute rows and columns evenly. *To make all the rows or columns the same height or width, click in the table, and then click the Distribute Rows Evenly or Distribute Columns Evenly button on the Tables And Borders toolbar.*

Set column widths to fit.
You can have Word set the column widths to fit the cells' contents or to fill the space between the document's margins. Click in the table, click the Insert Table button drop-down arrow on the Tables And Borders toolbar, and then click AutoFit To Contents or AutoFit To Window.

Insert Additional Cells

1. Select the cells where you want the new cells to appear.

2. Click the Table menu, point to Insert, and then click Cells.

3. Select the direction in which you want the existing cells to shift.

4. Click OK.

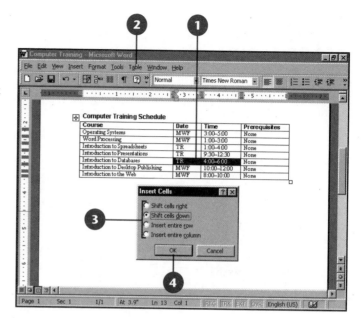

Delete Rows, Columns, or Cells

1. Select the rows, columns, or cells you want to delete.

2. Click the Table menu, point to Delete, and then click Columns, Rows, or Cells.

3. If necessary, select the direction in which you want the remaining cells to shift to fill the space, and then click OK.

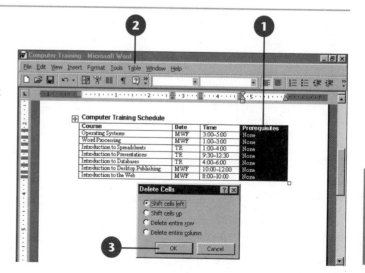

6

Adjusting Table Cells

Often there is more to modifying a table than adding or deleting rows or columns; you need to make cells just the right size to accommodate the text you are entering in the table. For example, a title in the first row of a table might be longer than the first cell in that row. To spread the title across the top of the table, you can *merge* (combine) the cells to form one long cell. Sometimes to indicate a division in a topic, you need to *split* (or divide) a cell into two. You can also split one table into two at any row. Moreover, you can modify the width of any column and height of any row to better present your data.

Merge and Split Table Cells and Tables

◆ To merge two or more cells into a single cell, select the cells you want to merge, click the Table menu, and then click Merge Cells.

◆ To split a cell into multiple cells, click the cell you want to split, click the Table menu, and then click Split Cells. Enter the number of rows or columns (or both) you want to split the selected cell into, deselect the Merge Cells Before Split check box, and then click OK.

◆ To split a table into two tables separated by a paragraph, click in the row that you want as the top row in the second table, click the Table menu, and then click Split Table.

◆ To merge two tables into one, delete the paragraph between them.

The four cells in this row will be combined into one.

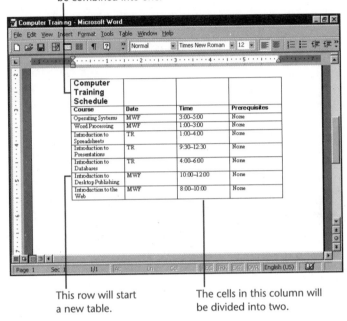

This row will start a new table.

The cells in this column will be divided into two.

Merged cells   Split cells

Computer Training Schedule			
Course	Date	Time	Prerequisites
Operating Systems	MWF	3:00–5:00	None
Word Processing	MWF	1:00–3:00	None
Introduction to Spreadsheets	TR	1:00–4:00	None
Introduction to Presentations	TR	9:30–12:30	None
Introduction to Databases	TR	4:00–6:00	None
Introduction to Desktop Publishing	MWF	10:00–12:00	None
Introduction to the Web	MWF	8:00–10:00	None

Split tables

Adjust Column Widths

1 Select the columns to change.

2 Click the Table menu, and then click Table Properties.

3 Click the Column tab.

4 To specify an exact width, click the Measure In drop-down arrow, and then click Inches.

5 Type an inch measurement.

6 Click OK.

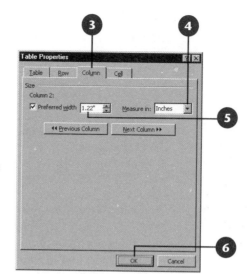

Adjust Row Heights

1 Select the rows to change.

2 Click the Table menu, and click Table Properties.

3 Click the Row tab.

4 Click the Row Height Is drop-down arrow, and then click Exactly or At Least.

5 Type an inch measurement.

6 Click OK.

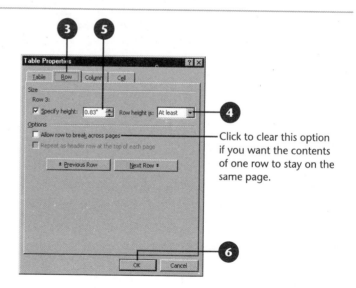

Click to clear this option if you want the contents of one row to stay on the same page.

6

Formatting a Table

Tables distinguish text from paragraphs. In turn, formatting, alignment, and text direction distinguish text in table cells. Start by applying one of Word's predesigned table formats. Then customize your table by realigning the cells' contents both horizontally and vertically in the cells, changing the direction of text within selected cells, such as the column headings, and resizing the entire table. You can also add borders and shading to make printed tables easier to read and more attractive.

TIP

Create nested tables. *You can move or copy a table from into a cell in another table. Select the table or cells to be nested, click the Edit menu, click Cut or Copy, right-click the table cell, and then click Paste As Nested Table on the Shortcut menu.*

Format a Table Automatically

1. Select the table you want to format.

2. Click the Table menu, and then click Table AutoFormat.

3. Click a format.

4. Preview the results.

5. When you find a format you like, click OK.

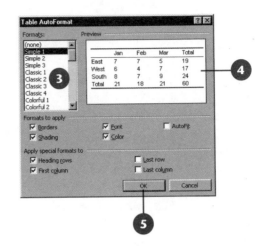

Align Text Within Cells

1. Click the Tables And Borders button on the Standard toolbar to display the Tables And Borders toolbar.

2. Select the cells, rows, or columns you want to align.

3. Click the Cell Alignment button drop-down arrow on the Tables And Borders Toolbar.

4. Click one of the nine alignment buttons.

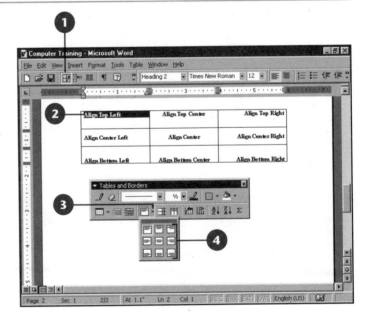

Change Text Direction Within Cells

1. Click the Tables And Borders button on the Standard toolbar to display the Tables And Borders toolbar.

2. Select the cells you want to change.

3. Click the Change Text Direction button on the Tables And Borders toolbar until the text is the direction you want.

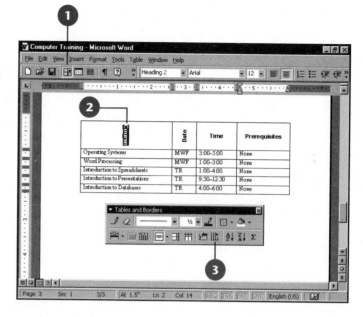

Resize the Entire Table Proportionally

1. Click to place the insertion point in the table.

2. Position the pointer over the table resize handle in the lower-right corner of the table.

3. Drag the resize handle until the table is the size you want.

Drag the table from here to move it to a new location.

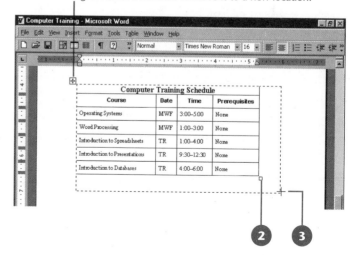

Creating a Form Letter

Did you ever send the same letter to several people and spend a lot of time changing personal information, such as names and addresses? If so, form letters will save you time. *Mail merge* is the process of combining names and addresses stored in a data file with a main document (usually a form letter) to produce customized documents. There are four main steps to merging. First, select the document you want to use. Second, create a data file with the variable information. Third, create the main document with the *boilerplate* (unchanging information) and merge fields. Finally, merge the two.

> ### TIP
>
> **Use existing data to create a form letter.** *You can select an existing data file instead of creating a new one. Click the Get Data button in the Mail Merge Helper dialog box, click Open Data Source, and then double-click the file.*

Select a Main Document

① Open a new or existing document you want to use as the main document.

② Click the Tools menu, and then click Mail Merge.

③ Click Create, and then select the type of document you want to create.

④ Click Active Window to make the current document the main document.

⑤ Verify the merge type and main document.

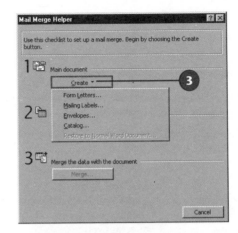

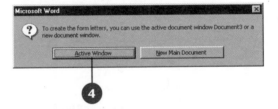

Create a New Data File

① If necessary, click the Tools menu, and then click Mail Merge to open the Mail Merge Helper dialog box.

② Click Get Data, and then click Create Data Source.

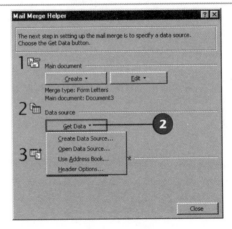

What are field names?

Information in a data file is stored in merge fields, *labeled with one-word names, such as FirstName, LastName, City, and so on. You insert merge field names in the main document as blanks, or placeholders, for variable information. When you merge the data file and main document, Word fills in the blanks with the correct information.*

Beware of those extra spaces.

Don't press the Spacebar after entering data in a field. Extra spaces will appear in the document between the data and the next word or punctuation, leaving ugly gaps or floating punctuation. Add spaces and punctuation to your main document instead.

Main document types.

In addition to form letters, you can create mailing labels, envelopes, and catalogs. Select these different document types as the main document and add boilerplate text and merge fields as usual.

3. To delete an unwanted field name, click it in the Field Names In Header Row list, and then click Remove Field Name.

4. To insert a new field name, type the field name in the Field Name box, and then click Add Field Name.

5. Click OK.

6. In the Save As dialog box, save the data file (which so far contains only field names) as you would any other document.

7. Click Edit Data Source to enter information into the data file.

8. Enter information for each field in the Data Form for one person or company record. Press Tab to move from one box to the next.

9. When you've typed all the data for one person or company, click Add New. Repeat step 8 for each record.

10. After you enter all the records you want, click OK.

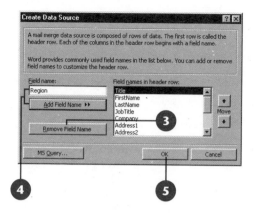

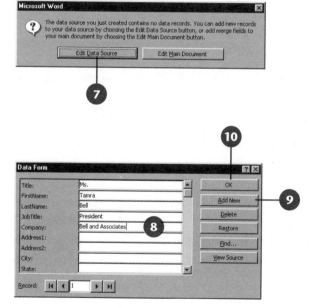

6

Merging a Form Letter with Data

Once you have selected a main document and created a data file, you insert the merge fields in the main document. The *merge fields* are those field names in the data source you created or selected for this merge. When you insert a merge field in the main document, make sure you insert the appropriate spacing and punctuation so the data merges correctly into the fields and document text.

Create the Main Document

1. If necessary, click the Tools menu, click Mail Merge, click Edit, and then click the name of your main document to display it and the Mail Merge toolbar.

2. Type and format the text you want to appear in every document, but leave the information that varies from letter to letter blank. (For example, type **Dear** :.)

3. Click the document where you want to insert a field name.

4. Click the Insert Merge Field button on the Mail Merge toolbar, and then click the field name.

5. When you're done, click the Save button on the Standard toolbar and save the document as usual.

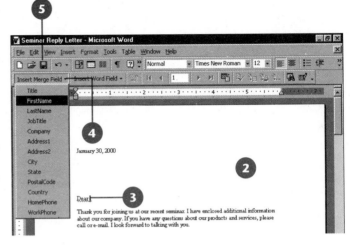

Field names inserted in the document. Word replaces these with names and addresses from the data file during the merge.

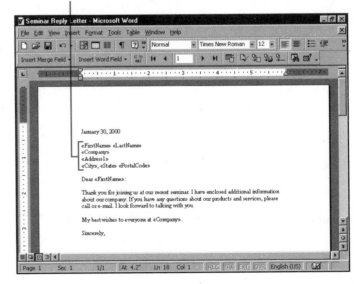

Check for errors before you start the mail merge. *Before you merge your form letter with your data file, click the Check For Errors button on the Mail Merge toolbar. Word checks the main document and the data file for errors that would prevent the merging.*

Send the merged documents directly to the printer. *If you don't want or need to create a new document with the merge data, you can send the merged documents directly to the printer by clicking the Merge To Printer button on the Mail Merge toolbar.*

Keep in touch. *Write a letter to friends and family catching them up on your life. Use fields for the variable information, such as names. Then merge the letter with a data file of the personal information.*

Merge the Main Document and Data File

1 Make sure the main document with field names inserted and the Mail Merge toolbar appear.

2 Click the Merge To New Document button on the Mail Merge toolbar.

Each letter is separated by a hard page break. For example, if you merged a one-page letter with ten records in data file, the merged document would contain ten pages.

3 Save and print the new document as usual.

4 Close the new document.

5 Close the main document.

6 Click Yes if you are asked to save changes to the data file or the main document.

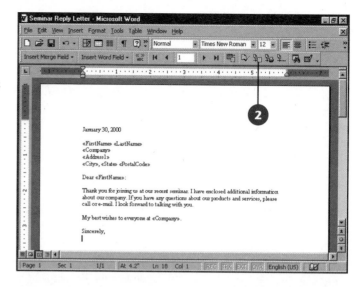

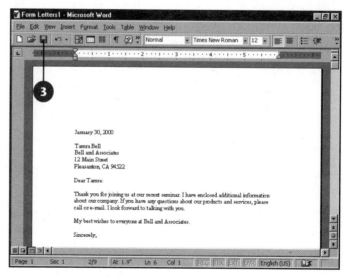

6

Tracking Changes

When you or others in your workgroup edit a document, track the changes so you can review every suggested text or formatting edit. You can review a document at any point to see what changes have been made and who made them.

> **TIP**
>
> **Select tracked changes options.** *Click the Tools menu, click Options, click the Track Changes tab, select the Mark and Color settings you want to use, and then click OK.*

> **TIP**
>
> **View tracked changes on screen or paper.** *Click the Tools menu, point to Track Changes, click Highlight Changes, then choose to see tracked changes on-screen, in the printed document or both, and then click OK.*

> **TIP**
>
> **Protect a document from changes.** *Click the Tools menu, click Protect Documents, select the protect options you want, enter a password, and then click OK.*

Track Changes

1 Right-click any toolbar, and then click Reviewing to display the toolbar.

2 Click the Save Version button on the Reviewing toolbar, and then click OK to save an unedited copy of the document.

3 Click the Track Changes button on the Reviewing toolbar.

4 Edit the text and formatting as usual.

Inserted text is underlined. Deleted text is crossed out.

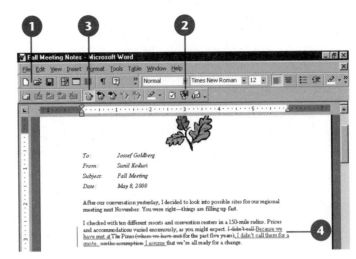

Review Tracked Changes

1 Right-click any toolbar, and then click Reviewing to display the toolbar.

2 Click the Previous Change or Next Change button on the Reviewing toolbar to select the next change.

3 Click the Accept Change button to leave the new text or formatting or click the Reject Change to return the original text or formatting.

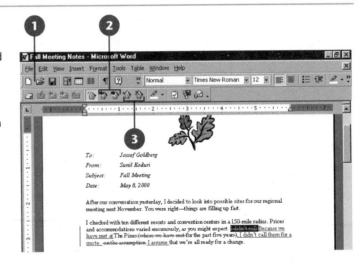

7

Creating a Worksheet with Excel 2000

Are you spending too much time number-crunching, rewriting financial reports, drawing charts, or searching for your calculator? Throw away your pencil, graph paper, and calculator, and start using Microsoft Excel 2000.

Calculating Quickly with Excel

Excel is a *spreadsheet program,* designed to help you record, analyze, and present quantitative information. With Excel you can track and analyze sales, organize finances, create budgets, and accomplish a variety of business tasks in a fraction of the time it would take using pen and paper. With Excel, you can create a variety of documents for analysis and record keeping, such as:

◆ Monthly sales and expense reports

◆ Charts displaying annual sales data

◆ An inventory of products

◆ A payment schedule for an equipment purchase

The file you create and save in Excel is called a *workbook.* It contains a collection of *worksheets,* which look similar to an accountant's ledger sheets, but can perform calculations and other tasks automatically.

Viewing the Excel Window

Title bar
The title bar contains the name of the active workbook. *Book1* is a temporary name Excel uses until you assign a new one.

Formula bar
The formula bar displays any data (labels, values, or formulas) contained in the active cell.

Menu bar
The nine menus give you access to all Excel commands.

Name box
The address of the currently selected (or active) cell appears here.

Active cell
The *active cell* is the currently selected cell into which you enter data.

Status bar
The status bar displays information about selected commands or procedures.

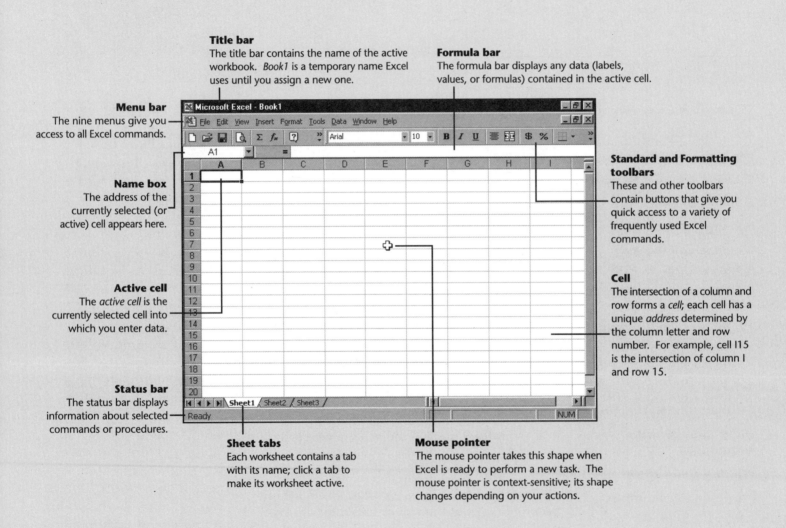

Standard and Formatting toolbars
These and other toolbars contain buttons that give you quick access to a variety of frequently used Excel commands.

Cell
The intersection of a column and row forms a *cell*; each cell has a unique *address* determined by the column letter and row number. For example, cell I15 is the intersection of column I and row 15.

Sheet tabs
Each worksheet contains a tab with its name; click a tab to make its worksheet active.

Mouse pointer
The mouse pointer takes this shape when Excel is ready to perform a new task. The mouse pointer is context-sensitive; its shape changes depending on your actions.

Selecting Cells

A *cell* is the intersection of a column and row. You must select a cell and make it *active* to work with it. A *range* is one or more selected cells that you can edit, delete, format, print, or use in a formula just like a single cell. The active cell has a dark border; selected cells have a light shading called a *see-through selection*. A range can be *contiguous* (all selected cells are adjacent) or *noncontiguous* (selected cells are not all adjacent). A *range reference* lists the upper-left cell address, a colon (:), and the lower-right cell address. Commas separate noncontiguous cells. For example, B4:D10,E7,L24.

> **TIP**
>
> **Deselect a range.** *Click anywhere on the worksheet.*

Select a Cell

1. Click a cell to select it.

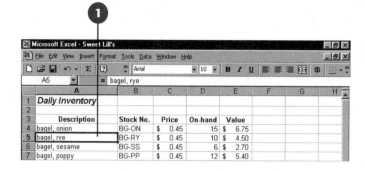

Select a Range

1. Click the first cell you want to include in the range.

2. Drag to the last cell you want to include the range. The upper-left cell of a selected range is active and the others are highlighted.

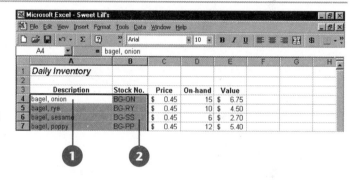

Select a Noncontiguous Range

1. Click the first cell or select the first contiguous range you want to include.

2. Press and hold Ctrl while you click additional cells and select other ranges.

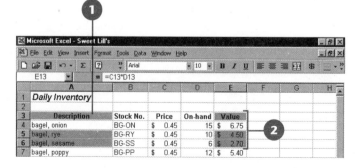

Working with Worksheets

Each new workbook opens with three *worksheets* (or *sheets*), in which you store and analyze values. You work in the *active*, or selected, worksheet. The default worksheet names are Sheet1, Sheet2, and Sheet3, which appear on the *sheet tab*, like file folder labels. As you create a worksheet, give it a meaningful name to help you remember its contents. The sheet tab size adjusts to fit the name's length. If you work on a project that requires more than three worksheets, add additional sheets to the workbook so all related information is stored in one file.

TIP

Move between cells. *Press Tab to move to the cell to right of the active cell. Press Enter to move to the cell below the active cell. Press the arrow keys to move to the next cell in the corresponding arrow key direction.*

Select a Worksheet

1 If necessary, click a sheet tab scroll button to display other tabs.

2 Click a sheet tab to make it the active worksheet.

3 To select multiple worksheets, press and hold Ctrl as you click other sheet tabs.

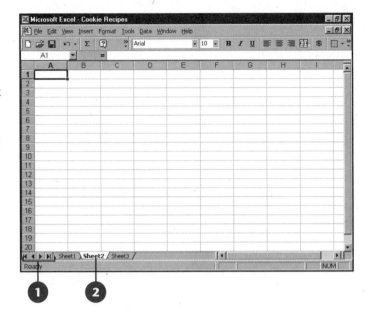

Name a Worksheet

1 Double-click the sheet tab you want to name.

2 Type a new name.

The current name, which is selected, is replaced when you begin typing.

3 Press Enter.

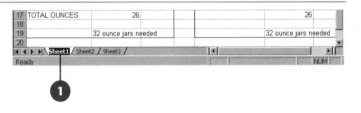

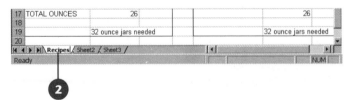

Insert a Worksheet

1. Click the sheet tab to the right of where you want to insert the new sheet.

2. Click the Insert menu, and then click Worksheet.

   A new worksheet is inserted to the left of the selected worksheet.

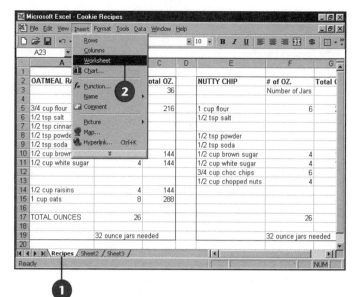

Delete a Worksheet

1. Click the sheet tab of the worksheet you want to delete.

2. Click the Edit menu, and then click Delete Sheet.

3. Click OK to confirm the deletion.

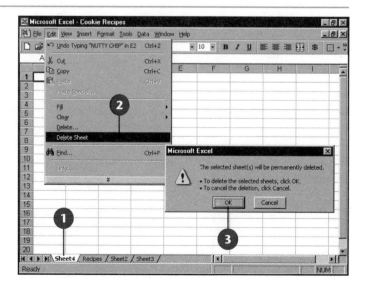

Entering Text and Numbers

Labels turn a worksheet full of numbers into a meaningful report by clarifying the relationship between the numbers. *Labels* are text or numbers that identify the data on the worksheet columns and rows; for example *Item* or *3-27-2000*. An apostrophe (') before the number label, such as the year 2000, prevents Excel from using that number in any calculations. The *PickList*, a list of labels you entered previously, helps keep your labels consistent. *Values* are the numbers you want to use in calculations. You can enter values as whole numbers, decimals, or dates.

> **TIP**
>
> **Different ways to accept an entry.** *Clicking the Enter button on the formula bar leaves the insertion point in the active cell; pressing Enter on the keyboard moves the insertion point down one cell.*

Enter a Text Label

1 Click the cell where you want to enter a text label.

2 Type a label.

A label can include uppercase and lowercase letters, spaces, punctuation, and numbers.

3 Click the Enter button on the formula bar, or press Enter.

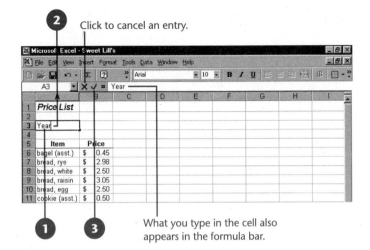

Click to cancel an entry.

What you type in the cell also appears in the formula bar.

Enter a Number as a Label

1 Click the cell where you want to enter a number label.

2 Type ' (apostrophe).

The apostrophe is a *label prefix* and does not appear on the worksheet.

3 Type a number.

Examples of number labels include a year, social security number, or telephone number.

4 Click the Enter button on the formula bar, or press Enter or Tab.

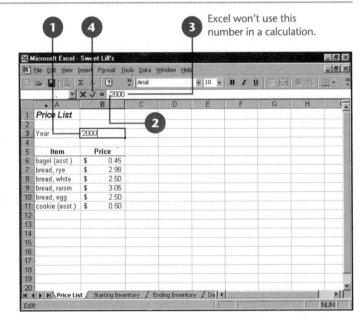

Excel won't use this number in a calculation.

7

Enter labels quickly with AutoComplete. *Type the first few characters of a label. If a previous entry in that column begins with the same characters, AutoComplete displays the entry. Press Enter or click the Enter button on the formula bar to accept the entry. Resume typing to ignore the AutoComplete suggestion.*

Enable AutoComplete for cell values. *Click the Tools menu, click Options, click the Edit tab, click to select the Enable AutoComplete For Cell Values check box, and then click OK.*

Long labels might appear truncated. *When you enter a label wider than the cell it occupies, the excess text appears to spill into the next cell to the right—unless there is data in the adjacent cell. If the adjacent cell contains data, the label appears* truncated—*you see only the portion of the label that fits in the cell's current width.*

Enter a Label from the PickList

1. Right-click the cell where you want to enter a label, and then click Pick From List.

2. Click an entry from the list.

Enter a Value

1. Click the cell where you want to enter a value.

2. Type a value.

   To simplify your data entry, type the values without commas and dollar signs and apply a numeric format to them later.

3. Press Enter or click the Enter button on the formula bar.

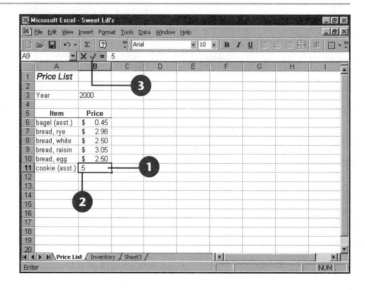

Editing Cell Contents

No matter how much you plan, you can count on having to make changes on a worksheet. Sometimes you'll need to correct an error; other times you'll want to add new information or see the results for different conditions, such as higher sales, fewer produced units, or other variables. You edit data just as easily as you enter it, using the formula bar or directly in the active cell.

TIP

Clear cell contents, formats, or both. *You can erase the contents or format of a cell. Select the cell, click the Edit menu, point to Clear, and then click Contents, Formats, or All (for both).*

TIP

Change editing options. *Click the Tools menu, click Options, click the Edit tab, and then change the editing options you want.*

Edit Cell Content

1 Double-click the cell you want to edit.

The status bar displays Edit instead of Ready.

2 Use the mouse pointer or the Home, End, and arrow keys to position the insertion point in the cell.

3 To erase characters, press Backspace or Delete.

4 To enter characters, type new characters.

5 Press Enter or click the Enter button on the formula bar to accept the edit, or click the Cancel button on the formula bar to cancel it.

Click to edit the cell content in the formula bar.

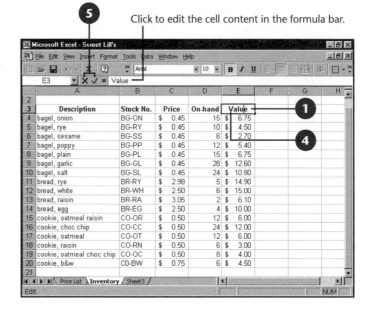

Naming Cells and Ranges

To make working with ranges easier, Excel allows you to name them. The name *Sales*, for example, is easier to remember than the coordinates B4:D10. You can use named ranges in formulas the same way you use cell references and range addresses. Named ranges can be used to navigate large worksheets.

TIP

Delete a named range. *If you want to delete unneeded named ranges, click the Insert menu, point to Name, click Define, click the name you want to delete, click Delete, and then click OK.*

TIP

Cell and range names are absolute addresses. *Unlike label ranges, which are relative, cell and range names are absolute.*

Name a Cell or Range

1. Select the cell or range you want to name.

2. Click the Name box on the formula bar.

3. Type a name for the range.

   A range name can include uppercase or lowercase letters, numbers, and punctuation. Try to use a simple name that reflects the information in the range, such as *Sales2000*.

4. Press Enter. The Name box shows the name whenever you select the range.

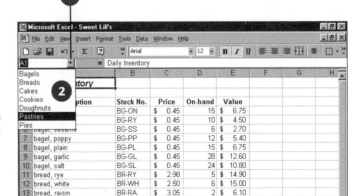

Select a Named Cell or Range

1. Click the Name box drop-down arrow on the formula bar.

2. Click the name of the cell or range you want to use.

   The range name appears in the Name box, and all cells included in the range are highlighted on the worksheet.

Inserting and Deleting Cells

You can insert new, blank cells anywhere on the worksheet, so you can enter new data exactly where you want it. Inserting cells moves the remaining cells in the column or row to the right or down as you choose and adjusts any formulas so they refer to the correct cells. You can also delete cells if you find you don't need them; deleting cells shifts the remaining cells to the left or up—just the opposite of inserting cells.

TIP

Deleting a cell vs. clearing a cell. Deleting *a cell removes the actual cell from the worksheet,* whereas clearing *a cell erases only the cell contents or format or both.*

SEE ALSO

See "Editing Cell Contents" on page 118 for information on clearing cell contents.

Insert One or More Cells

1. Select one or more cells where you want to insert new cell(s).

2. Click the Insert menu, and then click Cells.

3. To move the contents of the cells right, click the Shift Cells Right option button; to move the contents of the cells down, click the Shift Cells Down option button. Either way, two blank cells are inserted.

4. Click OK.

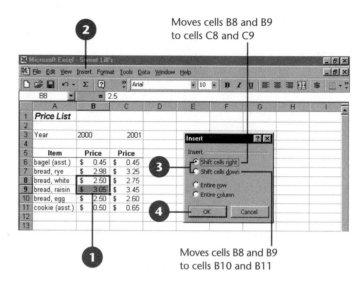

Moves cells B8 and B9 to cells C8 and C9

Moves cells B8 and B9 to cells B10 and B11

Delete One or More Cells

1. Select one or more cells you want to delete.

2. Click the Edit menu, and then click Delete.

3. To move the remaining cells left, click the Shift Cells Left option button; to move the remaining cells up, click the Shift Cells Up option button.

4. Click OK.

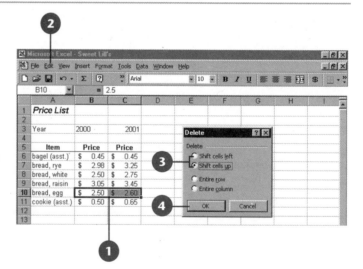

Inserting and Deleting Columns or Rows

You can insert one or more blank columns and rows on a worksheet between columns or rows that are already filled. The *header buttons* above each column and to the left of each row indicate the letter or number of the column or row. Inserted columns are added to the left of the selected columns. Inserted rows are added above the selected rows. Excel repositions existing cells to accommodate the new columns and rows and adjusts any existing formulas so that they refer to the correct cells.

Insert One or More Columns or Rows

1. To insert a column, click the column header button directly to the right of where you want to insert the new column.

    To insert a row, click the row header button directly below where you want to insert the new row.

2. To insert multiple columns or rows, drag to select the header buttons for the number of columns or rows you want to insert.

3. Click the Insert menu, and then click Columns or Rows.

Row header button   Column header button

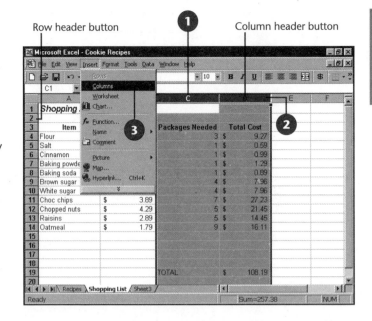

Delete One or More Columns or Rows

1. Select the columns or rows you want to delete.

2. Click the Edit menu, and then click Delete.

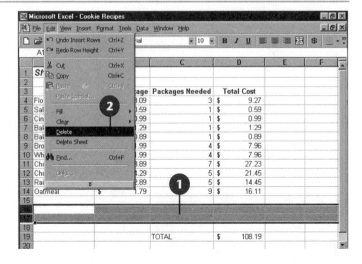

Adjusting Column Width and Row Height

You've entered labels and values, constructed formulas, and even formatted the cells. Only now some of your data isn't visible. You know it's there, but you just can't see it. Also, some larger sized labels are cut off. Narrow or widen each column width to fit its contents and adjust row heights as needed.

TIP

What is a point? *A point is a measurement unit used to size text and space on a worksheet. One inch equals 72 points. Apply different point sizes to your column width, row height, and text to determine which size is best for your worksheet.*

TIP

Adjust columns to fit. *Double-click the right border of a column header button to match the column width to the longest entry.*

Adjust Column Width or Row Height

1. Click the column or row header button for the first column or row you want to adjust.

2. If you want, drag to select more columns or rows.

3. Right-click the selected column(s) or row(s), and then click Column Width or Row Height.

4. Type a new column width or row height in points.

5. Click OK.

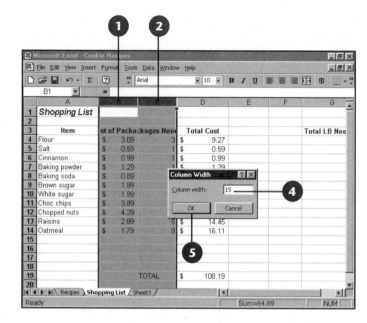

Adjust Column Width or Row Height Using the Mouse

1. Position the mouse pointer on the right edge of the column header button or the bottom edge of the row header button for the column or row you want to change.

2. When the mouse pointer changes to a double-headed arrow, click and drag the pointer to a new width or height.

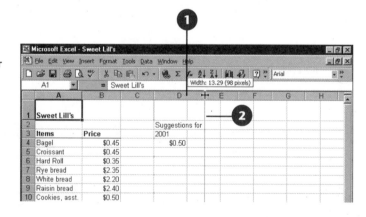

Freezing Columns and Rows

Once you've finished creating the worksheet structure—labels and formulas—you're ready to enter data. The first six columns and twelve rows or so are just fine, but as you scroll to enter data in later columns or rows, the labels shift out of view. Instead of memorizing the labels, freeze the label columns and rows, so they remain visible as you scroll through the rest of the worksheet. You can freeze just a row or a column as well.

Freeze Columns and Rows

1. Click the cell that intersects the rows and columns you want to remain visible on screen.

2. Click the Window menu, and then click Freeze Panes.

3. Edit and scroll the worksheet as usual.

Black lines indicate the edge of the frozen panes.

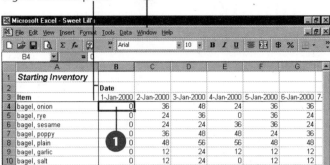

Unfreeze Columns and Rows

1. Click the worksheet that you want to unfreeze.

2. Click the Windows menu, and then click Unfreeze Panes.

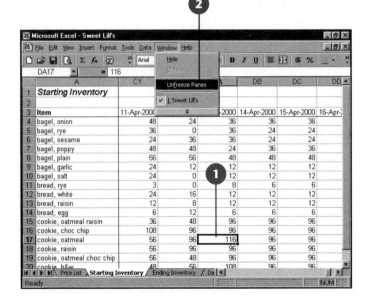

Creating a Formula

Instead of manually adding, subtracting, multiplying, or dividing, use formulas. A *formula* is an equation that analyzes values to return a result. All formulas begin with the equal sign (=) followed by *arguments*—values (such as 7.2) and cell references—connected by arithmetic operators (shown in the table). You enter and edit formulas just as you do labels and values—in the formula bar or in the cell. After you create a formula, you can quickly copy it to adjacent cells using AutoFill. Excel displays the formulas' results in cells, but you can change the view at any time to display the formulas themselves.

TIP

Select a cell to enter its address. *To avoid careless typing mistakes, click a cell to insert its cell reference in a formula rather than typing its address.*

Enter a Formula

1. Click a cell where you want to enter a formula.

2. Type an equal sign (=) to begin the formula. If you do not begin a formula with an equal sign, Excel displays the information you type; it does not perform the calculation.

3. Enter the first argument (a number or a cell reference). If the argument is a cell reference, type the cell reference or click the cell.

   If the formula can accept cell references, the cursor changes to a light gray cell-like shape to encourage you to select the cell on the worksheet.

4. Enter an arithmetic operator.

5. Enter the next argument.

6. Repeat steps 4 and 5 to complete the formula.

7. Click the Enter button on the formula bar, or press Enter.

   The cell displays the formula result, and the formula bar displays the formula.

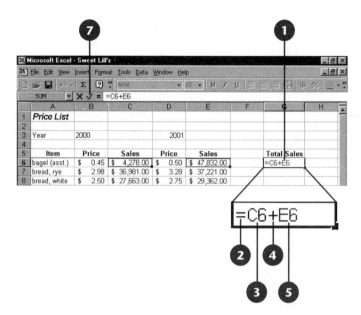

ARITHMETIC OPERATORS		
Symbol	**Operation**	**Example**
+	Addition	=E3+F3
−	Subtraction	=E3–F3
*	Multiplication	=E3*F3
/	Division	=E3/F3

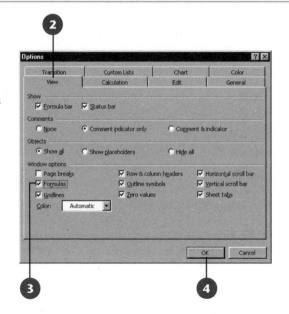

TIP

Use the order of precedence to create correct formulas. *Formulas containing more than one operator follow the order of precedence: exponentiation, multiplication and division, and then addition and subtraction. So, in the formula 5 + 2 * 3, Excel performs multiplication first and addition next for a result of 11. Excel calculates operations within parentheses first. The result of the formula (5 + 2) * 3 is 21.*

TIP

Copy a formula to a nonadjacent cell. *Select the cell whose formula you want to copy, click the Copy button on the Standard toolbar, select the cell where you want to paste the formula, and then click the Paste button on the Standard toolbar (or the icon on the Clipboard toolbar).*

TIP

Use Paste Special to copy only formulas. *Select the cells containing the formulas you want to copy, click where you want to paste the data, click the Edit menu, click Paste Special, click the Formulas option button, and then click OK.*

Copy a Formula Using AutoFill

1 Select the cell that contains the formula you want to copy.

2 Point to the fill handle in the lower-right corner of the selected cell (the pointer changes to a black plus sign).

3 Drag to select the adjacent cells where you want to paste the formula.

Display Formulas

1 Click the Tools menu, and then click Options.

2 Click the View tab.

3 Click to select the Formulas check box.

4 Click OK.

Simplifying a Formula with Ranges

Simplify your formulas by using ranges and range names. If 12 cells on your worksheet contain monthly budget amounts, and you want to multiply each amount by 10 percent, you can insert one range address in a formula instead of inserting 12 different cell addresses, or you can insert a range name. Using a range name in a formula helps to identify what the formula does; the formula =SALES2000*.10, for example, is more meaningful than =D7:O7*.10.

TIP

Guidelines for range names. *The first character must be a letter or underscore. The remaining characters can be letters, numbers, periods, or underscores, but not spaces. Although you can use uppercase and lowercase letters in names, Excel considers SALES, Sales, and sales the same name.*

Use a Range in a Formula

1. Type an equal sign (=) to begin the formula, and type the first part of the formula if necessary.

2. Click the first cell of the range and drag to the last cell in the range, or press and hold Ctrl as you click each cell in the range.

3. Complete the formula, and then press Enter.

Use a Range Name in a Formula

1. Type an equal sign (=) to begin the formula, and type the first part of the formula if necessary.

2. Press F3 to display a list of named ranges.

3. Click the name of the range you want to insert.

4. Click OK.

5. Complete the formula, and then press Enter.

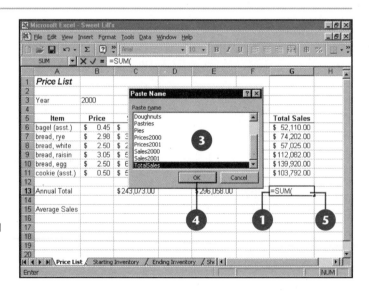

Understanding Relative and Absolute Cell References

7

Each cell, the intersection of a column and row on a worksheet, has a unique address, or *cell reference,* based on its column letter and row number. For example, the cell reference for the intersection of column D and row 4 is D4.

Cell References in Formulas

Excel's power lies in calculating data on a worksheet. To give you the most flexibility in analyzing your data, a formula combines arithmetic operators (+, −, /, *, ^) with values and cell references.

The simplest formula refers to a cell. If you want one cell to contain the same value as another cell, type an equal sign followed by the cell reference, such as =D4. The cell that contains the formula is known as a *dependent cell* because its value depends on the value in another cell. Whenever the cell that the formula refers to changes, the cell that contains the formula also changes. The formula =D4*7 multiplies the value in cell D4 by 7. The formula is recalculated whenever the value in cell D4 changes.

Depending on your task, you can use either *relative cell references*, which are references to cells relative to the position of the formula, or *absolute references*, which are cell references that always refer to cells in a specific location.

Relative Cell References

Using a relative cell reference is like giving a friend directions from their door to a specific destination: Go out your door, walk downhill three blocks, turn left, and then walk two blocks. Similarly, the cell with the formula is the door, or starting point. The relative cell reference specifies the directions to locate the value. For example, the formula =D4 in cell E5 tells Excel to go up one cell and left one cell from cell E5.

When you copy and paste a formula that uses relative references, the references in the pasted formula change to reflect cells that are in the same relative position to the formula. For example, if you copy the formula =D4 from cell E5 to cell F7, the pasted formula becomes =E6, which, like the original formula, refers to the cell that is one cell above and to the left of the formula.

Absolute Cell References

If you don't want a cell reference to change when you copy a formula, make it an absolute reference by typing a dollar sign ($) before each part of the reference that you don't want to change. For example, the formula =D4 changes as you copy it from cell to cell, but the formula =D4 always references the same cell. You can add a $ before the column letter, the row number, or both. To ensure accuracy and simplify updates, enter constant values (such as tax rates, hourly rates, and so on) in a cell, and then use absolute references to them in formulas.

Calculating with Functions

Functions are preset formulas that save you the time and trouble of creating commonly used equations. Excel includes hundreds of functions that you can use alone or with other formulas or functions. Functions perform a variety of tasks from adding, averaging, and counting to more complex tasks, such as calculating monthly loan payments.

TIP

Enter a function with the Paste Function. *Select the cell where you want to enter a function, click the Paste Function button on the Standard toolbar, click a function category, click a function, click OK, select cell references, and then click OK.*

TIP

Calculate totals with AutoSum. *Click the cell you want to display the AutoSum calculation, click the AutoSum button on the Standard toolbar, and then press Enter.*

Enter a Function

1 Click the cell where you want to enter the function.

2 Type an equal sign (=), type the name of the function, and then type (, an opening parenthesis. For example, to insert the AVERAGE function, type **=AVERAGE(**.

3 Type the argument or click the cell or range you want to insert in the function.

4 Click the Enter button on the formula bar, or press Enter. Excel adds the closing parenthesis to complete the function.

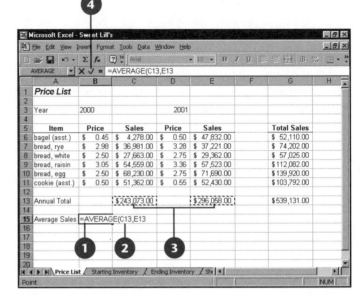

COMMONLY USED EXCEL FUNCTIONS		
Function	**Description**	**Sample**
SUM	Calculates the sum of the argument	=SUM(*argument*)
AVERAGE	Calculates the average value of the argument	=AVERAGE(*argument*)
COUNT	Calculates the number of values in the argument	=COUNT(*argument*)
MAX	Displays the largest value in the argument	=MAX(*argument*)
MIN	Displays the smallest value in the argument	=MIN(*argument*)
PMT	Determines the monthly payment in a loan	=PMT(*argument*)

Using AutoCalculate and AutoFill

Sometimes you want to see the results of a calculation but don't want to add a formula to the worksheet. *AutoCalculate* displays in the status bar the sum, average, maximum, minimum, or count of selected cells. This result doesn't print, but provides quick answers while you work. Another shortcut is *AutoFill*, which enters data based on the adjacent cells. Use the fill handle to extend data in series (such as dates), and copy values or formulas to adjacent cells. When you enter new data to a list, Excel applies the same formulas and formatting data as in the preceding cell.

Calculate a Range Automatically

1. Select the range (contiguous or noncontiguous). The sum of the selected cells appears in the status bar.

2. To change the type of calculation, right-click the AutoCalculate button in the status bar.

3. Click the type of calculation you want.

Fill In Data or Formulas Automatically

1. Select the first cell in the range you want to fill, enter the starting value for a series or a formula to copy, and then press Enter.

2. Right-click as you drag the fill handle of the selected cell (the pointer changes to a black plus sign) over the range.

3. Release the mouse button, and then click the type of series you want.

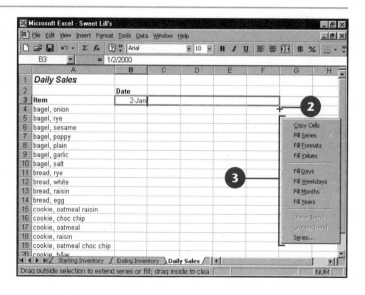

Printing a Worksheet

At some point you'll want to print your work so you can distribute it to others or use it for other purposes. You can print all or part—a print area—of any worksheet and control the page appearance. You can determine whether to print the gridlines, column letters, and row numbers that appear on the screen, or whether to repeat certain columns and rows on each page.

> **TIP**
>
> **Clear a print area.** *Click the File menu, point to Print Area, and then click Clear Print Area.*

> **TIP**
>
> **Preview before you print.** *You can preview what will print on paper. Click the Print Preview button on the Standard toolbar. To magnify a page, click Zoom. To preview the next page, click Next. To change the margins, click Margins and drag a dotted line. When you're done, click Close on the toolbar.*
>
>

Specify a Print Area

1. Select the range you want to print.

2. Click the File menu, point to Print Area, and then click Set Print Area.

   A dotted line indicates the area you set.

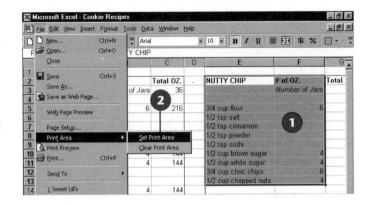

Print a Worksheet

1. Click the File menu, and then click Print.

2. If necessary, click the Name drop-down arrow, and then click the printer you want to use.

3. Select whether you want to print the entire document or only the pages you specify.

4. Select whether you want to print the selected text or objects, the selected worksheets, or all the worksheets in the workbook with data.

5. Click OK.

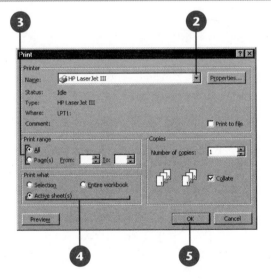

Print Row and Column Titles

1. Click the File menu, and click Page Setup.

2. Click the Sheet tab.

3. Enter the row numbers and column letters that you want to contain the titles, or click the appropriate Collapse Dialog Box button, select the title rows or columns, and then click the Expand Dialog Box button.

4. Click OK.

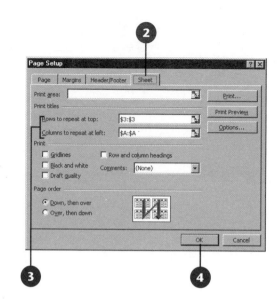

Add and Print Headers or Footers

1. Click the File menu, click Page Setup, and then click the Header/Footer tab.

2. Click Custom Header or Custom Footer.

3. Enter text, or insert the page number, date, time, filename, or tab name in the Left Center, or Right section.

4. Click OK.

5. Click OK or Print.

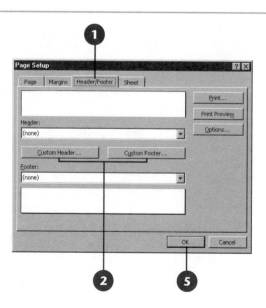

Previewing Page Breaks

If you want to print a worksheet that is larger than one page, Excel divides it into pages by inserting *automatic page breaks*. These page breaks are based on paper size, margin settings, and scaling options you set. You can change which rows or columns are printed on the page by inserting *horizontal* or *vertical page breaks*. In page break preview, you can view the page breaks and move them by dragging them to a different location on the worksheet.

TIP

Remove a page break.
Select the column or row next to the page break, click the Insert menu, and then click Remove Page Break.

Insert a Page Break

① To insert a horizontal page break, click the column header button to the right of where you want to insert a page break.

To insert a vertical page break, click the row header button below where you want to insert a page break.

To start a new page, click the cell below and to the right of where you want a new page.

② Click the Insert menu and then click Page Break.

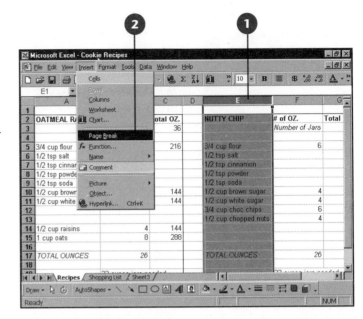

Preview and Move a Page Break

① Click the View menu, and click Page Break Preview.

Page breaks appear as a thick blue line.

② Drag a page break to a new location.

③ When you're done, click the View menu, and then click Normal.

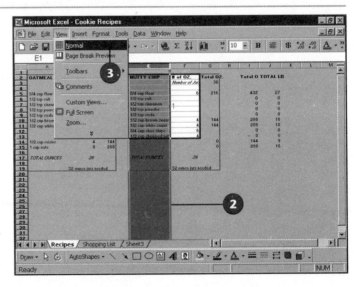

8

Designing a Worksheet with Excel 2000

In addition to using a worksheet to calculate values, you can also use it to manage a list of information, sometimes called a *database*. You can use an Microsoft Excel 2000 worksheet to keep an inventory list, a school grade book, or a customer database. Excel provides a variety of tools that make it easy to keep lists up-to-date and analyze them to get the information you want quickly. For example, you can use these tools to find out how many inventory items are out of stock, which students are earning an A average, or which product is the best-selling item.

Analyzing Worksheet Data

Excel's data analysis tools include alphanumeric organizing (called *sorting*), displaying information that meets specific criteria (called *filtering*), and summarizing data within a table (called a *PivotTable*) and chart (called a *PivotChart*). You can analyze data directly on a worksheet, or use a feature called a *Data Form*, an on-screen data entry tool similar to a paper form. A Data Form lets you quickly enter data by filling in blank text boxes, and then it adds the information to your database, also called a *list*. This tool makes entering information in a lengthy list a snap!

Formatting Text and Numbers

Sometimes you want to format cells with labels differently from cells with totals. You can change the appearance of data in selected cells without changing its actual label or value. Format text and numbers by using *font attributes*, such as boldface, italics, or underlines, to enhance data to catch the readers' eye and focus their attention. You can also apply *numeric formats* to values to better reflect the type of information they present— dollar amounts, dates, decimals, percentages. For example, you can format a number to display up to 15 decimal places or none at all.

TIP

Excel has formatting intelligence. *As you type at the end of a column or row, Excel extends the formatting and formulas you are using in that column or row.*

Format Text Quickly

1. Select a cell or range with the text you want to format.

2. Click one of the buttons on the Formatting toolbar to apply that attribute to the selected range.
   - ◆ Bold
   - ◆ Italic
   - ◆ Underline

3. Click the Font or Font Size drop-down arrow, and then select a font or size.

   You can apply multiple attributes to the range.

Format Numbers Quickly

1. Select a cell or range with the numbers to format.

2. Click one of the buttons on the Formatting toolbar to apply that attribute to the selected range.
   - ◆ Currency Style
   - ◆ Percent Style
   - ◆ Comma Style
   - ◆ Increase Decimal
   - ◆ Decrease Decimal

   You can apply multiple attributes to the range.

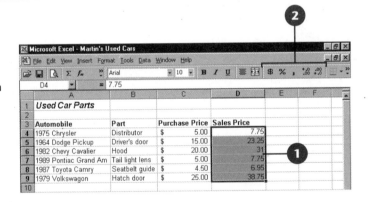

8

Copy cell formats with Format Painter. *You can copy formatting from one cell to another. Select the cell or range whose formatting you want to copy, double-click the Format Painter button on the Standard toolbar, select the cells you want to format, and then click the Format Painter button.*

Use AutoFormat to save time. *An* AutoFormat *is a combination of ready-to-use, designed formats. Select the cell or range you want to format, click the Format menu, click AutoFormat, click a format style in the AutoFormat dialog box, and then click OK.*

Current date and currency formats. *Excel includes global currency symbols and text (including the new Euro currency) so you and your money can be up to date. New date formats display four-digit years (such as 4/2/2000) to ease the millennium transition.*

Apply Numeric, Date, and Time Formats

1. Select a cell or range with the numbers to format.

2. Click the Format menu, and then click Cells.

3. Click the Number tab.

4. Click a numeric, date, or time category.

5. Select the formatting options you want to apply.

6. Preview the selections.

7. Click OK.

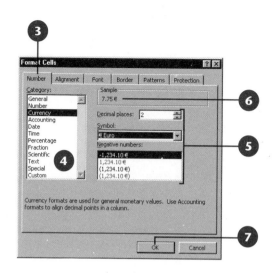

Change Font, Font Style, and Font Size

1. Select the cell or range containing the font to change.

2. Click the Format menu, and then click Cells.

3. Click the Font tab.

4. Select a font.

5. Select a font style.

6. Select a font size.

7. Select any additional formatting effects.

8. Click OK.

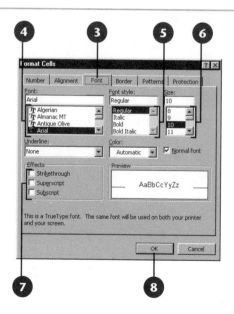

Designing Conditional Formatting

Make your worksheets more powerful by setting up *conditional formatting,* which lets you determine a cell's formatting based on its contents. For example, you might format this year's sales information in red italics if it's lower than last year's sales but in green bold if it's higher. Apply the first format directly to the cell. Then set up the second format to occur only if the condition is true. The condition can be based on a cell value or a formula. Each worksheet cell can have as many as three conditions.

TIP

Delete a condition. *To delete an unwanted condition, click the Delete button in the Conditional Formatting dialog box, click to select the check boxes next to the conditions you want to delete in the Delete Conditional Formatting dialog box, and then click OK.*

Create Conditions for Formatting

1. Select the cell or range to format conditionally.

2. Click the Format menu, and then click Conditional Formatting.

3. Select whether you want to test a cell value or formula.

4. For cell value, select a comparison operator.

5. Enter a value or formula for the condition. For the Between or Not Between operator, enter both an upper and lower cell value or range.

6. Click Format, select the format for when the condition is true, and then click OK.

7. Preview the results.

8. To add another condition, click Add and then repeat steps 3 through 7. You can set up to three conditions per cell.

9. Click OK.

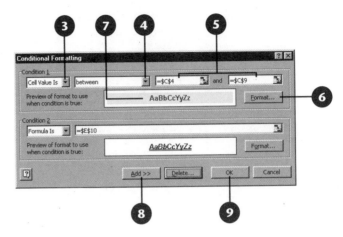

Controlling Text Flow and Alignment

A label might not always fit within its column width. If the cell to the right is empty, a label spills into it, but if that cell contains data, the label is *truncated* (or cut off). Rather than widen the column, you can wrap the text to multiple lines, shrink the text to fit the cell, merge cells, or angle the text orientation by degrees. When you enter data in a cell, labels align on the left edge of the cell and values and formulas align on the right edge. The placement of data relative to the left and right edges of a cell is called *horizontal alignment*, and the placement relative to the top and bottom is called *vertical alignment*. For example, the label *2000 Division 1 Sales* can be stacked 3 lines in a column as wide as *Division 1*.

Control Text Flow

1. Select a cell or range with the text you want to reflow.

2. Click the Format menu, click Cells, and then click the Alignment tab.

3. Click an orientation point by which to angle the text.

4. Click to select check boxes.
   - ◆ Wrap Text forces text to form multiple lines in the cell.
   - ◆ Shrink To Fit reduces font size to fit text in the cell.
   - ◆ Merge Cells combines selected cells into one.

5. Click OK.

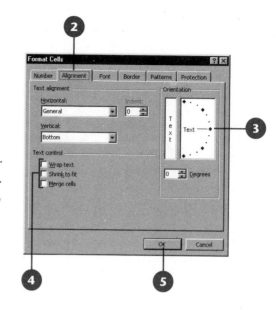

Align Data

1. Select a cell or range with data you want to align.

2. Click an alignment button on the Formatting toolbar.

ALIGNMENT TOOLBAR BUTTONS		
Button	**Name**	**Description**
≣	Align Left	Aligns cell contents on the left edge of the cell
≣	Center	Centers cell contents in the middle of the cell
≣	Align Right	Aligns cell contents on the right edge of the cell
⊞	Merge And Center	Combines selected cells and then centers cell content in the middle of the merged cell

Adding Color and Patterns to Cells

Colors and patterns added to the worksheet's light gray grid help identify data and streamline entering and reading data. If your data spans many columns and rows, color every other row light yellow to help readers follow the data. Or add a red dot pattern to cells with totals. *Color* adds background shading to a cell. *Patterns* add dots or lines to a cell in any color you choose.

TIP

Change the font color.
Select a range, click the Font Color drop-down arrow on the Formatting toolbar, and then click a color.

Apply Color and Patterns

1. Select a cell or range to which you want to apply colors and patterns.

2. Click the Format menu, and then click Cells.

3. Click the Patterns tab.

4. To add shading to the cell, click a color in the palette.

5. To add a pattern to the cell, click the Pattern drop-down arrow, and then click a pattern and color in the palette.

6. Click OK.

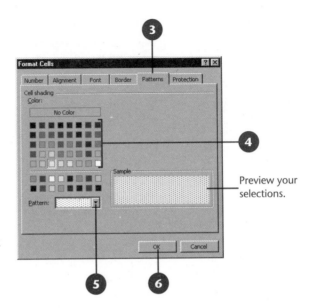

Preview your selections.

Apply Color Using the Formatting Toolbar

1. Select a cell or range.

2. Click the Fill Color drop-down arrow on the Formatting toolbar.

   If necessary, click the More Buttons drop-down arrow to display the button.

3. Click a color.

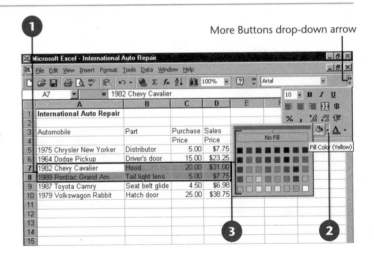

More Buttons drop-down arrow

Adding Borders to Cells

The light gray grid that appears on the worksheet helps your eyes move from cell to cell. Although you can print these gridlines, sometimes a different grid pattern better emphasizes your data. For example, you might put a decorative line border around the title, a double-line bottom border below cells with totals, or a thick border between sections of a complicated worksheet. You can add borders of varying colors and widths to any or all sides of a single cell or range.

TIP

Add a border quickly. *You can add a border to any or all sides of a cell in a range. Select the cell or range, click the Borders drop-down arrow on the Formatting toolbar, and then click the border you want.*

Apply a Border

1. Select a cell or range to which you want to apply borders, or click the Select All button to select the entire worksheet.

2. Click the Format menu, and then click Cells.

3. Click the Border tab.

4. Select a line style.

5. Click the Color drop-down arrow, and then click a color for the border.

6. If you want a border on the outside of a cell or range, click Outline. If you want a border between cells, click Inside. If you want to remove a border, click None.

7. To set a custom border, click a Border button or click the Preview Border box where you want to add a border.

8. Click OK.

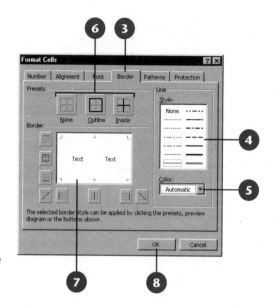

Creating a Chart

A *chart* provides a visual, graphical representation of numerical data. Whether you turn numbers into a bar, line, pie, surface, or bubble chart, patterns become more apparent. For example, the trend of annual rising profits becomes powerful in a line chart. A second line showing diminishing annual expenses creates an instant map of your business's success. *Titles* on the chart, horizontal or X-axis, and vertical or Y-axis identify the data. A *legend* connects the colors and patterns in a chart with the data they represent. *Gridlines* are horizontal and vertical lines to help the reader determine data values in a chart. Excel simplifies the chart-making process with the *Chart Wizard*, a series of dialog boxes that leads you through all the steps to create an effective chart on a new or an existing worksheet.

Create a Chart Using the Chart Wizard

1. Select the data range you want to chart.

   Make sure you include the data you want to chart *and* the column and row labels in the range. The Chart Wizard expects to find this information and incorporates it in your chart.

2. Click the Chart Wizard button on the Standard toolbar.

3. Click a chart type.

4. Click a chart sub-type.

5. Click the Click And Hold To View Sample button to preview your selection.

6. Click Next.

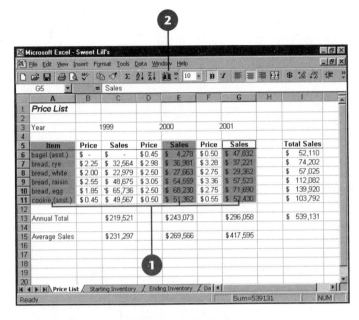

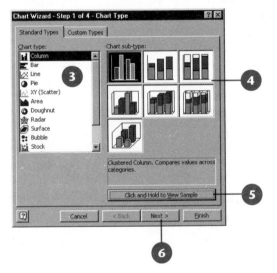

TIP

Major vs. minor gridlines.
Major gridlines *occur at each value on an axis;* minor gridlines *occur between values on an axis. Use gridlines sparingly and only when they improve the chart's readability.*

TIP

Change the chart type.
Select the chart, click the Chart menu, click Chart Type, click a new chart type, click a new chart sub-type, and then click OK.

TIP

Change chart options. *You can revise titles, gridlines, and legends at any time. Select the chart, click the Chart menu, click Chart Options, click the appropriate tab, select or change options, and then click OK.*

TIP

Explode a pie slice. *Select a pie chart, click to select the pie slice you want to explode, and then drag the slice away from the pie.*

SEE ALSO

See "Embedding and Linking Information" on page 282 for information on embedding.

7 Verify the data range.

8 Select to plot the data series in rows or in columns.

9 Click Next to continue.

10 Select chart options.

   ◆ **Titles tab**: Type titles for the chart, x-axis, and y-axis in the appropriate text boxes.

   ◆ **Gridlines tab**: Select the type of gridlines you want for the x-axis and y-axis.

   ◆ **Legend tab**: Click to select the Show Legend check box, and then select its location.

11 Preview the options.

12 Click Next to continue.

13 Select to place the chart on a new or existing sheet.

   A chart placed on an existing sheet is an *embedded object.*

14 Click Finish.

15 Drag the chart to a new location if necessary.

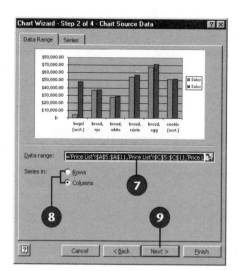

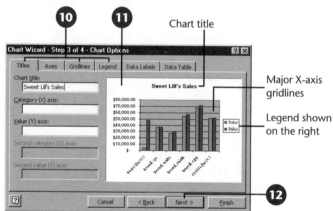

Chart title

Major X-axis gridlines

Legend shown on the right

Adding and Deleting a Data Series

Each range of data that comprises a bar, column, or pie slice is called a *data series;* each value in a data series is called a *data point.* You define the data series when you select a range and then open the Chart Wizard. But what if you want to add a data series to an existing chart? Add a data series by changing the data range information in the Chart Wizard, by using the Chart menu, or by dragging a new data series into an existing chart. You can delete a data series just as quickly as you add one.

TIP

Use the Chart toolbar to select chart elements. *Select a chart element by clicking the Chart Objects drop-down arrow on the Chart toolbar. Once an element is selected, double-click it to open a corresponding Format dialog box.*

Add a Data Series Quickly

1. Select the range that contains the data series you want to add to your chart.

2. Drag the range into the existing chart.

3. Release the mouse button to display the chart with the added data series.

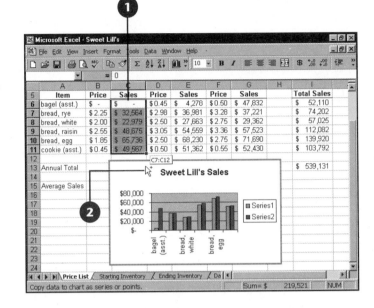

Delete a Data Series

1. Select the chart that contains the data series you want to delete.

2. Click any data point in the data series.

   The series is selected in the chart and the worksheet.

3. Press Delete.

   Excel removes the data series and displays the revised chart.

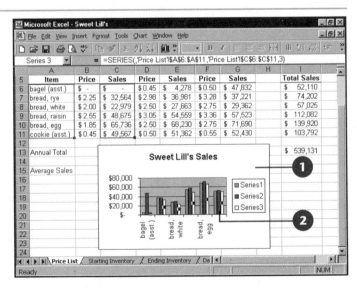

Change a Data Series

1. Select the chart that contains the data series you want to change.

2. Click the Chart menu and then click Source Data.

3. Click the Series tab.

4. Click the series name you want to change.

5. Click the Name or Values Collapse Dialog button to change the name or value, and then click the Expand Dialog button.

6. Click OK.

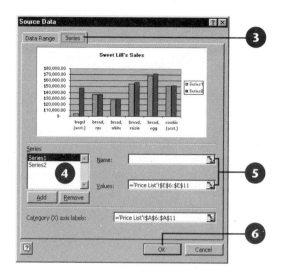

Change Data Series Order

1. Select the chart that contains the data series you want to delete.

2. Double-click any data point in the data series.

3. Click the Series Order tab.

4. Click the series you want to reorder.

5. Click Move Up or Move Down.

6. Click OK.

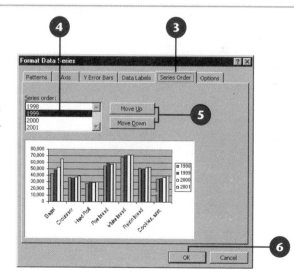

8

Enhancing a Chart

You can format or change any *chart object*—such as titles, legends, gridlines, data labels, data tables, and text annotations—to enhance the appearance of the chart and increase its overall effectiveness. A *chart title* identifies its purpose and *axis titles* identify the plotted data. Titles can be multiple lines and formatted like other worksheet text.

TIP

Add a text annotation. *A text annotation is separate text not attached to a specific axis or data point. Select the chart, type the annotation text, and then press Enter. The text appears in a text box. If you want, drag the text box to a new location. Press Esc to deselect the text box.*

TIP

Move and resize a chart. *Drag the selected chart from its center to a new location. Drag a resize handle to enlarge or shrink the chart's size.*

Format a Chart Object

1. Double-click the chart element you want to format.

2. Click the tab that corresponds to the type of change you want to make.

3. Select the formatting options you want to change or apply.

4. Click OK.

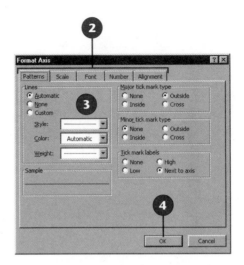

Change Chart Options

1. Select a chart you want to change.

2. Click the Chart menu, and then click Chart Options.

3. Click the chart option tab (Titles, Axis, Gridlines, Legend, Data Labels, or Data Table) you want to change.

4. Enter information and select the options you want.

5. Click OK.

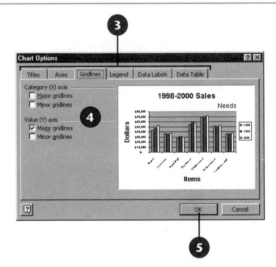

Auditing a Worksheet

When you create formulas on a worksheet, Excel can give visual cues to show the relationship between cells in the formula. With the Auditing toolbar, you can examine the relationship between cells and formulas on your worksheet and identify errors. When you use the auditing tools, tracer arrows point out cells that provide data to formulas and the cells that contain formulas that refer to the cells. A box is drawn around cell ranges that provide data to formulas.

TIP

Circle invalid data. *To circle invalid data in a formula, click the Circle Invalid Data button on the Auditing toolbar. Click the Clear Validation Circles button to hide the circles.*

Audit Cells in a Worksheet

1. Click the cell you want to audit.

2. Click the Tools menu, point to Auditing, and the click Show Auditing Toolbar.

3. To find cells that provide data to a formula, select the cell that contains the formula, and then click the Trace Precedents button.

4. To find out which formulas refer to a cell, select the cell and then click the Trace Dependents button.

5. If a formula displays an error value, such as #DIV/ 0!, click the Trace Error button to locate the problem.

6. To remove arrows, click the Remove Precedent Arrows button, Remove Dependent Arrows button, or Remove All Arrows button.

7. Click the Close button on the Auditing toolbar.

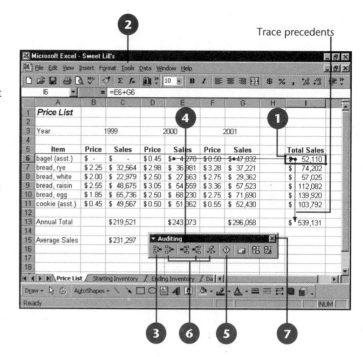

Trace precedents

Understanding Lists

A *database* is a collection of related records. Examples of databases are an address book, a list of customers or products, and a telephone directory. In Excel, a database is referred to as *list*.

Record
One set of related fields, such as all the fields pertaining to one customer or product. In a worksheet, each row represents a unique record.

Field name
The title of a field. In an Excel list, the first row contains the names of each field. Each field name can have up to 255 characters, including uppercase and lowercase letters and spaces.

List range
The block of cells that contains some or all of the list you want to analyze. The list range cannot occupy more than one worksheet.

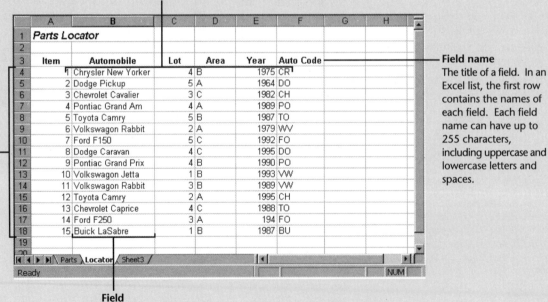

Field
One piece of information, such as customer's last name or an item's code number. On a worksheet, each column represents a field.

Creating a List

To create a list in Excel, you can enter data on worksheet cells, just as you do any other worksheet data, but the placement of the field names and list range must follow these rules.

- ◆ Enter field names in a single row that is the first row in the list.

- ◆ Enter each record in a single row.

- ◆ Do not include any blank rows within the list range.

- ◆ Do not use more than one worksheet for a single list range.

You can enter data directly in the list or in a data form, a dialog box in which you can view, change, add, or delete records in a list. Don't worry about entering records in any particular order; Excel tools organize an existing list alphabetically, by date, or in almost any order you can imagine.

Create a List

1 Open a blank worksheet, or use a worksheet that has enough empty columns and rows for your list.

2 Enter a label for each field in adjacent columns across the first row of the list.

3 Enter field information for each record in its own row; start with the row directly below the field names.

Enter Records with a Data Form

1 Enter a label for each field in adjacent columns across the first row of the list.

2 Click the Data menu, and then click Form.

3 Click OK to set the row as the column labels.

4 Enter information for each field, pressing Tab to move from one field to the next.

5 Click New and enter field information for each additional record.

6 When you're done, click Close.

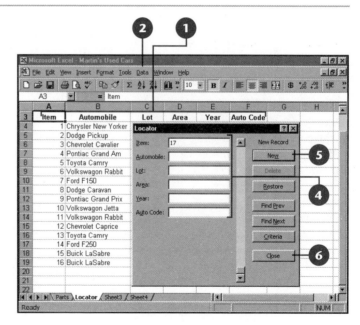

Sorting Data in a List

After you enter records in a list, you can reorganize the information by *sorting* the records. For example, you might want to sort records in a client list alphabetically by last name or numerically by their last invoice date. *Ascending order* lists records from A to Z, earliest to latest, or lowest to highest. *Descending order* lists records from Z to A, latest to earliest, or highest to lowest. You can sort the entire list or use *AutoFilter* to select the part of the list you want to display in the column. You can sort a list based on one or more *sort fields*, fields you select to sort the list. A simple sort, for example, might organize a telephone directory alphabetically by last name; a more complex sort might organize the telephone directory numerically by area code and then alphabetically by last name.

Display Parts of a List

1. Click in the list range.

2. Click the Data menu, point to Filter, and then click AutoFilter.

3. Click the drop-down arrow of the field you want to use.

4. Select the item that records must match to be displayed.

5. Click the Data menu, point to Filter, and then click Show All to redisplay all records in the list.

6. Click the Data menu, point to Filter, and then click AutoFilter to remove the field drop-down arrows.

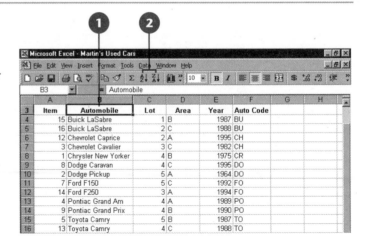

Sort Data Quickly

1. Click the field name by which you want to sort.

2. Click the Sort Ascending or the Sort Descending button on the Standard toolbar.

Sort a List Using More Than One Field

1. Click anywhere within the list range.

2. Click the Data menu, and then click Sort.

3. Click the Sort By drop-down arrow, and then click the field on which the sort is based (the *primary sort field*).

4. Click the Ascending or Descending option button.

5. Click the top Then By drop-down arrow, select a second sort field, and then click Ascending or Descending.

6. If necessary, click the lower Then By drop-down arrow, select a third sort field, and then click Ascending or Descending.

7. Click the Header Row option button to *exclude* the field names (in the first row) from the sort, or click the No Header Row option button to *include* the field names (in the first row) in the sort.

8. Click OK.

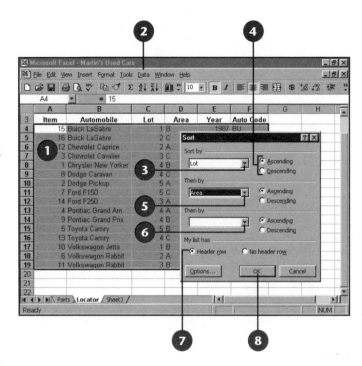

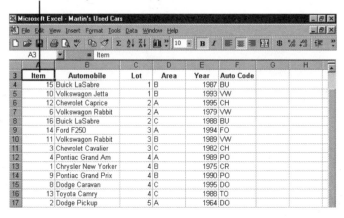

List sorted by lot and then by area

Analyzing Data Using a PivotTable

Your worksheet contains a long list of data in the order that was easiest to enter. But now, you want to view and analyze the data several ways. Try a *PivotTable*—an interactive table that quickly summarizes large or small amounts of data, which you can sort and filter, group by rows and columns, and total.

TIP

Update a PivotTable. *If you revise the data list upon which a PivotTable is based, click the Refresh Data button on the PivotTable toolbar.*

TIP

Add and remove PivotTable fields. *Drag field names from the PivotTable toolbar to the "drop-zones" in the table and from the table to the toolbar to change the data.*

Create a PivotTable

1. Click any cell in the list.

2. Click the Data menu, and then click PivotTable And PivotChart Report.

3. Click the Microsoft Excel List Or Database option button.

4. Click the PivotTable option button.

5. Click Next to continue.

6. Verify the range includes the correct data. If you want, click the Collapse Dialog Box button, select the list range with the field names, and then click the Expand Dialog Box button.

7. Click Next to continue.

8. Click Layout.

9. Drag field names to the ROW, COLUMN, and DATA areas.

10. Click OK.

11. Specify where to place the PivotTable.

12. Click Finish.

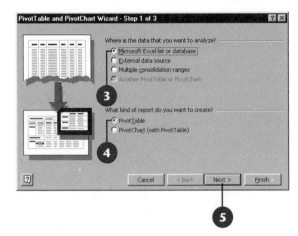

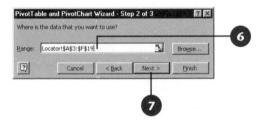

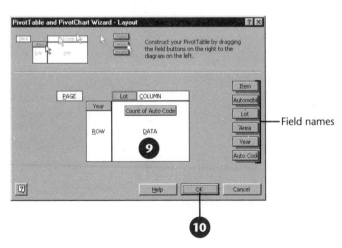

Field names

Charting a PivotTable

Data summarized in a PivotTable is ideal for a chart, because the table itself represents a tremendous amount of hard-to-read data. A *PivotChart* provides a visual tool for analyzing data. After you select data from the PivotTable, use the Chart Wizard to chart it like any other worksheet data. As you update a linked PivotTable and PivotChart, the associated table or chart updates and refreshes to reflect your changes.

TIP

Revise a PivotChart. *You can drag fields to and from a PivotChart to add and remove fields.*

TIP

View PivotTables and PivotCharts in a browser. *Users who view a PivotTable or PivotChart in Internet Explorer 4 or later can update and interact with the data. Users using other Web browsers can see the table or chart, but cannot make changes.*

Create a PivotChart

1. Click in the table you want to chart.

2. Click the Chart Wizard button on the Standard or PivotTable toolbar.

   Excel creates a chart from the PivotTable and places it in a new sheet tab, labeled Chart1.

3. Click the Chart Wizard button on the Standard or PivotTable toolbar to open the Chart Wizard.

4. Make selections from each of the four Chart Wizard dialog boxes.

5. Click Finish.

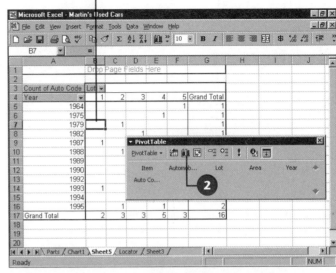

8

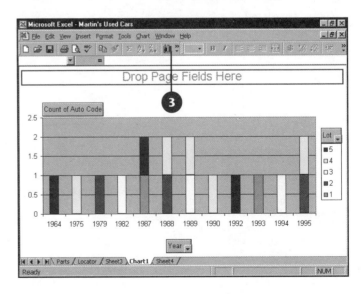

Modifying a PivotTable and PivotChart

You can modify PivotTable and PivotChart reports. With Excel's AutoFormat, you can quickly format a PivotTable to create professional-looking reports. You can also change field settings to format a number or show the data in a different form.

TIP

Change the layout of a PivotTable. *Click a field in the PivotTable, click the PivotTable Wizard button on the PivotTable toolbar, click Layout, make the changes you want, click OK, and then click Finish.*

TIP

View or hide field items. *Click a field's drop-down arrow to display a list of items. Click to select check boxes to include items, and clear them to remove items, and then click OK.*

AutoFormat a PivotTable Report

1. Click any field in the PivotTable report.

2. Click the Format Report button on the PivotTable toolbar.

3. Click the AutoFormat style you want.

4. Click OK.

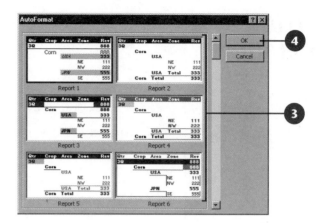

Change Field Settings in a PivotTable or PivotChart Report

1. Select the field you want to change.

2. Click the Field Settings button on the PivotTable toolbar.

3. To change the number format, click Number, select a format, and then click OK.

4. To show the data in a different form, click the Show Data As drop-down arrow, and select a form.

5. Click OK.

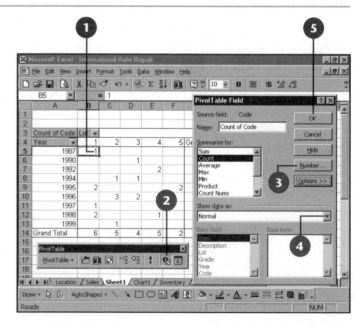

Tracking Data Changes

As you build a workbook you can keep track of all the changes you and others make. The Track Changes feature makes it easy to know who has made what changes and when the changes were made. To take full advantage of this feature, turn it on the first time you or a coworker edit a workbook. Then when it's time to review the workbook, all the changes will be recorded. Cells containing changes are surrounded by a blue border; you can view the changes instantly by moving your mouse pointer over any outlined cell. When you're ready to finalize the workbook, you can review it and either accept or reject the changes.

SEE ALSO

See "Inserting Comments" on page 37 for information on adding comments to a document.

Turn On Track Changes

1. Click the Tools menu, point to Track Changes, and then click Highlight Changes.

2. Click to select the Track Changes While Editing check box. If necessary, select when, who, and where to track changes.

3. Click OK.

4. Click OK to save the workbook.

5. Position the mouse pointer over an edited cell to view the tracked change.

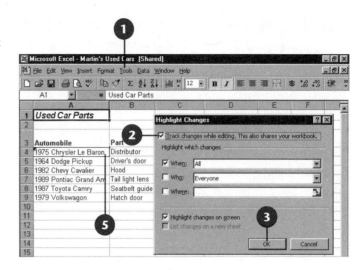

Accept or Reject Tracked Changes

1. Click the Tools menu, point to Track Changes, and then click Accept Or Reject Changes.

2. If necessary, click OK to save the workbook.

3. Click OK.

4. Review the changes. Click Accept or Reject to make or remove the selected change, or click Accept All or Reject All to make or remove all changes.

5. Click Close.

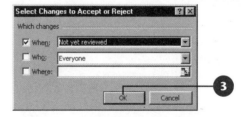

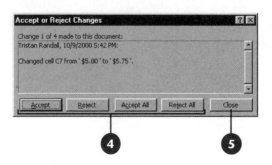

Protecting Your Data

You work very hard creating and entering information in a workbook. To preserve all your work—particularly if others use your files—you can password-protect its contents. You can protect a sheet or an entire workbook. In each case, you'll be asked to supply a password, and then enter it again when you want to work on the file.

TIP

Protect your password.
Make sure you keep your password in a safe place. Also, try to avoid obvious passwords like your name or your company.

TIP

You need your password to unprotect a worksheet. *To turn off protection, click the Tools menu, point to Protection, and then click Unprotect Sheet. Enter the password, and then click OK.*

Protect Your Worksheet

1 Click the Tools menu, point to Protection, and then click Protect Sheet.

You can protect an individual worksheet, the entire workbook, or you can protect and share a workbook. The steps for all are similar.

2 Click to select the check boxes for the options you want to protect.

3 Type a password.

A password can contain any combination of letters, numbers, spaces, and symbols. Excel passwords are case-sensitive so you must type uppercase and lowercase letters correctly when you enter passwords.

4 Click OK.

5 Retype the password.

6 Click OK.

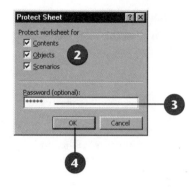

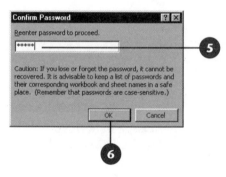

9

Communicating and Scheduling with Outlook 2000

If, like many people, you're juggling a scheduler, an address book, and an e-mail address list, and you're cluttering your desk and computer with reminder notes and to-do lists, help is here—Microsoft Outlook 2000.

Outlook, a messaging and personal information manager, integrates all the common messaging, planning, scheduling, organization, and management tools into one simple and flexible system.

◆ *Inbox* receives and stores your incoming messages.

◆ *Contacts* replaces your standard card file and stores multiple street addresses, phone numbers, e-mail and Web addresses, and any personal information you need about each contact.

◆ *Calendar* replaces your daily or weekly planner and helps you schedule meetings and block time for appointments and events.

◆ *Tasks* organizes and tracks your to-do list.

◆ *Notes* provides a place to jot random notes, which you can group, sort, and categorize.

◆ *Journal* automatically records your daily activities.

Outlook provides a single place to plan, organize, and manage every aspect of your work and personal life.

Setting Up Outlook

When you start Outlook for the first time, a setup wizard appears to step you through the process of setting up an e-mail service. A *service* is a connection to an e-mail server where you store and receive e-mail messages. Outlook can be used with more than one e-mail account on the most common e-mail servers. Outlook also works with other messaging services such as Microsoft Mail, CompuServe, and Lotus Notes. So whether you send e-mail messages, schedule meetings, or just need a personal information manager (PIM), Outlook provides the necessary tools for your information management needs.

Configure and Set Up Outlook

1. Click the Start button, point to Programs, and then click Microsoft Outlook to start the program for the first time.

2. Read the information in each setup wizard dialog box, and enter the required information. Click Next to continue.

3. Click Finish in the last wizard dialog box.

E-MAIL SERVICE OPTIONS	
Service	**Feature Summary**
Internet Only	Provides e-mail access; sends and receives meeting requests; works with Microsoft Exchange Server; manages personal tasks, contacts, appointments, and calendar
Corporate Or Workgroup	Works with Microsoft Exchange Workgroup Server; contains message recall and voting buttons; completes group scheduling interpretable with Schedule+; shares contact information; works with Microsoft Mail and third-party mail programs; manages personal tasks, contacts, appointments, and calendar
No E-Mail	Manages personal tasks, contacts, appointments, and calendar; does not provide e-mail or Internet access

Modify or Add Services

1. Click the Tools menu, and then click Services.

2. Select an available service, and then click Properties.

   To add a service, click Add, select a service, and then click OK.

3. Click the tabs to display the service information.

4. Enter the information you want for the service.

5. Click OK.

6. Click OK.

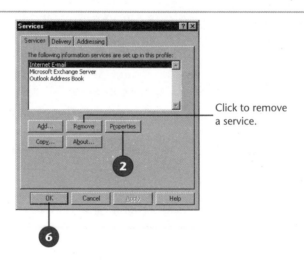

Click to remove a service.

Viewing the Outlook Window

Title bar
The title bar shows the program name, Microsoft Outlook, preceded by the current folder, in this case, Inbox.

Folder Banner
The name of the current folder appears here.

Standard toolbar
The toolbar contains the buttons you need to work in a particular view or folder. The toolbar you see depends on the view or folder you are using.

Menu bar
The menu bar contains menus that contain commands for using Microsoft Outlook. The commands you use most often appear when you first click a menu. Additional commands appear when you click the arrows at the bottom of the menu or wait a few sections.

Group buttons
Outlook items (Inbox, Calendar, Contacts, and so on) are organized into groups. Click a group button to display the shortcut icons for the items in that group.

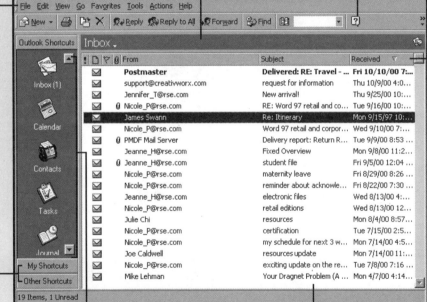

Column buttons
The column headings are actually buttons that you can click to change the order in which the items in the window are displayed. Click the button to switch between *ascending* order (low to high, A to Z, earliest to latest) and *descending* order (high to low, Z to A, latest to earliest).

Outlook Bar
The Outlook Bar is always visible. It contains shortcut icons you can click to move among all the groups and folders. You can create shortcut icons on the Outlook Bar so that you can quickly open other folders or Web pages on your computer or network.

Information viewer
This part of the window displays different views, depending on the folder you are using. This figure displays the Inbox containing e-mail messages.

Moving Around Outlook

As you work, you'll often need to switch between Outlook folders and to create new *items* such as tasks, contacts, messages, and appointments. A typical session in Outlook might involve revising your list of tasks, calling an associate, adding a new contact to your contact list, sending an e-mail message, and scheduling a meeting. To keep track of all this activity in Outlook, you can move among Outlook's folders—Tasks, Contacts, Inbox, Calendar—with a single click. Outlook folders are organized into groups—click a group button on the Outlook Bar to display related folder icons.

> **TIP**
>
> **Add a Web page shortcut icon to the Outlook Bar.**
> *Display the Web toolbar, open the Web page you want, click the File menu, point to New, and then click Outlook Bar Shortcut To Web Page.*

Display Folder Icons and Open a Folder

1 Click a group button on the Outlook Bar.

2 If necessary, click the scroll arrow to display the folder icon you want.

3 Click any folder icon that you want to open.

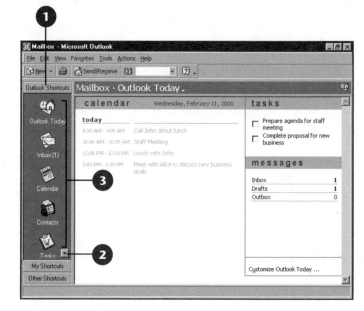

Create a New Item for Any Folder

1 Click the New drop-down arrow on the Standard toolbar.

The New button on the Standard toolbar changes to identify the kind of item you can create in the current folder. For example, if the Inbox is open, a mail message is created.

2 Click the type of item you want to create.

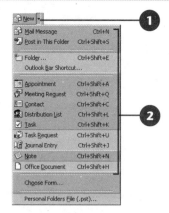

Using Outlook Today

If you like seeing all your appointments, tasks, and upcoming events in one summary view without having to switch between different views, you'll like Outlook Today. Outlook Today displays information using the style of a Web page, which makes it easy to open any piece of information by simply clicking it. You can easily customize Outlook Today, including options for how e-mail messages, calendar items, tasks, and Web page links are displayed.

TIP

Create your own Outlook Today view. *Outlook Today is defined using HTML, which allows you to create your own Outlook Today view like you would a Web page. The Outlook Today view could include specific company or workgroup information.*

View Outlook Today

1. Click Outlook Today on the Outlook Bar.

2. Click any item to view it in more detail or to change it.

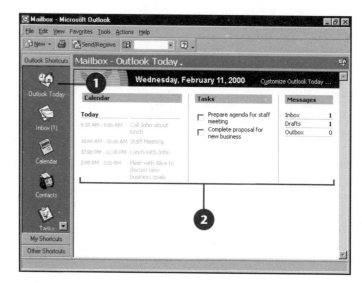

Customize Outlook Today

1. Click Outlook Today on the Outlook Bar.

2. Click Customize Outlook Today.

3. Set the options you want.
   - ◆ Display the Outlook Today page at startup
   - ◆ Display message folders
   - ◆ Set the number of days in the Calendar
   - ◆ Display and sort tasks
   - ◆ Choose the page style

4. Click Save Changes.

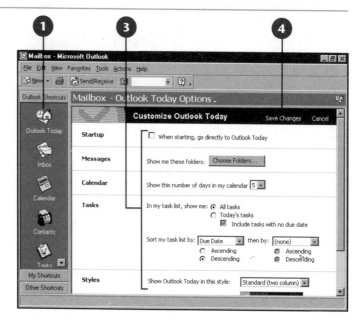

Creating a Contact

A *contact* is a person or company with whom you want to communicate. One contact can have several mailing addresses, various phone and fax numbers, e-mail addresses, and Web sites. You can store all this data in the Contacts folder along with more detailed information, such as job titles, birthdays, and anniversaries. When you double-click a contact, you open a dialog box in which you can edit the detailed contact information. You can also directly edit the contact information from within the Contacts folder. If you send the same e-mail message to more than one person, you can group contacts together into a distribution list.

TIP

Find a contact quickly.
Click Contacts on the Outlook Bar and start typing the name of the contact you want to find. The contact that best matches the text is displayed.

Create a New Contact

1. Click the New drop-down arrow on the Standard toolbar, and then click Contact.

2. Fill in information on the General tab. You can enter name, addresses (postal, e-mail, and Web page), phone numbers, and comments.

3. If you want, click Categories to organize the contact.

4. Click the Save And Close button.

Click to save the new contact and then open a new one.

Click to change the data field.

Change Contacts Views

1. Click Contacts on the Outlook Bar.

2. Click the View menu, point to Current View, and then click the view you want.

3. If you want, click the button for the first letter of the contact name to move to that section of your contact list.

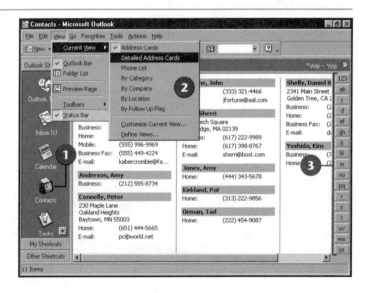

TIP

Edit a contact quickly. *Click Contacts on the Outlook Bar, change the current view to Detailed Address Cards, click the information you want to change, use normal editing commands, and then press Enter.*

TIP

Delete a contact. *Click Contacts on the Outlook Bar, click the contact you want to delete, and then click the Delete button on the Standard toolbar. Any journal entries that refer to that contact remain intact.*

TIP

Display a map of a contact's address. *Click Contacts on the Outlook Bar, double-click the contact for whom you want a map, click the Actions menu, and then click Display Map Of Address to open your Web browser and display a street map.*

SEE ALSO

See "Organizing Folders" on page 190 for information on flagging a contact for follow-up.

Open and Update an Existing Contact

1. Click Contacts on the Outlook Bar.

2. Double-click the contact you want to update.

3. Use the normal editing commands to update the information.

4. Click the Save And Close button.

Create a Distribution List from Contacts

1. Click Contacts on the Outlook Bar.

2. Click the Actions menu, and then click New Distribution List.

3. Type a name for the distribution list.

4. Click Select Members, select the members you want, and then click Add.

5. When you're done selecting names, click OK.

6. Click the Save And Close button.

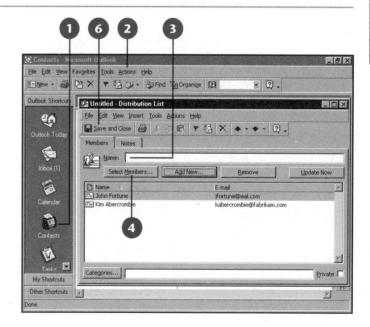

Creating and Sending an E-Mail Message

Sending mail messages is a quick and effective way to communicate with others. Mail messages follow a standard memo format in which you specify the recipient of the message, the subject of the message, and the message. To send a message, you need to enter the recipient's or recipients' complete e-mail addresses. Use the Address Book to make entering e-mail addresses quick and easy.

TIP

An important note about e-mail addresses. *An e-mail address is not case-sensitive (that is, capitalization doesn't matter), but an e-mail address cannot contain spaces.*

SEE ALSO

See "Managing E-Mail Messages" on page 168 for information on creating folders for your Outlook tasks.

Create and Send an E-Mail Message

1 Click the New drop-down arrow on the Standard toolbar, and then click Mail Message.

2 Click the To button or type the e-mail address (Use a semicolon to separate two or more addresses).

3 Select an Address Book.

4 Click a name. To select multiple names, press and hold Ctrl while you click other names.

5 Click the To, Cc, or Bcc button. (To sends the message to the selected names; Cc sends a courtesy copy; Bcc sends a blind courtesy copy.)

6 When you're done selecting names, click OK.

7 Type a brief description of your message.

8 Type the text of your message.

9 Click the Options button, specify the message settings you want, and then click Close.

10 Click the Send button.

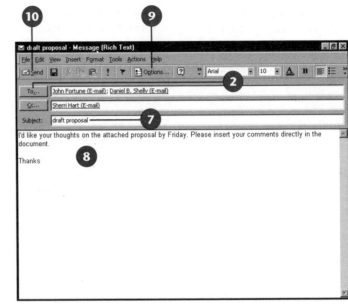

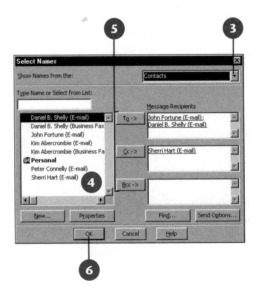

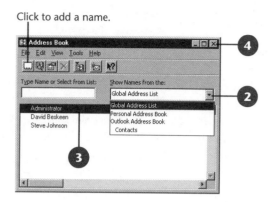

TIP

About the Address Book.
Use the Address Book to store e-mail and fax information and the Contacts folder to store all types of information. There are several types of address books, including the Personal Address Book and the Outlook Address Book (Contacts with e-mail or fax information).

TIP

Compose an e-mail message now but send it later. *To save a mail message without sending it, click the Save button, and then click the Close button. When you're ready to send the message, click the Drafts folder, double-click the message, edit it if necessary, and then click the Send button.*

TIP

Send e-mail with tracking and delivery options. *Create a new mail message, click the Options button on the Standard toolbar, select the delivery options or the tracking options you want, and then click Close.*

TIP

Change the e-mail format to a Web page format.
Click the Format menu, and then click HTML. The Format menu changes to provide Web page formatting commands.

Open the Address Book and View an Entry

1. Click the Tools menu, and then click Address Book.

2. Click the Show Names From The drop-down arrow, and then select the Address Book type you want.

3. Double-click an entry to view its details, and then click OK.

4. Click the Close button.

Click to add a name.

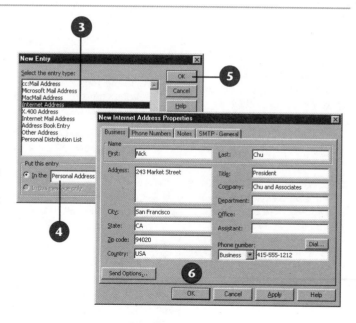

Add a Name to an Address Book

1. Click the Tools menu, and then click Address Book.

2. Click the New Entry button on the toolbar.

3. Click the type of entry you want to add.

4. Click the In The drop-down arrow, select the address location in which you want to store this name.

5. Click OK.

6. Enter the necessary information, and then click OK.

7. Click the Close button.

9

Using Stationery

There is no reason to limit your mail messages to black and white. Give your mail messages a dramatic appearance by writing them on stationery. Outlook comes with a variety of stationery, which includes background images and borders. You can customize the stationery to reflect your creative spirit or create your own stationery from scratch.

SEE ALSO

See "Creating a Signature" on page 165 for information on creating a signature and attaching a personal business card.

TIP

Create an e-mail message using any Office program. *Click Inbox on the Outlook Bar, click the Actions menu, point to New Mail Message Using, and then point to Microsoft Word (RTF) or point to Microsoft Office, and then click an Office program.*

Create an E-Mail Message Using Stationery

1. Click Inbox on the Outlook Bar.

2. Click the Actions menu, and then point to New Mail Message Using.

3. Click the stationery you want to use.

   If none is available, click More Stationery, click the stationery you want, and then click OK.

Create Stationery

1. Click the Tools menu, click Options, and then click the Mail Format tab.

2. Click Stationery Picker, and then click New.

3. Type a stationery name.

4. Click the stationery option button you want to use. Click Next to continue.

5. Select the font options and the background you want to use.

6. Click OK.

7. Click OK.

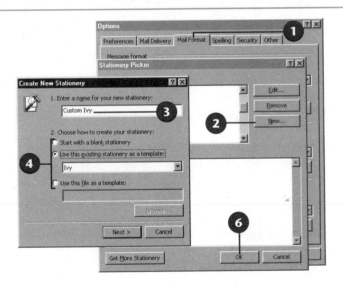

Creating a Signature

Give your message a personal touch by ending it with your unique signature. A *signature* is any file (a text file, graphic file, or a file that is a scanned image of your handwritten signature) that you choose to use in the closing of a mail message. A *business card* is your, or someone else's, contact information that comes directly from the Address Book.

TIP

Insert a signature in a new e-mail message. *Create a new mail message, click the Insert menu, point to Signature, click a signature, or click More to select another from the list of available signatures.*

TIP

Send a business card in a e-mail message. *Click Contacts on the Outlook Bar, click the contact you want to send, click the Actions menu, click Forward As vCard, select a recipient, type your message, and then click the Send button.*

Create a Signature and Attach a Business Card

1. Click the Tools menu, click Options, and then click the Mail Format tab.

2. Click Signature Picker and then click New.

3. Enter a name for your signature. Click Next to continue.

4. Type your signature text.

5. Select the signature, and then click the Font and Paragraph buttons to further customize the text.

6. To attach a business card, click the drop-down arrow, and then select a contact.

7. To create a new business card, click New vCard From Contact, click a contact, click Add, and then click OK.

8. Click Finish.

9. Click OK.

10. Click OK.

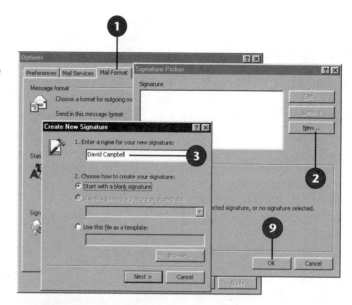

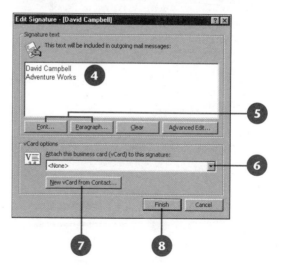

Reading and Replying to an E-Mail Message

You can receive an e-mail message anytime, day or night, even when your computer is turned off. New mail messages (which are displayed in bold text) appear in the Inbox along with mail messages you haven't yet stored or deleted. A *flag* next to a mail message indicates a specific level of importance or sensitivity. The message's flag, along with the sender's name and subject line, can help you determine which message you want to open, read, and respond to first. Whenever you reply to or forward a mail message, Outlook adds a note indicating when you replied or forwarded the mail message. If you are out of the office, you can have Outlook automatically respond to your incoming e-mail with a standardized message.

Preview and Open an E-Mail Message

① Click Inbox on the Outlook Bar.

② Click the View menu, and then click Preview Pane or AutoPreview (or both).

③ Double-click the message you want to open.

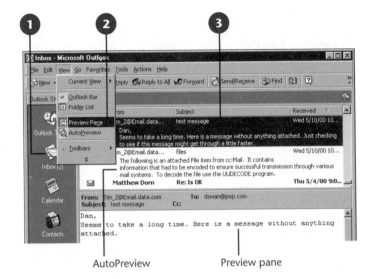

AutoPreview   Preview pane

Reply to an E-Mail Message

① Click Inbox on the Outlook Bar.

② Click the message to which you want to respond.

③ Click the Reply button to respond to only the message's sender, or click the Reply To All button to respond to the sender and all other recipients of the original mail message.

④ Type your message at the top of the message box.

⑤ Click the Send button.

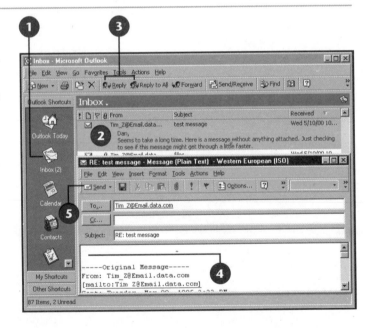

Forward an E-Mail Message

1. Click Inbox on the Outlook Bar.

2. Click the message you want to forward.

3. Click the Forward button on the Standard toolbar.

4. Click the To button or Cc button, and then select recipients for this mail message.

5. Type new text at the top of the message box, and attach any files if appropriate.

6. Click the Send button.

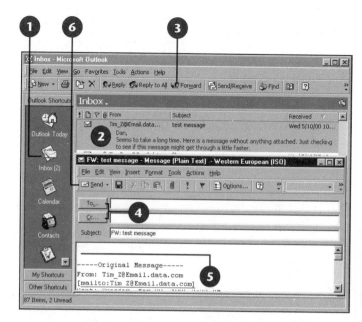

Create an Out of Office Message Reply

1. Click the Tools menu, and then click Out Of Office Assistant.

2. Click the I Am Currently Out Of The Office option button.

3. Type a message reply.

4. If you want, click Add Rule to apply criteria to incoming messages.

5. Click OK.

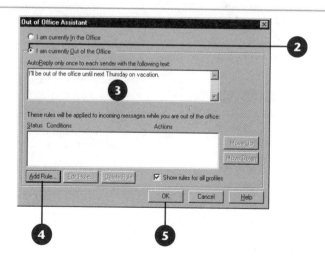

Managing E-Mail Messages

Instead of scrolling through your Inbox to find a mail message, you can use the Find button on the Standard toolbar. To avoid an overly cluttered Inbox, remember to routinely clear the Inbox of mail messages that you have read and responded to. You can delete mail messages you no longer need or move them to other folders. Storing your mail messages in other folders and deleting unwanted mail messages make it easier to see new mail messages and to clear your computer's resources for new activities.

TRY THIS

Select multiple e-mail messages at one time. *To select two or more adjacent mail messages, click the first mail message and press and hold Shift while you click the last mail message. To select two or more nonadjacent mail messages, click the first one and press and hold Ctrl while you click each additional one.*

Find E-Mail Messages

1. Click Inbox on the Outlook Bar.

2. Click the Find button on the Standard toolbar.

3. Enter the information you want to find in a message.

4. Click to select the Search All Text In The Message check box.

5. Click Find Now.

6. Click the Find button on the Standard toolbar to return to the Inbox.

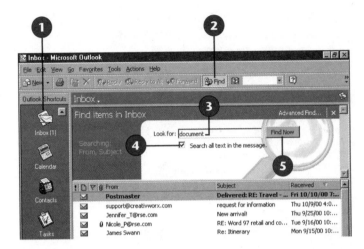

Delete Unwanted E-Mail Messages

1. On the Outlook Bar, click Inbox, Outbox, Sent Items, or the folder in which you store mail messages.

2. Select the mail message or messages you want to move to the Deleted Items folder.

3. Click the Delete button on the Standard toolbar.

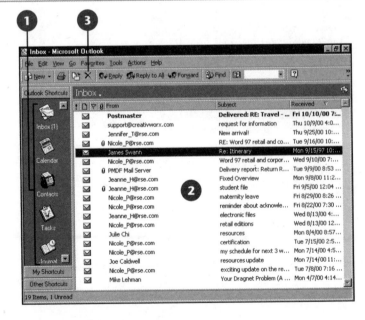

9

TIP

Retrieve e-mail messages from the Deleted Items folder. *Items remain in the Deleted Items folder until you empty it. To retrieve e-mail messages from the Deleted Items folder, click the My Shortcuts group button on the Outlook Bar, and then click Deleted Items. Drag an item to the Inbox or to any other folder icon on the Outlook Bar.*

TIP

Empty the Deleted Items folder. *To empty the Deleted Items folder and permanently delete its contents, right-click Deleted Items on the Outlook Bar, click Empty "Deleted Items" Folder, and then click Yes to confirm the deletion.*

TIP

Sort items within a folder. *If available, click a column button to sort items in the folder by that column in either ascending or descending order.*

TIP

Save a e-mail message as a file. *Click the e-mail message you want to save, click the File menu, click Save As, click the Save As Type drop-down arrow, click a file type, type a new filename, and then click Save.*

Create a New Folder

1. Click the File menu, point to Folder, and then click New Folder.

2. Type a name for the new folder.

3. Click the Folder Contains drop-down arrow, and then click the type of item you want to store here.

4. Click the folder in which you want to file this subfolder.

5. Click OK, and then click Yes or No to create a shortcut.

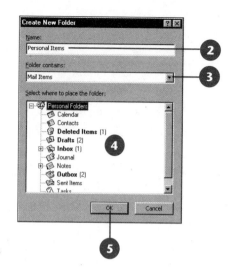

Move E-Mail Messages to a Different Folder

1. Click Inbox on the Outlook Bar.

2. Select the mail message or messages you want to move.

3. Click the Move To Folder button on the Standard toolbar, and then click Move To Folder or a folder name.

4. Click the folder where you want to move the mail messages.

5. Click OK.

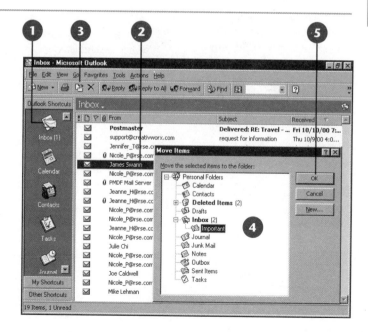

Attaching a File to an E-Mail Message

File sharing is a powerful feature of e-mail. You can attach one or more files, such as a picture or a document, to a mail message. The recipient of the mail message then opens the attached file in the program in which it was created. For example, suppose you are working on a report that a colleague needs to present today in another part of the country. After you finish the report, you can attach the file to a mail message and send the message with the attached file directly to your colleague.

TIP

Save attachments to your hard disk. *Open the e-mail message with the attachment, click the File menu, click Save Attachments, select the location where you want to save the file, and then click Save.*

Attach a File to an E-Mail Message

1. Compose a new message, or open an existing message.

2. Click the Insert File button.

   If necessary, click the More Buttons drop-down arrow on the Standard toolbar.

3. Click the Look In drop-down arrow, and then select the drive and folder that contains the file you want to attach.

4. Click the file.

5. Click Insert.

6. Send the mail message, or save it to send later.

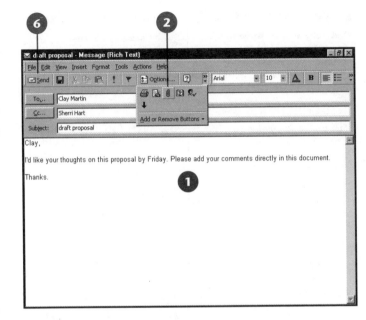

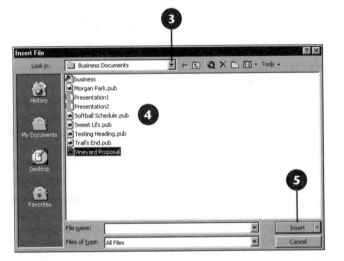

Viewing the Calendar

The *Calendar* is an electronic version of the familiar paper daily planner. You can schedule time for completing specific tasks, meetings, vacations, holidays, or for any other activity with the Calendar. Outlook and Schedule+ users can import and export messages, meeting requests, and appointments. However, neither can read the other's calendar. To view Schedule+ calendar information, you'll need to import it into Outlook.

TIP

Save your Calendar as a Web page. *Switch to the Calendar view you want to save, click the File menu, click Save As Web Page, select the duration and publishing options you want, enter a title and filename, and then click Save. Once the Calendar is published, you can open the file in a Web browser.*

Change the Calendar View

The Calendar displays your schedule in a typical daily planner format or in list format. You can change the Calendar view in several ways.

◆ Click the View menu, point to Current View, and then click the view option you want.

◆ Click one of the Calendar view buttons on the Standard toolbar.

◆ Click the left arrow or right arrow on the Date Navigator to change the current month.

◆ Click a date on the Date Navigator to view that day's schedule. The date highlighted in red is today's date.

◆ Click to the left of a week on the Date Navigator to view that week's schedule.

Calendar views   Date Navigator

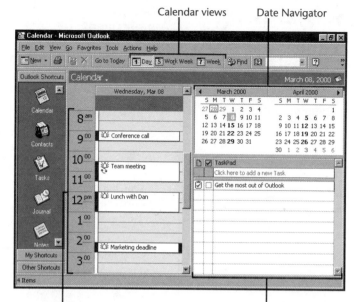

Appointment area
The appointment area shows the hours in day view (as in the figure) or days in weekly and monthly views. It also displays scheduled appointments and meetings.

TaskPad
The TaskPad lists the tasks you need to complete. Completed tasks are crossed out.

9

Scheduling an Event and Appointment

In Outlook, an *appointment* is any activity you schedule that doesn't include other people or resources. An *event* is any appointment that lasts one or more full days (24-hour increments), such as a seminar, a conference, or a vacation. You can mark yourself available (free or tentative) or unavailable (busy or out of the office) to others during a scheduled appointment or an event. You enter appointment or event information in the same box; however, when you schedule an event, the All Day Event check box is selected; the check box is cleared when you schedule an appointment.

TIP

Edit an appointment or event. *Click Calendar on the Outlook Bar, double-click the appointment or event, make changes, and then click the Save And Close button.*

Schedule an Appointment

1 Click Calendar on the Outlook Bar.

2 Drag to select a block of time in the appointment area.

3 Right-click the selected block, and then click New Appointment.

4 Type the subject of the appointment.

5 Type the location of the appointment, or click the drop-down arrow and select a location from the list.

6 Specify the start and end times.

7 Type any information needed for the appointment, or insert a file.

8 Click Categories to help you sort, group, or filter your appointments.

9 Click the Private check box if you do not want others to see this appointment.

10 Click the Save And Close button.

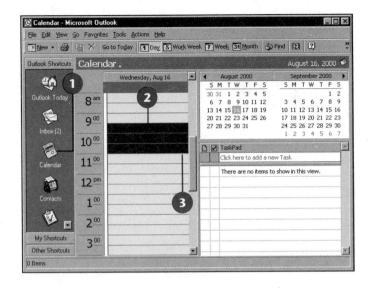

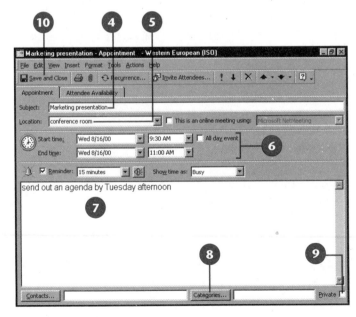

Switch between an event and appointment. *To change an event to an appointment or vice versa, click to clear or select the All Day Event check box.*

Schedule a recurring appointment. *In Calendar, select a block of time, click the Actions menu, click New Recurring Appointment, fill in the appointment times and recurrence information, click OK, and then click the Save And Close button.*

See "Changing a Meeting" on page 176 for information on rescheduling an appointment or event.

Request a reminder. *Click Calendar on the Outlook Bar, double-click the appointment or event you want a reminder for, click to select the Reminder check box, specify how far in advance you want to be reminded, and then click Save And Close. A reminder notice will appear at the scheduled time.*

Schedule an Event

1. Click Calendar on the Outlook Bar.

2. Double-click the date heading.

3. Type the subject of the event.

4. Type the location of the event, or click the drop-down arrow, and select a location from the list.

5. Specify the start and end times of the event.

6. Click to select the Reminder check box, specify an amount of time before the event that you want to notified.

7. Click the Show Time As drop-down arrow, and select an option that indicates your availability.

8. Type any notes or details regarding the event, or attach a file if necessary.

9. Click Categories to help you sort, group, and filter your events.

10. Click the Save And Close button.

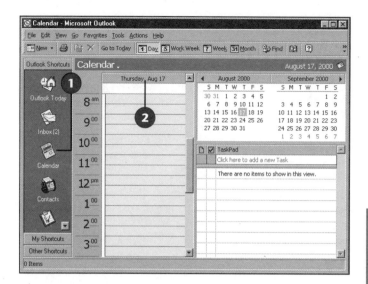

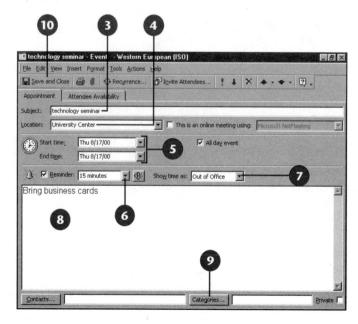

9

Planning a Meeting

The Calendar's *Meeting Planner* helps you to organize meetings quickly, send mail messages to all recipients announcing the meeting, and track their responses. As long as everyone is connected to the same network or the Internet, you can use their Calendars to determine when other people and resources are available so that you can select the best time to schedule a meeting. If you invite people who live in other time zones, Calendar converts their schedule times to your time zone. To facilitate meeting planning and scheduling, Outlook keeps track of your availability. Using Outlook's Free/Busy options, you can decide how your availability information is displayed to others.

Create and Send a Meeting Request

1. Click Calendar on the Outlook Bar, and then select the meeting time you want in the appointment area.

2. Click the Actions menu, and then click Plan A Meeting.

3. Click Invite Others.

4. Select an Address Book.

5. Click a name, and then click the Required or Optional button. Click the Resources button if you're selecting a resource, such as a conference room.

6. Click OK.

7. Click AutoPick to find the first common available time for all participants.

8. Click Make Meeting.

9. Type a brief description of the meeting.

10. Type any notes or attach files as needed.

11. If you want a recurring meeting, click Recurrence, select the schedule pattern, and then click OK.

12. Click the Send button.

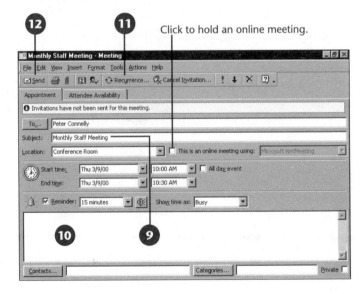

Use to select the meeting start and end times.

Click to update Free/Busy.

Click to hold an online meeting.

What is an iCalendar? *An iCalendar is a standard format for sharing free/busy time information in Calendar over the Internet.*

Hold a meeting over the Internet. *Using Microsoft NetMeeting, you can hold a meeting over the Internet. In the Appointment tab of the Meeting window, click to select the This Is An Online Meeting Using check box, select a directory server, and then enter the organizer's e-mail address.*

Respond to a meeting request. *Click Inbox on the Outlook Bar, double-click the meeting request e-mail message, and then click the Accept button on the Standard toolbar. Outlook schedules it in your Calendar.*

Set the Free/Busy Options

① Click the Tools menu, and then click Options.

② Click the Preferences tab, and then click Calendar Options.

③ For Internet users, click to select the Send Meeting Requests Using iCalendar By Default check box.

For network server users, click to clear this check box.

④ Click Free/Busy Options.

⑤ Enter the number of months you want to publish on the Web.

⑥ Enter how often to update the information.

⑦ Click to select the Publish My Free/Busy Information check box.

⑧ Enter the Web location where you want the information published.

You must have Internet access to the Web location to store the iCalendar.

⑨ Click OK.

⑩ Click OK.

⑪ Click OK.

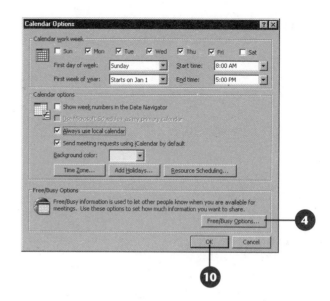

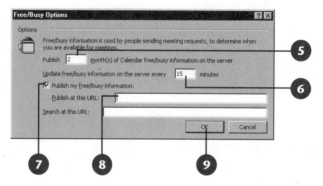

Changing a Meeting

A basic fact of life is that things change—appointments, events, or meetings may need to be moved to another day or time or even relocated. Outlook lets you easily revise your Calendar as your schedule changes so you can change the date of a meeting, switch the time, move the location, revise the attendees list, reserve a certain resource, or even cancel the meeting if necessary. When you do this from Outlook's Calendar, you can be assured that everyone who has been invited to the meeting receives an update.

TIP

Cancel an appointment or event. *Click Calendar on the Outlook Bar, click the appointment or event, and then click the Delete button on the Standard toolbar.*

Reschedule a Meeting, Appointment, or Event

1. Click Calendar on the Outlook Bar.

2. Double-click the meeting, appointment, or event that you want to change.

3. Make your changes.

4. Click the Save And Close button.

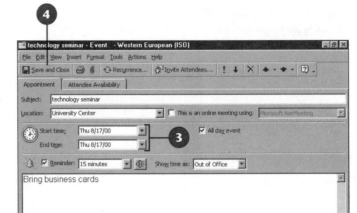

Cancel a Meeting

1. Click Calendar on the Outlook Bar.

2. Click the scheduled meeting that you want to cancel.

3. Click the Delete button on the Standard toolbar.

4. Click the Send Cancellation And Delete Meeting option button.

5. Click OK.

Convert an appointment into a meeting. *Open the appointment, click the Invite Attendees button on the Standard toolbar, add people and resources, enter a location if necessary, and then click the Send button on the Standard toolbar.*

What happens when you delete a meeting? *When you cancel a meeting, you must decide whether to send a cancelation notice as you delete the meeting. The cancelation notice sends an e-mail message to all invited people notifying them that the meeting is canceled and frees any reserved resources.*

Drag an appointment to reschedule it quickly. *Reschedule an appointment or event quickly by dragging it to a new time on the Time Bar or to a new day in the Date Navigator in Day/Week/Month view. Press and hold Ctrl as you drag the appointment or event to copy it to another date or time.*

Change a Meeting Attendees List or Resources

1 Click Calendar on the Outlook Bar.

2 Switch to the view that shows the meeting you want to change.

3 Double-click the meeting in the appointment area.

4 Click the Attendee Availability tab.

5 Select the name of the person you no longer want at the meeting, or select the resource you no longer want reserved, and then click the option to not include this person or resource.

6 Click Invite Others.

7 Click the name of the person you want to invite, or click the resource you need at the meeting.

8 Click the Required, Optional, or Resources button.

9 Click OK.

10 Click the Send button.

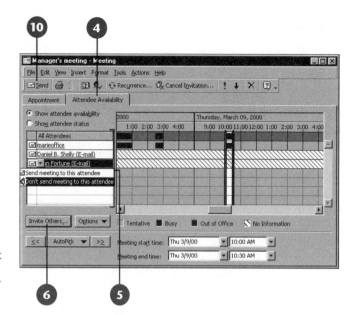

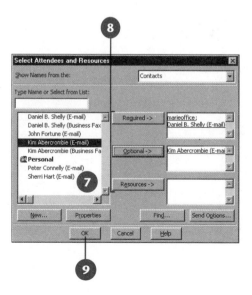

Customizing the Calendar

You can adjust the current view to display different Calendar options. From the View menu, you can display your schedule in a planner format: daily, weekly, or monthly. With AutoPreview turned on, you see the first three lines of the appointment. You can view all the appointments and meetings scheduled from the current day forward, or view current and future events, including those that occur only once a year. You also can view all appointments that take place regularly. In addition you can display all appointments by category.

TIP

Open a calendar from Schedule+. *Click the File menu, click Import And Export, double-click Import From Another Program Or File, double-click Schedule+, click Browse, double-click the file you want to open, select the options you want, and then click Finish.*

Customize the Calendar View

1. Click the Tools menu, and then click Options.

2. Click the Preferences tab, and then click Calendar Options.

3. Click the Calendar Work Week options you want to customize.

4. Click the Calendar Options check boxes you want.

5. Click the Background Color drop-down arrow, and then select a color you want for your calendar.

6. Click the Time Zone, Add Holidays, or Resource Scheduling button to customize these options.

7. Click OK.

8. Click OK.

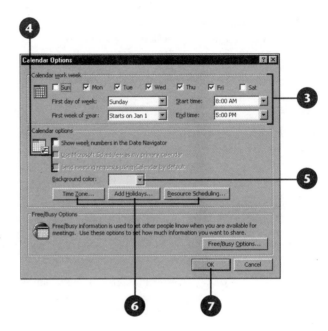

Managing Information with Outlook 2000

Microsoft Outlook 2000 provides an easy and efficient way to track and organize all the information that lands on your desk. You can use Outlook to create a to-do list and assign the items on the list to others as needed from *Tasks*. Rather than cluttering your desk or obscuring your computer with sticky pad notes, use *Notes* to jot down your immediate thoughts, ideas, and other observations. With everything related to your work in one place, you can always locate what you need—files, notes for a project, or even the time of a phone call with a certain contact. Just check the *Journal* timeline to find it.

To help organize and locate information, Outlook allows you to group, sort, and filter items. *Group* organizes items based on a particular *field* (an element for storing a particular type of information). *Sort* arranges items in ascending or descending order according to a specified field. *Filter* shows items that match specific criteria, such as "High Priority." You can group, sort, and filter by more than one field.

If you are interested in communicating with people around the world about things that interest you, you will have fun with newsgroups. A *newsgroup* is a forum where people can share common interests, communicate ideas, ask and answer questions, and comment on a variety of subjects. You can find a newsgroup on almost any topic, from the serious to the lighthearted, from educational to controversial, from business to social.

Managing Tasks

A common Monday chore is creating a list of activities that you should accomplish that week. Outlook *Tasks* is better than that traditional to-do list, because you can track a task's status and progress, estimated and actual hours, mileage, and other associated billing costs. You can create a to-do list with deadlines and cross off items as you complete them. Overdue tasks remain on your list until you finish them or delete them. You can also delegate a particular task to someone by sending a *task request*, complete with deadlines and related attachments. You can see an outstanding task in the Calendar TaskPad and in the tasks list until you check it off or delete it.

SEE ALSO

See "Viewing the Calendar" on page 171 for information about the Calendar TaskPad.

Create a New Task

1. Click the New drop-down arrow on the Standard toolbar, and then click Task.

2. Type a description of the task.

3. Set the time frame, status, priority, alarm, categories, or any other option.

4. Type any relevant notes, or attach related files.

5. Click the Save And Close button.

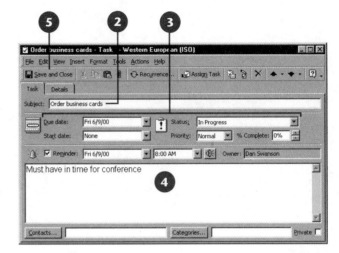

Assign a New Task to Someone Else

1. Click the New drop-down arrow on the Standard toolbar, and then click Task Request.

2. Type the name or e-mail address of the person you are assigning the task to, or click the To button and select a recipient from the list.

3. Type the subject, and then set the time frame, status, priority, alarm, categories, or any other option.

4. Click the Send button.

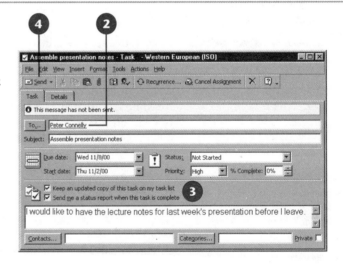

Make a task recurring.
Double-click an existing task on the tasks list or Calendar TaskPad to edit it, or create a new task. Click the Recurrence button on the Standard toolbar, set a recurrence pattern, and then click OK. When the task is set up the way you'd like, click the Save And Close button.

Insert a file into a task.
Double-click an existing task to open it, or create a task. Click the Insert File button on the Standard toolbar. Click the Insert drop-down arrow, select one of the Insert options, and then double-click the file you want to insert.

Enter a new task quickly.
To add a task quickly in either the Calendar TaskPad or the tasks list, click the Click Here To Add A New Task box, type a name or a brief description of the task, enter a deadline, enter any information necessary, and then press Enter.

See "Organizing Information by Categories" on page 186 for information about categories.

Delete a Task from the Task List

1. Click Tasks on the Outlook Bar.

2. Click the task you want to delete.

3. Click the Delete button on the Standard toolbar.

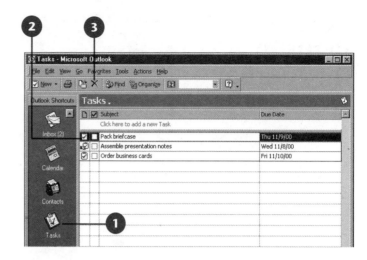

Review and Stop a Contact Activity

1. Click Contacts on the Outlook Bar.

2. Double-click the contact whose activity you want to review.

3. Click the Activities tab to display activities associated with the contact.

4. To stop an activity, select the activity, and then click Stop.

5. Click the Save And Close button.

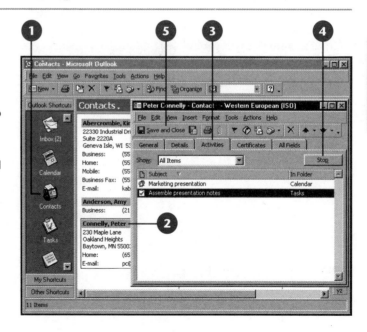

10

Recording Items in the Journal

The Outlook *Journal* is a diary of all the activities and interactions from your day. With everything organized on a timeline, you can see an overview of what you accomplished and when and how long certain activities took. The Journal also provides an alternate way to locate a particular item or a file. You can have the Journal automatically record entries of your phone calls, e-mail messages, meeting requests and responses, tasks, faxes, and documents on which you've worked. You must record tasks, appointments, personal conversations, and existing documents manually.

SEE ALSO

See "Creating a Contact" on page 160 for information about the Contact window.

Automatically Record New Items and Documents

1. Click the Tools menu, and then click Options.

2. Click Journal Options.

3. Click to select the check boxes for the items you want to record in the Journal automatically.

4. Click to select the check boxes of the contacts for whom you want to record the selected items.

5. Click to select the check boxes of the programs that you want recorded.

6. Click OK

7. Click OK.

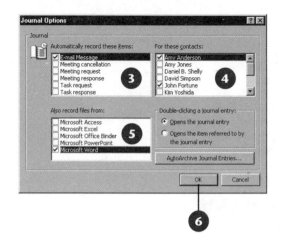

Manually Record a Personal Transaction

1. Click the items or the files you want to record.

2. Click the File menu, point to New, and then click Journal Entry.

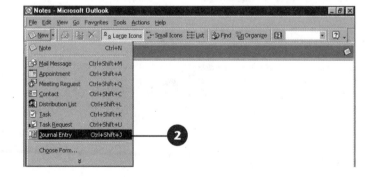

SEE ALSO

See "Working with Journal Entries" on page 184 for more information on journal entries.

SEE ALSO

See "Organizing Information by Categories" on page 186 for more information on categories.

3 Type a description of the journal entry.

4 Enter a company, select a start time and duration, and enter any notes.

5 Click Contacts, select a contact, and then click OK.

6 Click Categories, select one or more categories, and then click OK.

7 Click the Save And Close button.

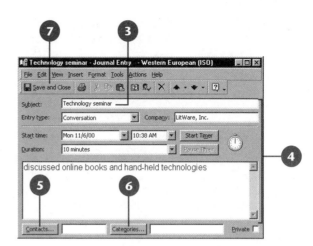

TRY THIS

Manually record an existing document in the Journal. *Display the My Documents folder or the folder that contains your file. Drag the file from its folder in the Information viewer to the Journal icon on the Outlook Bar. Make any changes necessary in the Journal Entry window, and then click the Save And Close button.*

Manually Record a Contact Activity

1 Click Contacts on the Outlook Bar, and then double-click an existing contact.

2 Click the Action menu, and then click New Journal Entry For Contact.

3 Type a description.

4 Click the Entry Type drop-down arrow, and then select an interaction type.

5 Enter a company, select a start time and duration, and then enter any notes.

6 Click the Save And Close button.

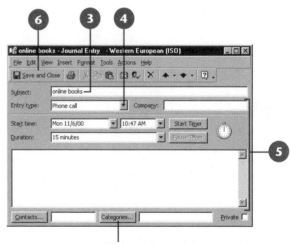

Click to select activity categories.

Working with Journal Entries

Journal entries and their related items, documents, and contacts are easy to open, move, and even delete. When you modify a journal entry, its associated item, document, or contact is not affected. Likewise, when you modify an item, document, or contact, any existing related journal entries remain unchanged. If you no longer need a journal entry, you can select the entry and press Delete or click the Delete button to remove it.

TIP

Expand and collapse entry types. *When you switch to the Journal to view recorded items, some types of entries might be expanded to show all items and others might be collapsed to hide all items. You can easily switch between expanded and collapsed views by double-clicking the Entry Type bar.*

Open a Journal Entry and Its Recorded Item

1. Click the My Shortcuts group on the Outlook Bar.

2. Click Journal on the Outlook Bar.

3. If necessary, click the plus sign (+) double-click the Entry Type bar to display its items.

4. Double-click the journal item, document, or contact name you want to open.

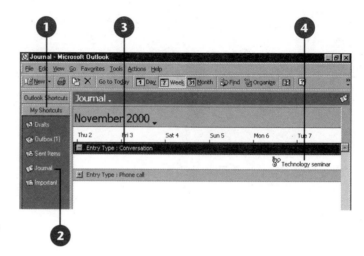

View Journal Entries for a Contact

1. Click Contacts on the Outlook Bar.

2. Double-click a contact name.

3. Click the Activities tab.

4. Click the Show drop-down arrow, and then click Journal.

5. Read the entries for the selected contact.

6. Click the Save And Close button.

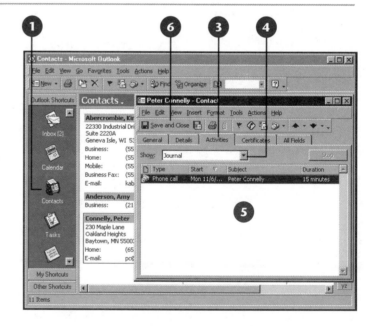

Viewing Information on a Timeline

A *timeline* is an easy way to view the chronological order of recorded items, documents, and activities in the Journal. Each item appears next to the date and time it originated. A solid bar indicates the duration of any activity. You can move items and documents by changing the start time. You can also change the time scale to see items by day, week, and month.

Change the Location of Items and Documents in a Timeline

1. Click Journal on the Outlook Bar.

2. If necessary, click the appropriate entry type.

3. Double-click the journal entry you want to move.

4. Click the Start Date drop-down arrow, and then click a new day.

5. Click the Start Time drop-down arrow, and then click a new time.

6. Click the Save And Close button.

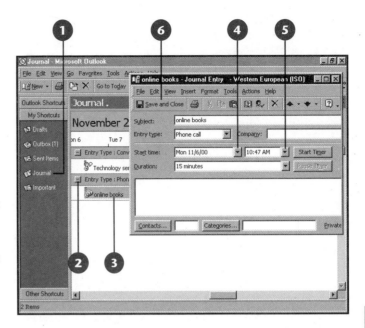

Change Time Scales

◆ Click the Go To Today button on the Standard toolbar to move to the current day.

◆ Click the Day button on the Standard toolbar to see one day at a time.

◆ Click the Week button on the Standard toolbar to view a week at a time.

◆ Click the Month button on the Standard toolbar to look at 30 days.

Time scale buttons

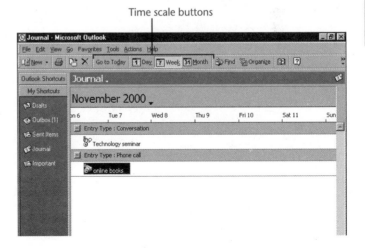

Organizing Information by Categories

A *category* is one or more keywords or phrases you assign to items so you can later find, group, sort, or filter them. Categories provide additional flexibility in how you organize and store items and files. By using categories you can store related items in different folders or unrelated items in the same folder, and still compile a complete list of items related to a specific category. Outlook starts you off with a *Master Category List* of some common categories, but you can add or remove them to fit your purposes.

TIP

Create a mailing list. *You can export a specific category of contacts using Microsoft Word's Mail Merge to create a mailing list.*

Assign and Remove Categories to and from an Outlook Item

1. Click any Outlook item to select it.

2. Click the Edit menu, and then click Categories.

3. Click to select or clear check boxes to assign or remove categories.

4. Click OK.

Categories currently assigned to the selected item

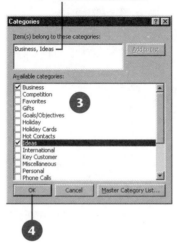

Add or Remove a Master Category

1. Click any item to select it.

2. Click the Edit menu, and then click Categories.

3. Click Master Category List.

4. To add a category, type a new category name, and then click Add.

5. To remove a category, click the category you want to remove, and then click Delete.

6. Click OK.

7. Click OK.

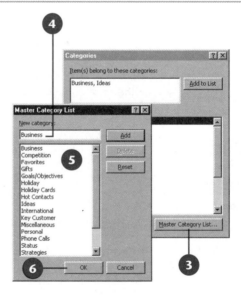

Viewing Items in Groups

As the number of items in Outlook grows, you'll want to be able to view related items. A *group* is any set of items with a common element, such as an assigned category, priority level, or associated contact name. You can group items only in a table or timeline view. If an item has more than one entry in the field by which you are grouping (for example, three categories), that item appears in every relevant group. The changes you make to the item in one group will appear in all copies of that item.

Group Items

1. Right-click a column button, and then click Group By Box.

2. Drag the column button to the Group By Box.

3. Drag any subsequent headings to the Group By Box in the order by which you want to group them.

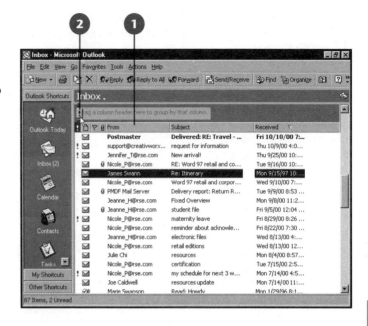

View Grouped Items or Headings

Refer to the table for commands to show or hide grouped items and headings.

VIEWING GROUPED ITEMS AND HEADINGS	
To	**Click**
Show group items	The Expand button
Hide group items	The Collapse button
Show all group items	The View menu, point to Expand/Collapse Groups, and then click Expand All
Show only group headings	The View menu, point to Expand/Collapse Groups, and then click Collapse All
Save new view settings	The View menu, point to Current View, click Edit Current View, click Group By, click the Expand/Collapse Defaults drop-down arrow, select As Last Viewed, click OK, and then click OK

10

Sorting Items

Sometimes you'll want to organize items in a specific order—for example, tasks from high to low priority or in alphabetical order by category. A *sort* arranges items in ascending (A to Z, lowest to highest, recent to distant) or descending (Z to A, highest to lowest, distant to recent) alphabetical, numerical, or chronological order. You can sort items by one or more fields; you can also sort grouped items. Items must be in a table view for you to sort them.

Sort a List of Items in a Table

1. Click the View menu, point to Current View, and then click Customize Current View.

2. Click Sort.

3. Click the Sort Items By drop-down arrow, and then click a field.

4. Click the Ascending or Descending option button.

5. Click the Then By drop-down arrow, and then click a second sort element and order, if necessary.

6. Click OK.

7. Click OK.

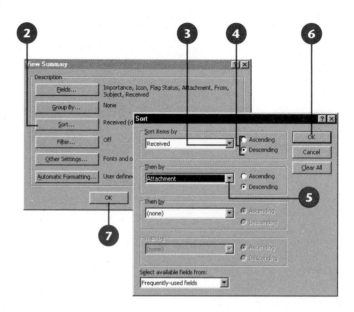

Remove a Sort

1. Click the View menu, point to Current View, and then click Customize Current View.

2. Click Sort.

3. Click Clear All.

4. Click OK.

5. Click OK.

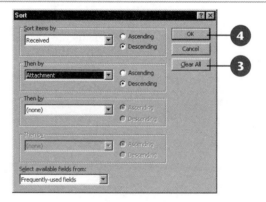

Viewing Specific Files Using Filters

A *filter* isolates the items or files that match certain specifications, such as all appointments with a certain contact or any documents you created last week. If you select two or more filter criteria, only those items and files that meet all the criteria are listed. "Filter Applied" appears in the lower left corner of the status bar as a reminder that you filtered the items and files you are viewing.

Set a Filter to Show Certain Items and Files

1. Click the View menu, point to Current View, and then click Customize Current View.

2. Click Filter.

3. Type a word to search for.

4. Click the In drop-down arrow, and then click a field.

5. Enter in the sender, recipient, and time frame as necessary.

6. Click OK.

7. Click OK.

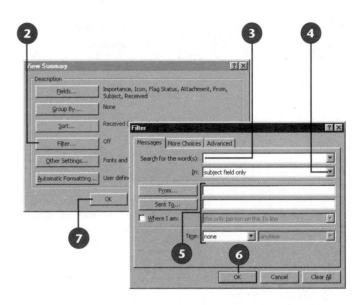

Remove a Filter

1. Click the View menu, point to Current View, and then click Customize Current View.

2. Click Filter.

3. Click Clear All.

4. Click OK.

5. Click OK.

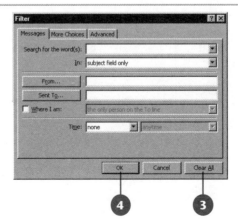

10

Organizing Folders

As you become more dependent on using e-mail for communicating, you need to logically organize the volumes of e-mail messages that you receive. Outlook provides a way to organize each of your folders using specific criteria, known as *rulers,* that you set. For example, you can set your Inbox to store incoming messages from a particular organization in an existing folder (such as Important) or in a folder that you create. You can even specify a way to identify the junk mail that comes into your Inbox.

TIP

Organize folders by color.
Click the Organize button on the Standard toolbar, click Using Colors, and then make the color selections you want.

SEE ALSO

See "Managing E-Mail Messages" on page 168 for information on moving an e-mail message to a folder.

Organize Your Inbox Folder

1. Click Inbox on the Outlook Bar.

2. Click the Organize button on the Standard toolbar.

3. Click an e-mail message in the Information viewer.

4. Click Using Folders.

5. To move the selected message, click the drop-down arrow, click a folder in the folder list, and then click Move.

6. To create a rule to move new messages, click the drop-down arrow, click a folder in the folder list, and then click Create.

   Click Yes or No to apply the rule to the current contents of the folder.

7. Click the Organize button on the Standard toolbar to remove the organize pane.

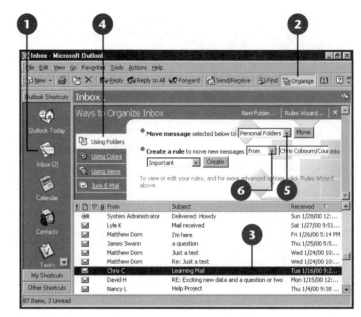

Add to junk senders list.
Click the e-mail message you want to add to the junk senders list, click the Actions menu, point to Junk E-Mail, and then click Add To Junk Senders List or Add To Adult Content Senders List.

Use the Rules Wizard to set criteria for incoming messages. *Click the Tools menu, and then click Rules Wizard, or click the Rules Wizard button when the Organize feature is on.*

Archive all folders using AutoArchive. *Click the Tools menu, click Options, click the Other tab, click AutoArchive, set the archive duration, select the location in which to save the archive, and then click OK. To archive a single folder, click the File menu, and then click Archive.*

File Junk E-Mail

1. Click Inbox on the Outlook Bar.

2. Click the Organize button on the Standard toolbar.

3. Click Junk E-Mail.

4. Click the first Automatically drop-down arrow, and then select Color or Move.

5. Click Turn On, and then click OK to create a Junk E-Mail folder.

6. If necessary, click Yes or click No to create a shortcut icon on the Outlook Bar.

7. Right-click an e-mail message, point to Junk E-Mail, and then click Add To Junk Senders List.

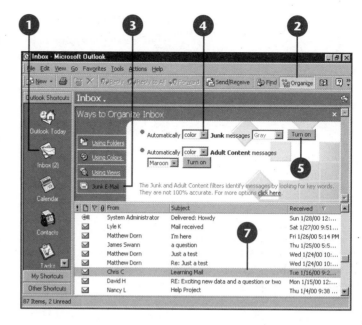

Flag an E-Mail Message for Follow Up

1. Click the e-mail message you want to flag.

2. Click the Actions menu, and then click Flag For Follow Up.

3. Click the Due By drop-down arrow, and then select a date.

4. Click OK.

Click to clear flag.

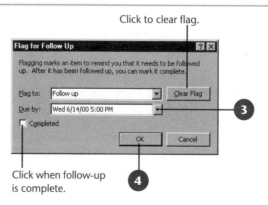

Click when follow-up is complete.

Writing Notes

Notes replace the random scraps of paper on which you might jot down reminders, questions, thoughts, ideas, or directions. Like the popular sticky notes, you can move an Outlook note anywhere on your screen and leave it displayed as you work. Any edits you make to a note are saved automatically. The ability to color-code, size, categorize, sort, or filter notes makes these notes even handier than their paper counterparts.

> **TIP**
>
> **Change the look of Notes.**
> *To change the note color, size, font, and display, click the Tools menu, click Options, and then click Notes Options. Select the options you want to change.*

> **TIP**
>
> **Delete a note.** *Select the note or notes you want to delete, and then click the Delete button on the Standard toolbar.*

Write a New Note

1 Click the New drop-down arrow on the Standard toolbar, and then click Note.

2 Type the text of the note.

3 Click the Close button.

Open and Close a Note

1 Click Notes on the Outlook Bar.

2 Double-click the note you want to open and read.

3 Drag the note to any location on your screen.

4 Click the Close button.

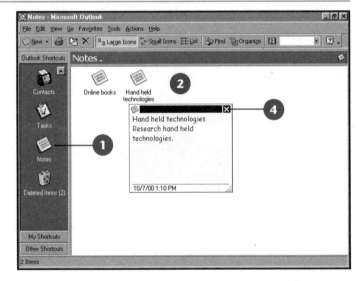

Printing Items from Outlook

You can print any item in Outlook. You can click the Print button on the Standard toolbar to print the selected item using the default print settings. The default or preset printing style is different for each view depending on what type of information you are printing. There are other printing options available in table, calendar, and card views. To choose a printing option, use the Print command on the File menu. You cannot print from a timeline or an icon view.

TIP

Preview your print results.
Click the File menu, and then click Print Preview. Use the Print Preview toolbar buttons to preview your print results, and then click the Close button.

Print an Item or View

1. Click the item you want to print.

2. Click the File menu, and then click Print.

   Printing options change depending on the item and view. Refer to the table for information on the printing options available for different views.

3. If necessary, click the Name drop-down arrow, and then select a printer.

4. Select a print style.

   If you want, click Define Styles to specify the print style settings you want.

5. Click the Number Of Pages drop-down arrow, and select All, Odd, or Even.

6. Specify print options or a print range. Options vary depending on the item you selected.

7. Click OK.

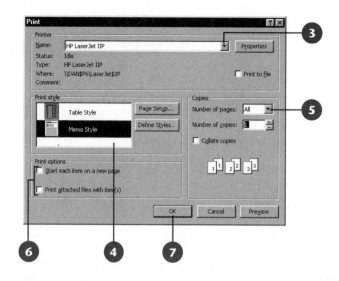

PRINTING OPTIONS		
View	**Style**	**Prints**
Table	Table	All items in a list in the visible columns
Calendar	Daily	Each day from 7 A.M. to 7 P.M. on a separate page with tasks and notes
	Weekly	Each week from midnight to midnight on a separate page
	Monthly	Each month on a separate page
	Tri-Fold	Three equal columns containing one day, one week, one month, or tasks
Card	Card	All contact cards with letter tabs and headings and six blank cards at the end
	Phone Directory	Names and phone numbers for all contacts with letter tabs and headings

10

Viewing the News Window

Toolbar
The toolbar contains buttons for commands you can use while you read your mail messages.

Menu bar
The menu bar gives you access to all Outlook Newsreader options.

Folder bar
The Folder bar displays the newsgroup currently selected in the Folder list.

Folder list
The Folder list contains all the folders in Outlook Newsreader. Both news servers and newsgroups are listed here.

Message list
The message list displays newsgroup messages from the currently selected group in the Folder list.

Preview pane
The preview pane displays the contents of the message currently selected in the message list.

Status bar
The status bar indicates how many newsgroup messages there are, indicates the progress of downloading news, shows that you are connected to the Internet, and provides other information.

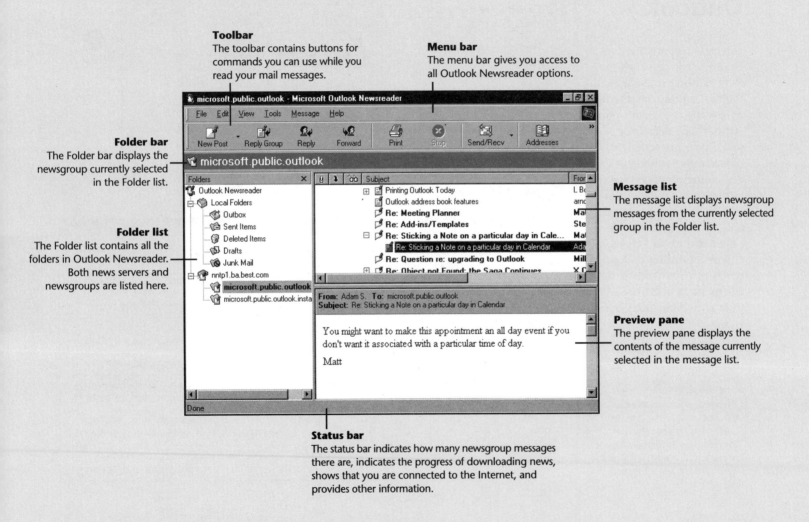

Subscribing to a Newsgroup

Before you can participate in a newsgroup, you need a *newsreader program*, such as Outlook Newsreader, that allows you subscribe to newsgroups. *Subscribing* to a newsgroup places a link to a group in the Folder list, providing easy access to the newsgroup. Before subscribing to a newsgroup, read some messages (called *articles*) and get a feel for the people and content. If you like what you read and want to participate regularly in the series of conversations related to specific topics (called *threads*), you can subscribe to that newsgroup.

TIP

Set up Outlook newsgroup account. *On the Outlook Newsreader start page, click the Setup A Newsgroup Account link, and then follow the wizard instructions.*

View and Subscribe to a Newsgroup

1. Click the View menu, point to Go, and then click News.

2. Click a news server in the folder list.

3. Click the Newsgroups button.

4. Click a newsgroup you want to view.

5. If you want to subscribe, click Subscribe.

6. Click Go To.

News server

Type a topic to find a newsgroup.

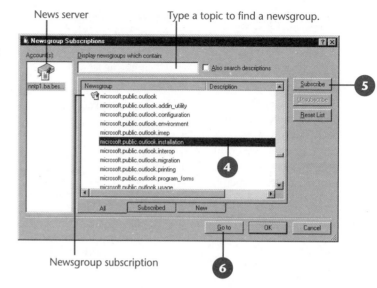

Newsgroup subscription

Unsubscribe to a Newsgroup

1. Right-click the newsgroup to which you want to unsubscribe.

2. Click Unsubscribe on the shortcut menu.

Current newsgroup subscription

Click to display newsgroups.

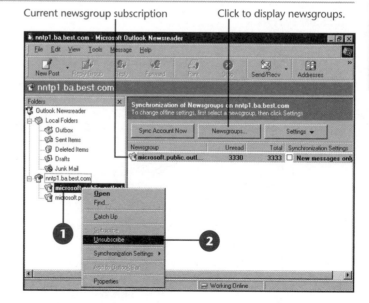

10

Reading and Posting News

Once you have subscribed to a newsgroup, you will want to retrieve new newsgroup messages (or at least the message headers), open the messages, and read them. If you want, you can save a message to your hard disk for future reference. Part of the fun of newsgroups is that you can participate in an ongoing discussion, respond privately to a message's author, or start a new conversation thread yourself by posting your own message on a topic. A *conversation thread* consists of the original message on a topic along with the responses that include the original message title preceded by *RE:*.

Open and Read News Messages

1. Click the news server icon in the folder list.

2. Click the newsgroup whose messages you want to read.

3. If necessary, click the plus sign (+) to the left of a message header to display all the reply headers for that message.

4. When you see a message or reply you want to read, click its header in the message list.

5. Read the message in the preview pane.

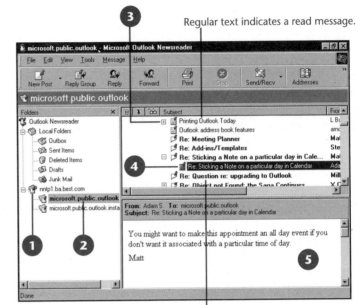

Regular text indicates a read message.

Bold text indicates an unread message.

Post a New Message

1. Select the newsgroup to which you want to post a message.

2. Click the New Post button on the toolbar.

3. Type a subject for your message.

4. Type your message.

5. Click the Send button on the toolbar.

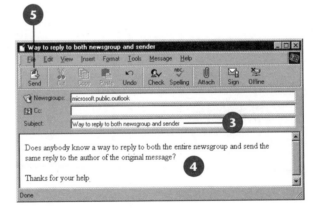

11

Creating a Publication with Publisher 2000

When you need to create a great looking publication, such as a business card, letterhead, newsletter, Web page, or brochure, use Microsoft Publisher 2000 to get the job done quickly and easily.

Publisher is a *desktop publishing program*—software you can use to combine text, graphics, and original drawings with sophisticated formatting, all in one easy-to-use package. With Publisher you can use creative layout and design techniques that were once the exclusive realm of high-priced publishers or graphics designers.

By far the most popular and useful tools in Publisher are the wizards. A wizard guides you through the process of completing a task. For example, when you use a publication wizard, you answer a few simple questions about your design preferences for your publication and the wizard creates it according to your specifications. After the wizard completes the publication, you can use other Publisher tools to add finishing touches. You can preview hundreds of professionally designed publications (invitations, announcements, business cards, newsletters, brochures, awards, and many others), and choose from dozens of creative and coordinated designs. You just choose the design elements you want.

Viewing the Publisher Window

Title bar
The title bar contains the name of the active publication. *Unsaved Publication* is a temporary name Publisher uses until you assign a new one.

Menu bar
The ten menus give you access to all Publisher commands.

Objects toolbar
The toolbar contains buttons to create and select objects, such as text or picture frames.

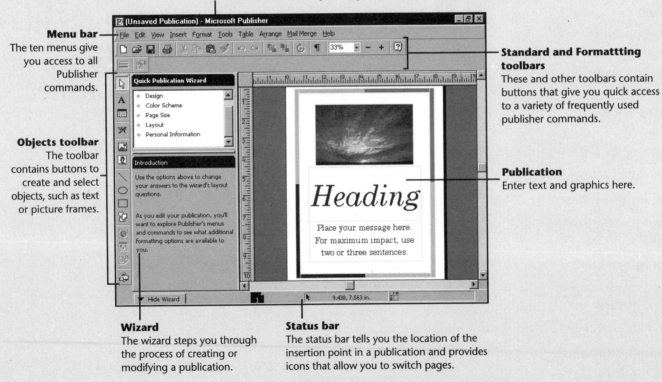

Standard and Formattting toolbars
These and other toolbars contain buttons that give you quick access to a variety of frequently used publisher commands.

Publication
Enter text and graphics here.

Wizard
The wizard steps you through the process of creating or modifying a publication.

Status bar
The status bar tells you the location of the insertion point in a publication and provides icons that allow you to switch pages.

Creating a Quick Publication

Occasionally you'll want to create a one-page publication that does not fit into any of the categories listed in Publisher's Catalog—for example, a title page for a report. When you want to create a page quickly, use the Quick Publications Wizard. After Publisher creates a page based on your selection, you can use the list of wizard options as a guide for customizing the page.

TIP

Don't display Catalog at startup. *Click the Tools menu, click Options, click the General tab, click to clear the Use Catalog At Start check box, and then click OK.*

TIP

Turn off AutoSave as a reminder. *Click the Tools menu, click Options, click the User Assistance tab, click to clear the Remind To Save Publication check box, and then click OK.*

Create a New Quick Publication

1. Start Publisher.

   If you have already started Publisher, click the File menu, and then click New.

2. Click the Publications By Wizard tab.

3. Click Quick Publications.

4. Click the thumbnail that displays the design for the publication you want.

5. Click Start Wizard.

6. Answer the wizard questions as you step through them.

   Click Next to continue or click Back to review your answers.

7. When you're done, click Finish.

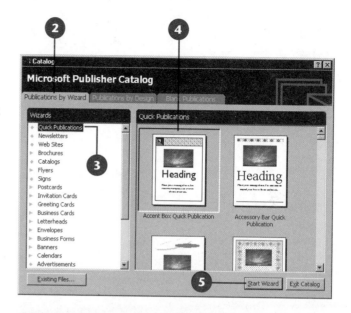

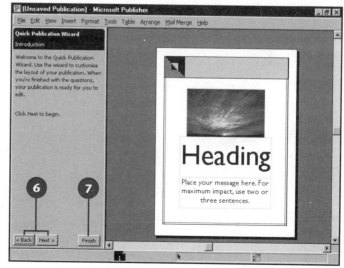

Creating a New Publication

When you first start Publisher, you see a Catalog dialog box you can use to create a new publication or open an existing publication. You have several options for creating a new publication. You can choose a wizard to help you, or you can start from a blank publication. Because you can work on only one publication at a time, Publisher closes the current publication before opening a new one. Publisher reminds you to save your changes before closing a publication.

Create a New Publication By Wizard

1. Start Publisher.

   If you have already started Publisher, click the File menu, and then click New.

2. Click the Publications By Wizard tab.

3. Click the type or category of publication you want.

   Click a category identified with an arrow to see its subcategories.

4. Click the thumbnail that represents the kind of publication you want to create.

5. Click Start Wizard.

6. Answer the wizard questions as you step through them for color scheme, page size, layout, personal information, and other options.

   Click Next to continue or click Back to review your answers.

7. When you're done, click Finish.

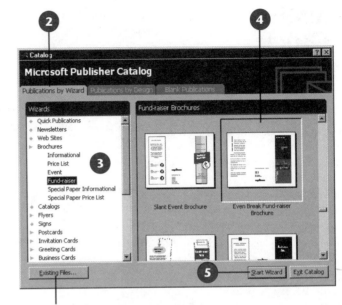

Click to open existing publications.

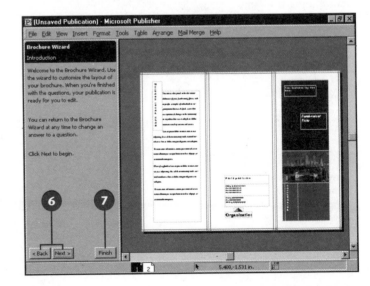

Bypass wizard questions without changing user assistance options. *Click the Finish button in the wizard window to complete the wizard without stepping through the remaining questions. Publisher creates your publication using default settings.*

Step through the wizard. *You can have the wizard ask you a series of questions about your formatting and design options. These questions correspond to the categories you see in the wizard area of the Publisher window. Click the Tools menu, click Options, click the User Assistance tab, click to select the Step Through Wizard Questions check box, and then click OK.*

Change your mind when stepping through a wizard. *Click the Back button to return to a previous wizard question and make different selections.*

Create a New Publication By Design

1. Start Publisher.

   If you have already started Publisher, click the File menu, and then click New.

2. Click the Publications By Design tab.

3. Click a design set, and then click a specific design.

4. Click the thumbnail that represents the kind of publication you want to create.

5. Click Start Wizard.

6. Answer the wizard questions as you step through them for design, color scheme, orientation, logo, printing, and other options.

   Click Next to continue or click Back to review your answers.

7. When you're done, click Finish.

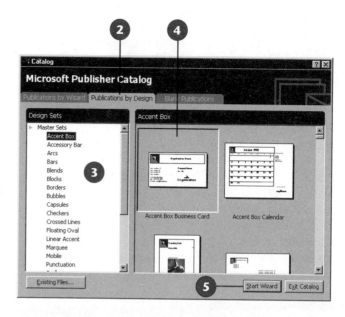

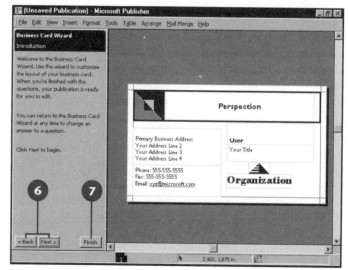

11

Creating a Blank Publication

Publisher's wizards can be a big help in getting you started when you create a new publication. Every so often, however, you want to create a unique publication and none of wizards will do the job. In that case, you can start a blank publication. If you know how to create and use frames, you can create a publication from scratch. Nevertheless, you can still display the wizard in the window to help you think of design elements and options, including orientation and layout. If none of the sample blank publications meets your needs, you can also create a custom page.

> **TIP**
>
> **See more of the window at one time.** *Click the Hide Wizard button to hide the wizard area at the bottom of the wizard panel, giving yourself more space to work.*

Create a Blank Publication

1. Start Publisher.

   If you have already started Publisher, click the File menu, and then click New.

2. Click the Blank Publications tab.

3. Click the kind of publication you want.

4. Double-click the thumbnail that displays the page layout for the publication you want.

5. In the wizard panel, click Design, and then choose a design.

6. In the wizard panel, click Color Scheme, and then choose a set of colors.

7. In the wizard panel, click Page Size, and then choose the orientation of the page.

8. In the wizard panel, click Layout, and then choose the arrangement of text and graphics on the page.

9. Click Personal Information, and then choose the name and address information that you want to appear.

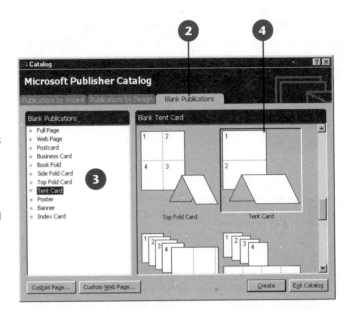

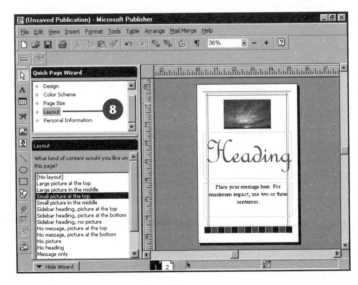

Choose a special paper size. *If you have special sized paper you want to use to print a publication, click the Special Size option button in the Page Setup dialog box. In the Choose A Special Size area, choose the type of paper stock, and if necessary specify the size of the paper.*

Choose a special fold. *When you are creating a publication with a page folded in an unusual way, click the Special Fold option button in the Page Setup dialog box. In the Choose A Special Fold area, choose the type of folds for your publication.*

Create labels for applying name and address information to an envelope or brochure. *Click Labels in the Page Setup dialog box. In the Choose A Label area, choose the brand and item number of the labels you are using.*

Create a Custom Blank Page

1. Start Publisher.

   If you have already started Publisher, click the File menu, and then click New.

2. Click the Blank Publications tab.

3. Click Custom Page.

4. Choose the layout for the publication.

5. Choose an orientation.

6. Click OK.

7. Begin designing your publication.

   No wizard options appear when you create a custom blank publication.

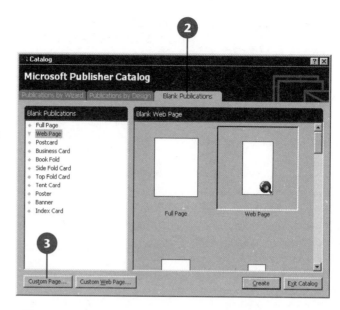

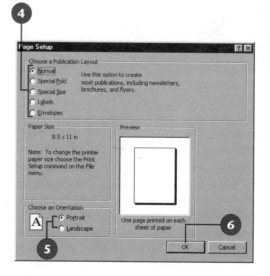

Creating a Newsletter

A newsletter is a great way to communicate information on a regular basis. Businesses can use newsletters to inform customers about new products and services, answer frequently asked customer support questions, or generate interest in upcoming events. For personal use, you can distribute a newsletter to update family members on family matters or use a newsletter as a creative alternative to the typical holiday letter. Using the Newsletter Wizard in Publisher, you can create a multiple-page newsletter formatted with one, two, three, or a combination of columns. You can also include forms, calendars, and other inside pages formatted for text and graphics. After you create the newsletter, use additional wizards to create inside pages and insert new pages.

Step Through a Wizard to Create a Newsletter

1. In the Catalog, click the Publications By Wizard tab.

2. Click Newsletters.

3. Double-click the thumbnail that displays the design for your newsletter.

4. Click Next to continue.

5. Choose a color scheme for your newsletter. Click Next to continue.

6. Indicate the number of columns you want. Click Next to continue.

7. Click Yes if you want to allow space for a customer address. Click Next to continue.

8. Indicate whether you want one-sided or two-sided printing. Click Next to continue.

9. Choose the name and address information that you want to appear.

10. Click Finish to create a newsletter based on your responses to the wizard.

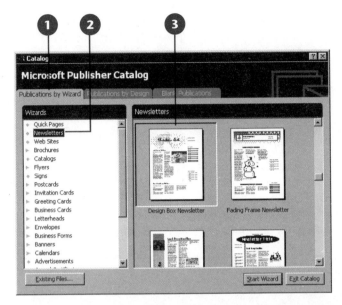

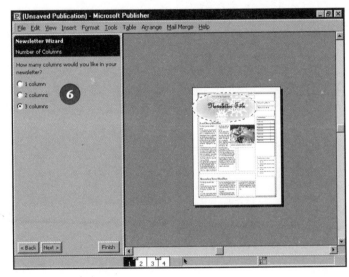

Use the Wizard to Create Inside Pages in a Newsletter

1. In the status bar, click the number of an inside page.

2. In the wizard panel, click Inside Page Content.

3. Click the drop-down arrow and choose the page for the new content.

4. Click the content option to include on this page.

   Repeat steps 2 and 3 for each inside page.

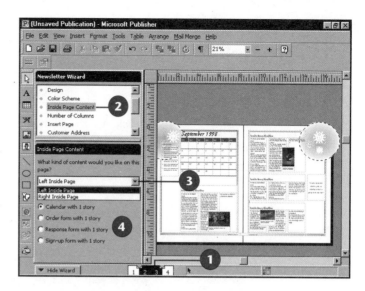

Use the Wizard to Insert a Page in a Newsletter

1. In the status bar, click the number of an inside page.

2. In the wizard panel, click Insert Page.

3. Click the Insert Page button.

4. Click the drop-down arrow, and then select a content option for this page.

5. Click OK.

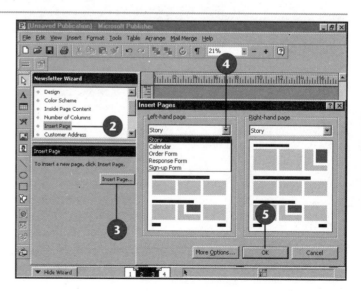

11

Creating a Web Site

The World Wide Web is your path to communicating with the greatest number of people without incurring printing and mailing costs. Use Publisher to create publications for your Web site. You can create Web pages that include text, calendars, schedules, special offers, price lists, and forms. You can use text and objects in your Web site to create hyperlinks to other Web pages. When you have completed your Web site, you can preview the Web pages as they will appear on the World Wide Web. Once you are satisfied with the Web site, you can use the Save As Web Page feature to save the publication for the Web.

TIP

Get Web site properties.
Open the Web site, click the File menu, click Web Properties, click the Site or Page tab, make any changes, and then click OK.

Step Through a Wizard to Create a Web Site

1 In the Catalog, click the Publications By Wizard tab.

2 Click Web Sites.

3 Double-click the thumbnail that displays the design for your Web site.

4 Click Next to continue.

5 Choose a color scheme for your Web site. Click Next to continue.

Publisher displays the first page (called the *home page*) of your Web site.

6 Click a check box for each of the pages you want to include as part of your Web site. Click Next to continue.

Each option will appear on its own page.

7 Indicate whether you want to include a form. Click Next to continue.

8 Indicate how you want the navigation bar to appear. Click Next to continue.

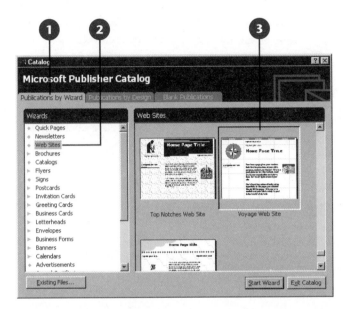

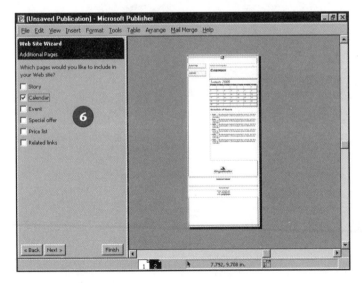

TIP

Create a custom Web site.
If you want to create a Web site from scratch, click the Blank Publications tab in the Catalog, and then click the Custom Web Page button.

TRY THIS

Convert your Web site to a newsletter or brochure.
Reuse the information in a Web site for a newsletter or brochure. Click Convert To Print in the wizard area of the window, and then choose to create a newsletter or a brochure. This starts the wizard for the publication you chose.

SEE ALSO

See "Previewing Web Pages" on page 265 and "Saving Documents as Web Pages" on page 266 for information on previewing and saving your Web page.

SEE ALSO

See "Inserting Hyperlinks" on page 260 and "Using and Removing Hyperlinks" on page 262 for information on inserting hyperlinks in text and on entire object.

(9) Click Yes if you want a background sound to play when the home page opens. Click Next to continue.

(10) Click Yes if you want the background to appear textured. Click Next to continue.

(11) Choose the name and address information that you want to appear.

(12) Click Finish to create a Web site based on your responses to the wizard.

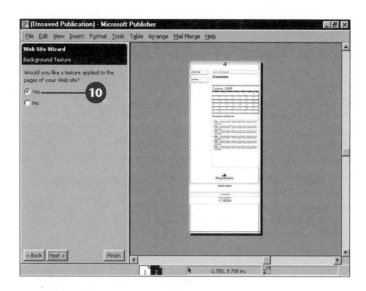

Create a Hyperlink on a Hot Spot

(1) Open the Web page in which you want to add a hyperlink on a hot spot.

(2) Click the Hot Spot Tool button on the Objects toolbar.

(3) Drag to create a rectangle around the area you want a hot spot.

(4) Click the hyperlink option button you want.

(5) Enter the Internet address.

(6) Click OK.

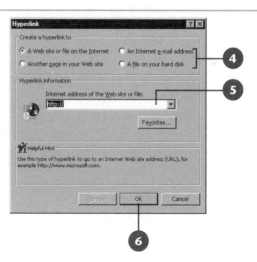

Changing Your View

You can view the pages in your publication in a one-page spread or a two-page spread. A two-page spread mimics the layout of a book or magazine that is lying open in front of you, where two pages face each other. You can also switch among various magnification levels. Viewing the page at a reduced size allows you to see an overview of your design. Zooming in on the pages makes type legible and provides a higher degree of accuracy when creating or positioning frames.

> **TIP**
>
> **Switch between two different view sizes.** *Press F9 to toggle back and forth between actual size (100%) and the current view size.*

> **TIP**
>
> **Zoom and scroll using Microsoft IntelliMouse.** *Roll the wheel to scroll, or press and hold Ctrl and roll the wheel to zoom.*

View a Publication in One- or Two-Page View

1. Click the View menu, and then click Two-Page Spread.

   A check mark next to Two-Page Spread indicates two-page view. No check mark indicates one-page view.

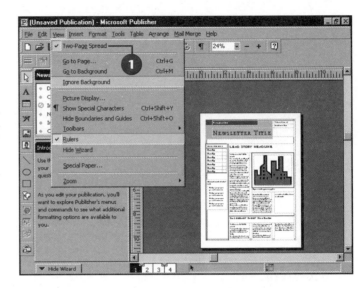

Change the View Size of a Page

1. Click the Zoom drop-down arrow on the Standard toolbar.

2. Select the view percentage you want.

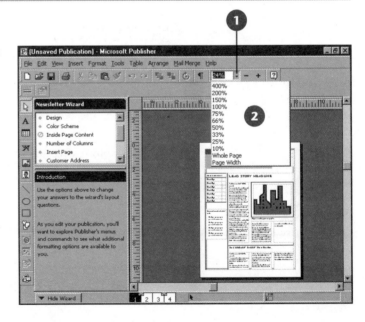

Inserting and Deleting Pages

You can add one or more pages to your publication at any time during the design process. However, you can delete only one page or one spread at a time.

TIP

Move from page to page. *You can see information on the other pages of a publication by clicking the page thumbnail on the status bar at the bottom of the window. Each thumbnail corresponds to a page in your publication.*

TIP

Go to a specific page. *Click the View menu, click Go To Page, enter the page where you want to go, and then click OK.*

TIP

Insert page numbers. *Click in the text or table frame where you want to insert a page number, click the Insert menu, and then click Page Number.*

Insert One or More Pages

1. Display the page before or after the one you want to insert.

2. Click the Insert menu, and then click Page.

3. If necessary, select the type of left-hand and right-hand page you want to insert, and then click More Options.

4. Type the number of pages you want to add.

5. Click the option button to indicate the location of the new pages.

6. Click OK.

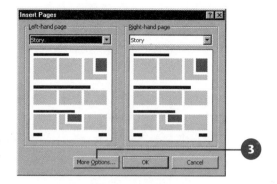

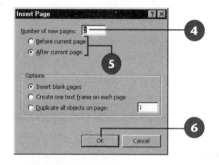

Delete a Page

1. Move to the page you want to delete.

2. Click the Edit menu, and then click Delete Page.

   In one-page view, Publisher deletes the page.

3. In two-page view, click the option button to indicate the pages you want to delete.

4. Click OK.

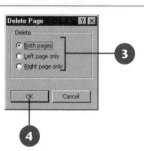

11

Inserting and Editing Text

When you create a publication with a wizard, Publisher places generic text in a text frame. Text in a text frame is also called a *text object*. The frame serves as a container in which you can easily format, move, and resize an area of text. The generic text acts as a placeholder. Replace the placeholder text with your own text. The *insertion point* indicates where text appears when you type. To place the insertion point in your text, move the mouse pointer over the text and then click.

You can automatically insert and update information, such as your name and address. If you change the information, Publisher updates it throughout the publication.

SEE ALSO

See "Editing Text" on page 28 for information on selecting, moving, and copying text.

Insert and Edit Text in a Frame

1. Click the text in a frame if it isn't already selected.

   The small boxes on the frame indicate that it is selected.

2. Click to place the insertion point where you want to enter or edit text.

3. To delete text, press Delete or Backspace.

4. Type the text you want to enter.

5. Click outside the text frame to deselect it.

Generic text

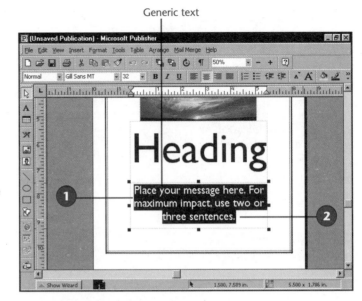

Change Edit Options

1. Click the Tools menu, and then click Options.

2. Click the Edit tab.

3. Click to select the editing check boxes you want.

   ◆ Drag-and-drop editing

   ◆ Automatic selecting or formatting entire word

   ◆ Automatic hyphenating in new text frame

   ◆ Use single-clicking object creation

4. Click OK.

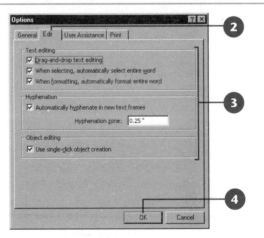

TIP

Clear or delete personal information. *To clear the personal information text throughout the publication, select the text and then press Delete. To delete the personal information in an individual text object, click to select the text object, click the Edit menu, and then click Delete Object.*

TIP

Check spelling in a publication. *Click the Spelling button on the Standard toolbar, click Ignore, or click the correct spelling, and then click Change. When you're done, click OK.*

SEE ALSO

See "Selecting, Moving, and Resizing Objects" on page 38 for information on selecting, moving, and resizing text objects.

SEE ALSO

See "Making Corrections" on page 36 and "Correcting Text Automatically" on page 34 for information on using the Undo and Redo command and AutoCorrect.

Enter or Update Personal Information

1. Click the Edit menu, and then click Personal Information.

2. Click the personal information set you want to edit.

3. Enter the personal information for that set.

4. Click Update.

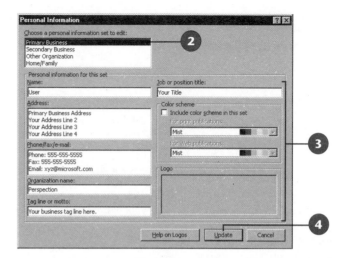

Insert Personal Information

1. Click the Insert menu, and then point to Personal Information.

2. Click the personal information set you want.

   A new text frame is created. Each personal information component must remain in its own separate text frame.

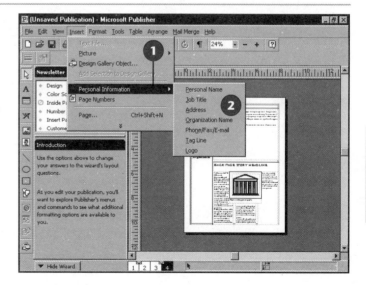

11

Merging Information in a Publication

Postcards, brochures, and newsletters provide space for mailing information. Instead of creating a new publication for each recipient, you can use Publisher's Mail Merge feature to enter all the names and addresses (called *fields*) in a list, called the *data source*, such as an Outlook contact list, an Excel worksheet, an Access database file, or a Publisher address list. Then you can merge the data source into whichever publications you choose. You can even reuse the same list with other publications.

Create an Address List

1. Click the Mail Merge menu, and then click Create Publisher Address List.

2. Enter the information you want to use when merging.

3. Click New Entry to add more entries.

4. After you have completed your entries, click Close.

5. Specify the location and the name for this data source.

6. Click OK.

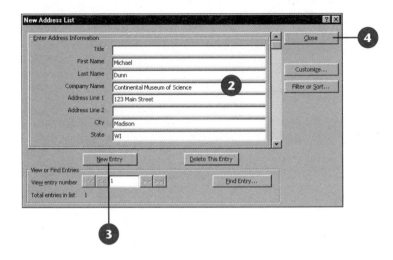

Insert Merge Fields from Different Sources

1. Open the publication in which you want the address information to appear.

2. Place the insertion point in the text box where you want address information.

3. Click the Mail Merge menu, and then click Open Data Source.

4. Click the button with the data source you want to merge in the publication.

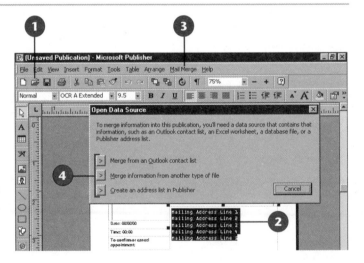

Preview merge results.
Click the Mail Merge menu, and then click Show Merge Results. Click one of the Page buttons to page through the merged publication or enter a number to view the corresponding entry.

Print merge results. *After you merge information in the publication, click the File menu, click Print Merge, select the print settings you want, and then click OK.*

Filter and sort merge results. *Click the Mail Merge menu, click Filter Or Sort, click the Filter or Sort tab, select the filter or sort settings you want, and then click OK.*

Save disk space. *Because it is so fast and easy to merge information from an address list, you can save a lot of disk space by not saving each of your merged publications. If you need to re-create the mailing in the future, merge the publication with the data source again.*

5 Click the Files Of Type drop-down arrow, and then select a file format. Locate and double-click the file that you want merge.

6 Select the field you want to insert.

7 Click Insert.

A field code (which serves as a placeholder) appears in the text box.

8 Type any spaces, punctuation, or returns to format or separate the fields.

9 Repeat steps 6 through 8 for each field you want to insert.

10 Click Close.

Merge Information

1 Open the publication that contains merge fields.

2 Click the Mail Merge menu, and then click Merge.

The data source information replaces the field codes.

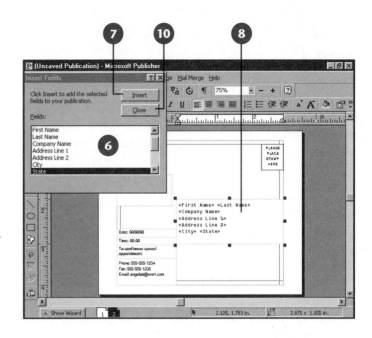

Current record   Click to review each merged document.

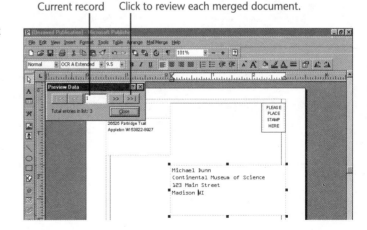

Setting Up the Page

Page layout determines the general size and orientation of your publication and affects how the pages will be arranged when you print. Paper size refers to the physical dimensions of the paper in your printer. Publisher's page size refers to the dimensions of your publication, which can be the same, smaller, or larger than the paper size.

TIP

Automatically display the Print Troubleshooter. *Click the Tools menu, click Options, click the Print tab, click to select the Automatically Display Print Troubleshooter check box, and then click OK.*

TIP

Improve printer color matching. *Click the Tools menu, click Options, click the General tab, click to select the Improve Screen And Printer Color Matching check box, and then click OK.*

Set Up the Page

1. Click the File menu, and then click Page Setup.

2. Click the publication layout option button you want.

   ◆ Normal

   ◆ Special Fold or Special Size

   ◆ Labels or Envelopes

3. Specify the options you want for the publication layout.

4. Click OK.

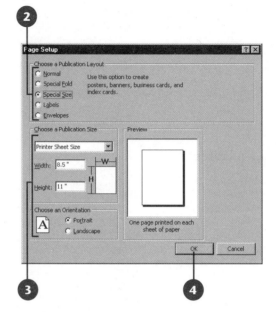

Set Up the Printer

1. Click the File menu, and then click Printer Setup.

   Each printer displays a different Print Setup dialog box.

2. Specify the print setup options that you want.

3. Click Properties, change the specific printer settings you want, and then click OK.

4. Click OK.

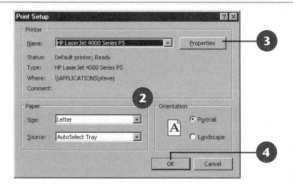

Using Commercial Printing Tools

Publisher provides full support for commercial printing, including automatic conversion to spot or process color with automatic color separation. In addition, advanced tools such as trapping (overlapping the edges of different colors), graphic link management, and font lists provide commercial printers with the features they need to print high-quality publications.

TIP

Get an embedded font list.
An embedded font is attached to the document. Embed a font when the printer doesn't have it. Click the Tools menu, point to Commercial Printing Tools, and then click Fonts.

TIP

Check links to graphics.
Click the Tools menu, point to Commercial Printing Tools, and then click Graphic Manager. Select a link, click Details, click OK, and then click Close.

Change Color Print Settings

1. Click the Tools menu, point to Commercial Printing Tools, and then click Color Printing.

   Check with your commercial printer for details.

2. Click the color option button you want.

3. Click OK.

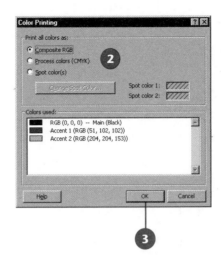

Change Trapping Preferences

1. Click the Tools menu, point to Commercial Printing Tools, point to Trapping, and then click Preferences.

   Check with your commercial printer for trapping options.

2. Click to select the trapping and black overprinting check boxes you want.

3. If necessary, click Reset All to restore settings.

4. Click OK.

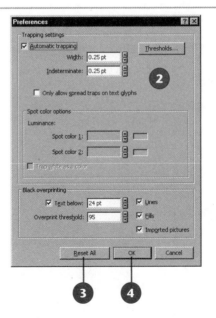

11

Printing Publications

The whole point of creating publications is to publish them, which—except for Web pages—means printing the publications you've created. If you have a printer connected to your computer you can print publications right away. If you have special printing needs, however, you might want to use a commercial printer who can deliver high-quality color documents. The *Pack And Go Wizard* compacts all the information a printer needs across multiple disks. Whatever your printing requirements, Publisher makes it easy to get the results of your labors onto the printed page.

TIP

Unpack the Pack And Go file. *In Windows Explorer, double-click the Unpack.exe file to open a Pack And Go file.*

Print a Publication on Your Printer

1. Click the File menu, and then click Print.

2. Specify the pages that you want to print.

3. If necessary, click Advanced Print Settings to select resolution, printer's marks, bleeds, font substitution, and special print output.

4. Click OK.

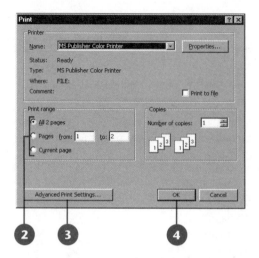

Create a File for Commercial Printing

1. Click the File menu, point to Pack And Go, and then click Take To A Commercial Printing Service.

2. Click Next to begin creating the file.

3. Specify the drive and directory where you want to save the file. Click Next to continue.

4. Click the graphics and font information you want to include. Click Next to continue.

5. Click Finish.

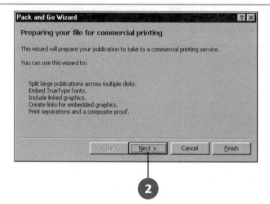

12

Designing a Publication with Publisher 2000

After you create a publication, you can modify any design element you see. Each element in a publication is enclosed in a *frame*. The frame serves as a container to hold objects, such as a block of text, a picture, or a graphic element you've created yourself. If you created a publication with a wizard, you see placeholder text, which you replace with your own text in the frame. You can add more elements by adding new frames. For example, to add a new heading (or some other text) to a brochure, you create a text frame. To add a graphic, you create a picture frame and then insert a graphic. You create new frames using the corresponding frame tool located on the toolbar at the left side of the window. After you create a frame, you can move it or change its size to allow for more text (in the case of a text frame) or a larger or smaller image (as in a picture frame). You can rotate frames or change their order when you want to place different pictures or text on top of or behind each other. And with the Design Gallery you can add ready-made elements such as mastheads, calendars, and coupons.

If you already know how to use Microsoft Word's text and picture frames, you'll be on familiar ground with Publisher's frames. If using frames is new to you, you will find working with frames a snap to learn.

Checking Your Design

You can check the design of your publication for errors. The Design Checker looks over your publication for problems, such as empty frames, text in overflow areas off the page, covered objects, objects in nonprinting regions, disproportional pictures, and poor spacing between sentences.

TIP

Make changes as you check. *The Design Checker uses a special kind of window called a* modeless dialog box, *which means you don't need to close the Design Checker dialog box while you work on your document. Drag the title bar to see your document.*

TIP

Use the Design Checker for your Web documents. *The Design Checker can search for specific problems related to Web pages, such as hyperlinks that can't be reached or graphics that will take a long time to download.*

Check Your Design

1. Click the Tools menu, and then click Design Checker.

2. Specify the pages you want to check.

3. To check the background, click to select the Check Background Page(s) check box.

4. Click Options.

5. Click to select the check boxes for the types of errors you want to find.

6. Click OK.

7. Click OK.

8. If Publisher finds a problem, it describes it in a dialog box and suggests ways to fix it.

   ◆ If you don't understand how to fix the problem, click Explain.

   ◆ Click Continue to proceed with checking your document.

   ◆ Click Ignore to not fix the problem.

9. Click OK.

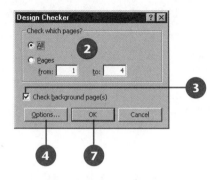

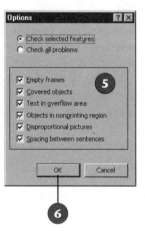

Creating a Frame

Before you can type text, insert a table, import a picture, design WordArt, or insert an OLE object, you must draw the appropriate frame for that type of object.

TIP

Show or hide frame boundaries and guides. *You can show or hide frame boundaries. To show boundaries, click the View menu, and then click Show Boundaries And Guides. To hide boundaries, click the View menu, and then click Hide Boundaries And Guides.*

TIP

Get tips and tricks on using Publisher. *Click the Help menu, and then click Publisher Tutorial. Click a link to the topic you want learn about. When you're done, click the Close button.*

SEE ALSO

See Section 3, "Using Shared Office 2000 Tools," for information on adding pictures, WordArt, and media clips.

Create a Frame

1 Click the corresponding toolbar button to create the type of object you want.

Refer to the table for information on the different tools.

2 Position the pointer on the page where you want the frame.

3 Press and hold the mouse button while you drag diagonally.

The frame boundary will appear.

4 Release the mouse button when you have created a rectangle the size you want.

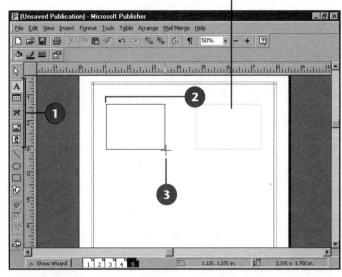

Previously created frame

TOOLBAR BUTTONS

Icon	Button Name	Purpose
A	Text Frame Tool	Create a frame for text
	Table Frame Tool	Create a frame for a table
	WordArt Frame Tool	Create a frame for stylized text
	Picture Frame Tool	Create a frame for a picture
	Clip Gallery Tool	Create a frame for a picture, sound, or video.

12

Working with Text

When you want to add new text to your publication, you need to create a text frame. Using the Text Frame tool, you drag a rectangle that will contain your text. When you release the mouse, the insertion point blinks inside the frame, indicating that you can start typing. You can add ready-made elements such as calendars, ads, and coupons with the Design Gallery. After entering text, you can format the text to change its font, size, and color. Similarly, you can change the color of the background of the frame (behind the text) and add interesting borders to the frame.

TIP

Use the Snap features to arrange objects. *With the Snap features turned on, you can align objects to the ruler, guides or other objects. Click the Tools menu, and then click to check Snap To Ruler Marks, Snap To Guides, or Snap To Objects.*

Create a Text Frame

1. Click the Text Frame Tool on the Objects toolbar.

2. Position the mouse pointer where you want the frame to start.

3. Drag diagonally to create a rectangle the size you want.

4. Type the text you want in the frame.

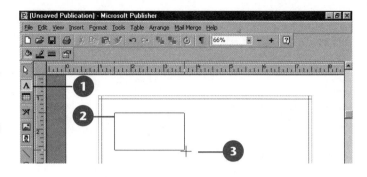

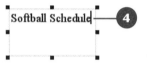

Insert an Object from the Design Gallery

1. Click the Design Gallery Object on the Objects toolbar.

2. Click a tab to choose how you want to display the objects (by category or by design).

3. Click a category or design.

4. Double-click a thumbnail.

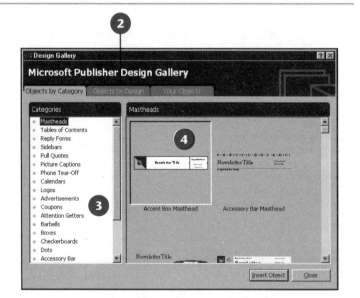

Improve the appearance of large fonts by changing character spacing. *Characters formatted in very large fonts often look too far apart. To adjust the space between characters, click the Character Spacing command on the Format menu.*

Change line spacing. *You can adjust the amount of space between lines of text with the Line Spacing command on the Format menu.*

Separate ideas with bullets or numbers. *Emphasize each idea or stress a sequence with the Bullets And Indents command on the Format menu.*

Get creative with borders and shading. *Highlight important text by applying shading or borders to a text frame. Use the Fill Color command to change the background color. Use the Line Color command to change the color of a line. Use the Line/ Border Style command to choose from a variety of line styles to surround the text frame.*

Format Text in a Frame

1. Select the text that you want to format.

2. Right-click the selected text.

3. Point to Change Text.

4. Point to a command to change a specific characteristic of the text in the selected frame.

5. Select the format options you want.

6. Click OK.

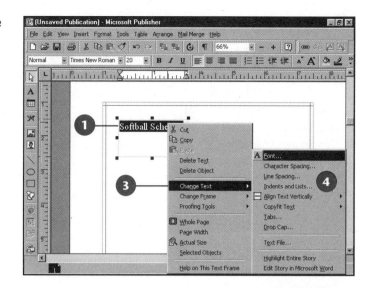

Format a Text Frame

1. Right-click the text frame.

2. Point to Change Frame.

3. Point to a command to change a specific characteristic of the selected frame.

4. Select the format options you want.

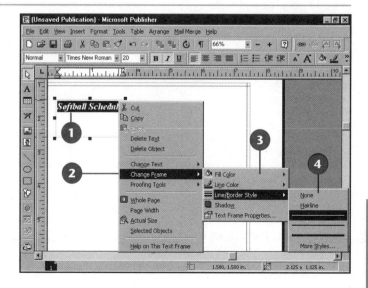

Connecting Text Frames

You can control the way the text flows in your publications. You can link and unlink frames that are adjacent to each other on the same page or different pages. Special text frame buttons appear when text is in the overflow area or when two or more text frames are linked in a chain. You can insert *Continued* notices to help readers follow text from page to page. In addition, you can use *AutoFit Text* to resize text to fit the size of the text frame.

TIP

Create multiple text frames. *Press and hold Ctrl, and then click the Text Frame Tool button. After you draw a text frame, the pointer doesn't revert to the arrow pointer. Click another tool when you're done.*

TIP

Delete a text frame from a chain. *Select the text frame you want to delete, click the Edit menu, and then click Delete Object.*

Connect Text Frames

1. Select the first text frame you want to connect.

   This frame can be empty or it can contain text.

2. Click the Connect Text Frames button on the Connect Frames toolbar.

3. Position the pitcher pointer over the empty text frame you want to connect.

4. Click the empty text frame to connect the two frames.

   If the overflow area of the first frame contains any text, the overflow text will flow into the newly connected text frame.

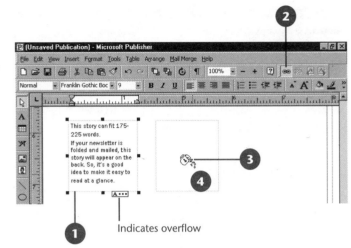

Indicates overflow

Disconnect a Text Frame

1. Select the text frame you want to disconnect.

2. Click the Disconnect Text Frames button on the Connect Frames toolbar.

Click to go to the previous text frame.

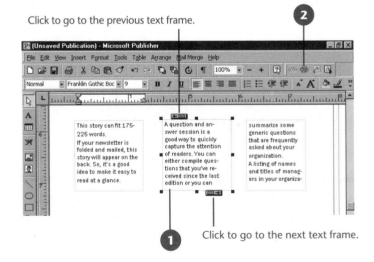

Click to go to the next text frame.

What's the difference between the pitcher pointers. *The upright pitcher indicates that the pointer is not positioned over a text frame. The tilted pitcher indicates that the pointer is over a text frame.*

Connecting text on different pages. *After you click the Connect Text Frames button, position the pointer over the page controls (the pitcher pointer changes the arrow pointer) at the bottom of the window. Click the page to which you want to move, and then click the text frame to which you want to connect.*

Flow text automatically. *When you insert a text file, you can have Publisher use AutoFlow to insert the text in frames. Select an unlinked text frame or the first frame in a linked chain, click the Insert menu, click Text File, double-click the text file you want to insert, and then click Yes twice.*

Insert a Continued Notice

1. Select the text frame in which you want to add a notice.

2. Click the Format Menu, and then click Text Frame Properties.

3. Click to select one or both of the Include Continued On Page and Include Continued From Page check boxes.

4. Click OK.

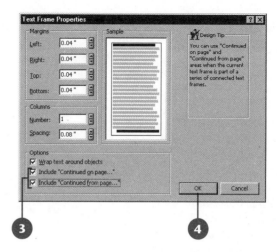

AutoFit Text

1. Click to select the text frame you want to format automatically.

2. Click the Format menu, and then point to AutoFit Text.

3. Click Best Fit or Shrink Text On Overflow.

   To turn off AutoFit Text, click None.

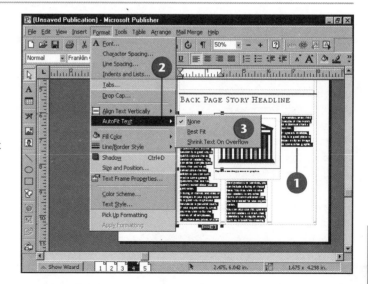

12

Creating a Consistent Look

When you create a collection of related publications, such as those for a specific event or organization, make sure that all the publications look similar. By using consistent choices of colors, design elements, and text formatting, your readers will instantly recognize that all your publications are related to the same effort or company. Publisher's Catalog and color schemes can help you achieve consistent designs and colors. Use *text styles*, which store text formatting settings, to ensure your text formatting is consistent in all your publications. After creating a text style in a publication, you can import the style to other publications.

Create a New Style by Example

1. Select the text with the style you want.

2. Click the Format menu, and then click Text Styles.

3. Click Create A New Style.

4. Enter a name for the new style.

    At first, the new style's settings are the same as the settings in the selected text frame.

5. Click each of the formatting options and change the formatting settings for the new style.

6. Click OK.

7. Click Close.

    You now need to apply the style to the selected text.

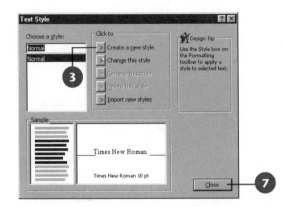

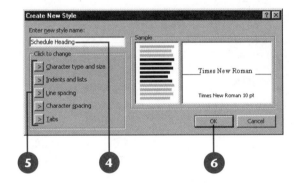

Apply a Style

1. Select the text or text frame to which you want to apply a style.

2. Click the Style drop-down arrow on the Formatting toolbar.

3. Select a style.

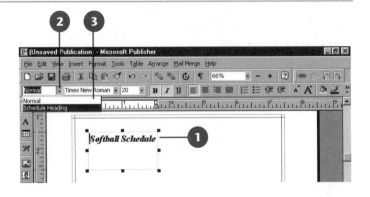

Create styles based on existing formatting in a text frame. *A new text style is initially formatted with the same settings as the selected text frame. To save time when creating a style, select a text frame with a format close to the one you want.*

Pick up and apply a style. *Select the word or text object whose format you want to use. Click the Format Painter button on the Formatting toolbar, and then select the text to which you want to apply the format.*

Change a style. *Click the Format menu, click Text Styles, click the style you want to change, click Change This Style, change the style, and then click Close.*

Rename a style. *Click the Format menu, click Text Styles, click the style you want to rename, click Rename This Style, type the new name, and then click Close.*

Import a Style

1. Click the Format menu, and then click Text Styles.

2. Click Import New Styles.

3. Double-click the publication that contains the styles you want to import.

4. Click Close.

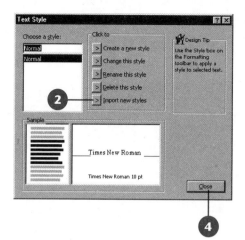

Delete a Style

1. Click the Format menu, and then click Text Styles.

2. Click the style you want to remove.

3. Click Delete This Style.

4. Click Yes to confirm that you want to delete the style.

5. Click Close.

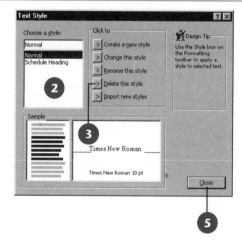

12

Creating Tables

A *table* is an arrangement of text in a grid of rows and columns. Within a table, the intersection of a row and a column is a called a *cell*. In Publisher you can use tables to align text. Tables are a convenient way to create schedules, calendars, and forms. You create a table with the Table Object Tool button on the Objects toolbar. After you create a table, you can format the color, line and border style, or shadow of individual cells or the entire table. You can also use the Table AutoFormat feature to apply sets of lines and borders to rows and columns or individual cells.

SEE ALSO

See Section 6, "Enhancing a Document with Word 2000," for information on entering text in tables, and modifying, formatting, and adjusting tables cells.

Create a Table Frame

1. Click the Table Frame Tool button on the Objects toolbar.

2. Position the mouse frame where you want the object to start.

3. Drag to create a rectangle the size you want.

4. Enter the number of rows and columns you want the table to have.

5. Click the formatting you want.

    You can preview your selections in the Sample box.

6. Click OK.

    Click in a cell to begin entering text in the table.

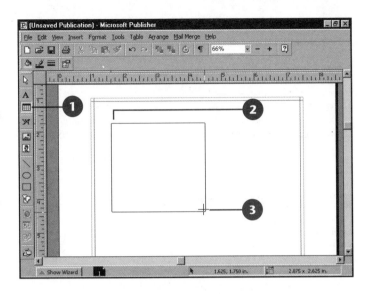

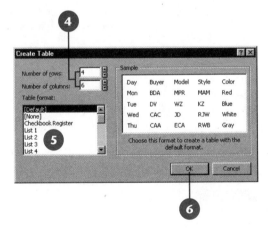

Format Text in a Cell

1. Right-click the selected text you want to format.

2. Point to Change Text.

3. Click a command to change a specific characteristic of the text in the selected frame.

4. Select the format options you want.

5. If necessary, click OK.

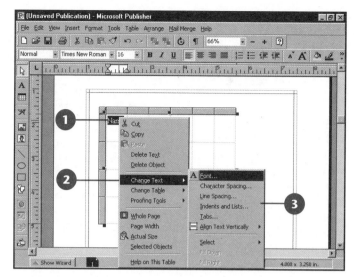

Format a Table

1. Select the rows, columns, or cells you want to format, and then right-click the selection.

2. Point to Change Table.

3. Point to a command to change a specific characteristic of the selected frame.

4. Click a command or select the format options you want.

5. If necessary, click OK.

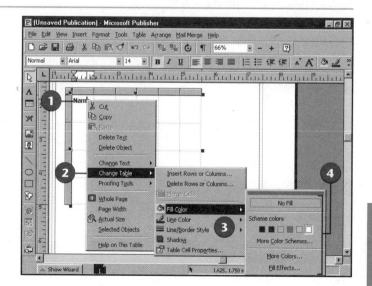

Working with Pictures and Shapes

When you want to insert a picture from a file or a clip art picture from the Clip Gallery, you need to create a picture frame. Using the Picture Frame Tool or Clip Gallery Tool button, you create a rectangle that will contain your picture. Then you can modify the picture. You can also create your own original drawing. Using the drawing tools on the Objects toolbar, you can create lines and basic shapes, as well as custom shapes that include stars, cartoon balloons, arrows, and many more elements that are sure to add interest to your publication.

SEE ALSO

See "Modifying Media Clips" on page 46 for information on cropping a picture. The Crop button is located on the Formatting toolbar in Publisher.

Create a Picture Frame

1. Click the Picture Frame Tool on the Objects toolbar.

2. Position the mouse pointer where you want the picture frame to start.

3. Drag to create a rectangle the size you want.

4. Double-click the frame to insert a picture from a file.

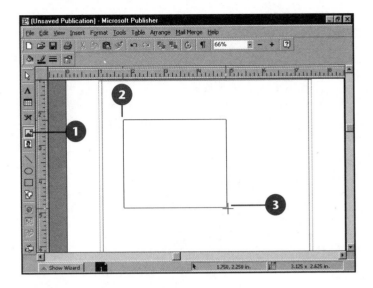

Change the Picture Color

1. Right-click the picture frame, point to Change Picture, and then click Recolor Picture.

2. Click the Color drop-down arrow, and then select a new color.

3. Click OK.

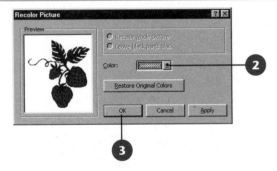

Create a Line, Oval, or Rectangle

1 Click the Line Tool, Oval Tool, or Rectangle Tool button on the Objects toolbar.

2 Position the mouse pointer where you want the object to start.

3 Drag to create an object the size you want.

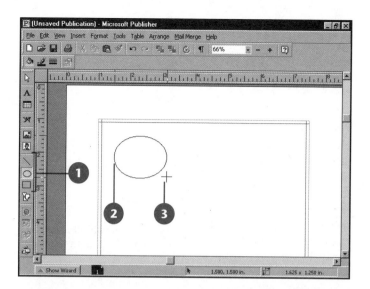

Create a Custom Shape

1 Click the Custom Shapes button on the Objects toolbar.

2 Click the shape you want to create.

3 Position the mouse pointer where you want the shape to start.

4 Drag to create a shape the size you want.

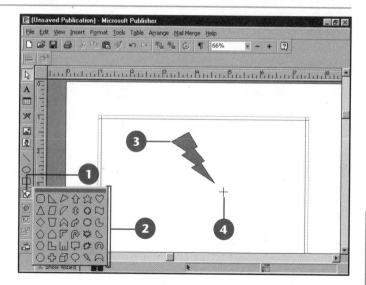

12

Wrapping Text Around an Object

You can wrap text around an object, such as a graphic, to attractively integrate text and objects in a publication. By default, Publisher flows text around an object's rectangular frame. So that there are no unsightly gaps between text and nearby graphics, you can wrap the text to flow tightly around irregularly shaped or round objects. Use the Text Wrap feature in Publisher to have text follow the outlines of the object itself. Brochures and news-letters often use this technique to combine text and graphics.

> **TIP**
>
> **Drawn objects must be filled to wrap text around them.** *If you want text to wrap around a shape you've drawn, fill the shape with a color. Publisher won't flow text around a transparent shape. By default, Publisher wraps tightly around drawn shapes.*

Wrap Text Around an Object

1. Select the text frame that you want to wrap.

2. Click the Format menu, and then click Text Frame Properties.

3. Click to select the Wrap Text Around Objects check box.

4. Click OK.

5. Click the object around which you want the text to flow.

6. Click the Bring To Front button on the Standard toolbar.

   The text object must be under the graphic object.

7. Click the Wrap Text To Picture button on the Formatting toolbar.

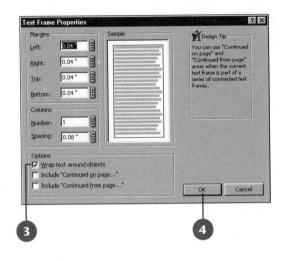

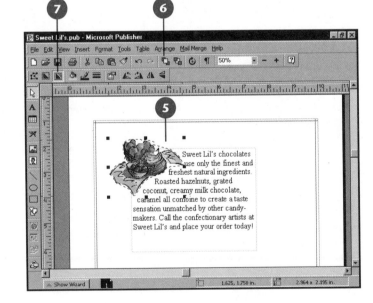

Fine-tune Text Flow Around an Object

1. Click the object around which you want the text to flow.

2. Click the Wrap Text To Picture button on the Formatting toolbar.

3. Click the Edit Irregular Wrap button on the Formatting toolbar.

4. Position the pointer over an adjust handle until you see the adjust pointer, and then drag the handle to change the shape of the boundary.

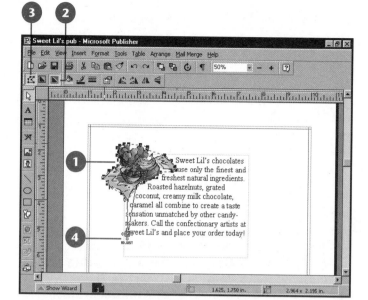

Add an Adjust Handle

1. Click the object around which you want the text to flow.

2. Click Wrap Text To Picture button on the Formatting toolbar.

3. Click the Edit Irregular Wrap button on the Formatting toolbar.

4. Press and hold Ctrl as you click the dotted-line boundary.

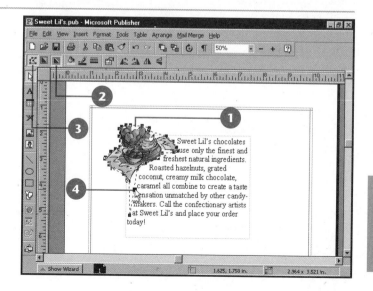

12

Layering Objects

Like pieces of paper arranged on your work surface, you can arrange objects in a publication on top of each other. The object you created or edited last appears on top of the stack of other objects. Layering objects allows you to achieve effects like shadows and complex designs that include many shapes. You can rearrange the order of the objects in the stack by sending individual objects behind one another or to the back of the stack, or by bringing other objects in front of one another or to the front of the stack.

TIP

Ungroup objects before changing the order. *If you see no change in the order of the objects in the stack, click the Ungroup Object button, and then select the object you want to move. Be sure to regroup the objects after you are satisfied with the layers.*

Send an Object Behind or Bring an Object to the Front of the Stack

1. Click to select the object you want to change.

2. Click the Send To Back or Bring To Front button on the Formatting toolbar.

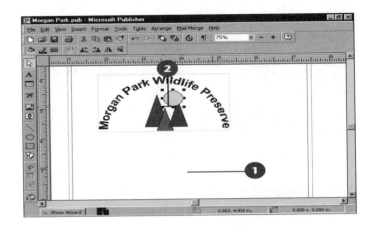

Send an Object Behind or Bring an Object in Front of Another Object

1. Click to select the object you want to change.

2. Click the Arrange menu, and then click Send Backward or Bring Forward.

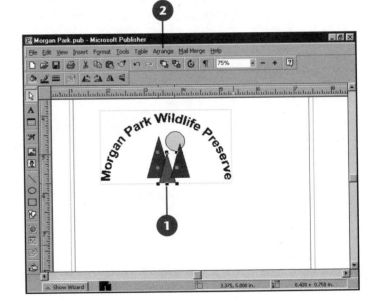

Rotating and Flipping Objects

To fit objects together in a specific way or to achieve a dramatic effect, consider rotating an object. Flipping objects, either vertically or horizontally, is a fast way to change their position. You can flip an object horizontally or vertically to create a mirror image of it along its vertical or horizontal axis.

TIP

Rotate an object directly. *Select the object, and press and hold Alt as you point to a sizing handle. When you see the rotate pointer, drag the object in the direction you want. Press Alt+Ctrl to rotate objects in 15-degree increments.*

ROTATE

TIP

Remove an object's rotation. *Select the object, click the Rotate button on the Standard toolbar, click No Rotation, and then click Close.*

Rotate an Object

1. Click to select the object you want to rotate.

2. Click Rotate on the Standard toolbar.

3. Click Rotate Left or Rotate Right until the object is oriented the way you want.

Click to rotate left or right in 90-degree increments.

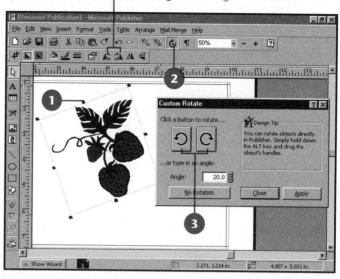

Flip an Object Horizontally or Vertically

1. Click to select the object you want to flip.

   You can flip all Publisher object, except for text objects.

2. Click the Flip Horizontally or Flip Vertically button on the Formatting toolbar.

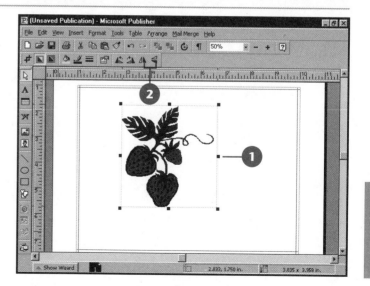

12

Grouping Objects Together

Often you want Publisher to treat several objects as a single one. That way, if you decide to move one object, you can also move other objects. In Publisher, you can accomplish this with the *grouping* feature. Group objects when you want to move, resize, or format a set of objects as a single object. If you decide that you want to work with each object independently, you can ungroup them.

TIP

Sizing handles help identify grouped objects.
When you click an object and you see multiple highlighted frames but only one set of sizing handles, it means that the object is part of a group.

Group Objects

1. Click to select the object you want to group.

2. Press and hold Shift while you click the other objects that you want to group together.

3. Click the Group Objects button.

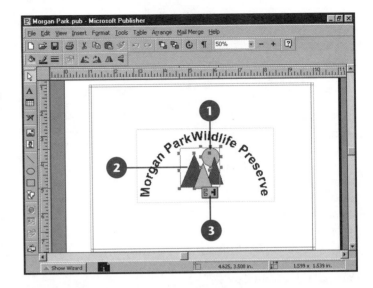

Ungroup Objects

1. Click to select the object you want to ungroup.

2. Click the Ungroup Object button.

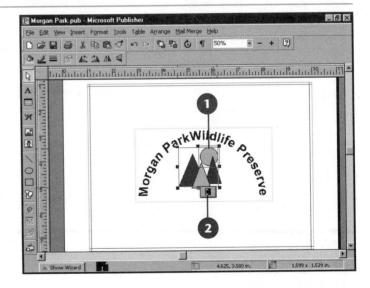

13

Browsing the Web with Internet Explorer 5

Microsoft Internet Explorer 5 is more than a traditional Web browser program. It is a flexible tool you can use to navigate your computer, network, or company intranet, as well the Internet. By integrating Internet Explorer with the Windows operating system and its Office 2000 suite of programs, Microsoft has opened new windows to the Internet from which you can:

- ◆ Easily set up your connection to the Internet.

- ◆ Jump directly to your favorite Web sites from your desktop.

- ◆ View Web pages as wallpaper—even have the content updated automatically.

- ◆ Use the same "Explorer" to view Web pages, folders on your hard disk, or your Office documents.

Learn One Method to Work Efficiently

With Internet Explorer, you can browse your hard disk with the same ease that you browse the Internet. And most content is only a click away—whether you're opening a Word document or a site on the Web.

Getting Started with the Internet Explorer Suite

The Internet Explorer Suite is a variety of programs that work together to provide you the simplest and most efficient way to create and view content, as well as to communicate with others on the Internet. Each program serves a distinct purpose, but their features all function similarly, so learning the entire suite is easy. The suite includes:

Connection Wizard—A program that enables you to get connected to the Internet. The Connection Wizard walks you through setting up a new or existing Internet account.

Internet Explorer—A browsing program for exploring content on the World Wide Web, a network or intranet, or your computer's hard drives. With Internet Explorer, you can view Web content online or offline, and protect yourself and your computer with features such Microsoft Wallet and the Content Advisor.

Outlook Express—A messaging program for sending or reading e-mail or newsgroup messages. Outlook Express accesses and manages multiple e-mail and newsgroup accounts, provides offline reading and composing capabilities, and offers security options.

Address Book—A program that enables you to keep track of names, street and e-mail addresses, personal and business Web sites, and other related information. Address Book is also used by other programs, such as Outlook Express.

NetMeeting—A program that allows you and your multimedia PC to communicate and collaborate with people around the world through voice (with speakers and a microphone) or video conferencing (with a connected video camera), and through data conferencing using a shared Whiteboard and Chat features.

NetShow—A program that enables you to receive multimedia shows from the Internet or a local intranet. NetShow content might come from a video or audio program or a slide show with a soundtrack. Like other programs in the Internet Explorer Suite, NetShow allows you to listen to or view this content online or offline.

FrontPage Express—A WYSIWYG HTML editor based on the Web authoring and management tools in Microsoft FrontPage. FrontPage Express walks you through creating new Web pages and editing existing HTML documents. When you use the Web Publishing Wizard, your Web pages are easily transferred to a server on the Internet.

Personal Web Server—A network file and application server that enables you to publish Web pages. You can use a Personal Web Server to publish your Web pages on the Internet or over a local area network (LAN) on an intranet and to transmit or receive files using an FTP (File Transfer Protocol) service.

Windows Media Player—A program that enables you to receive audio, video, and mixed-media files in most popular formats—including streaming media. You can use Media Player to listen to or view live news updates or broadcasts of your favorite sports teams, music videos or concerts, and movies on the Web.

Active Channels—A feature that turns your desktop into a virtual television for Web sites. For those upgrading from Internet Explorer 4 or installing on Windows 98, channels feature specialized content developed especially for Internet Explorer that you can display as wallpaper on your desktop, as Web pages, or as a screen saver. When you add an active channel, Internet Explorer downloads new content to you as it's made available from the channel provider.

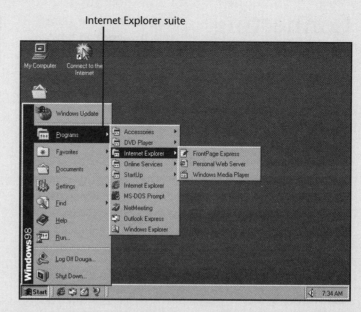
Internet Explorer suite

Connecting to the Internet

Sometimes connecting your computer to the Internet can be the most difficult part of getting started. Internet Explorer's Connection Wizard simplifies the process, whether you want to set up a new connection using an existing account, or you want to select an Internet service provider (ISP) and set up a new account. You may need to obtain connection information from your ISP or your system administrator.

Connect To The Internet

Get Connected Using the Internet Explorer Connection Wizard

1. Double-click the Connect To The Internet icon on the desktop.

   Or click the Start button on the taskbar, point to Programs, point to Accessories, point to Communications, and then click Connection Wizard.

2. Click the option button for the setup you want to use. Click Next to continue.

3. Read the information in each wizard dialog box, and then enter the required information. Click Next to move from one wizard dialog box to another.

4. In the final wizard dialog box, click Finish.

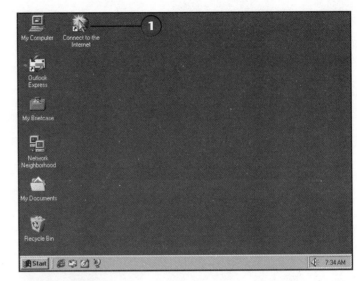

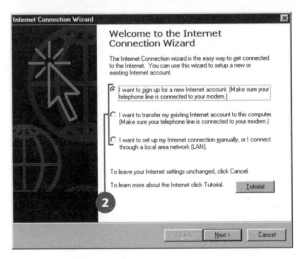

Viewing the Internet Explorer Window

Menu bar
Contains all the commands you need to access and move around Web pages, customize Internet Explorer, and get Help

Title bar
Displays the name of the Web page you are viewing

Standard toolbar
Provides buttons to locate and move around Web pages, as well as work in Internet Explorer

Address bar
Displays the address of the current Web page or document you are viewing or trying to access

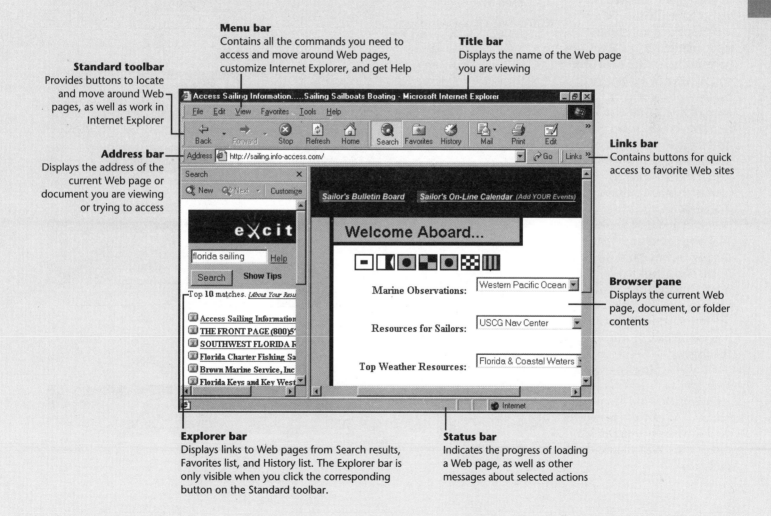

Links bar
Contains buttons for quick access to favorite Web sites

Browser pane
Displays the current Web page, document, or folder contents

Explorer bar
Displays links to Web pages from Search results, Favorites list, and History list. The Explorer bar is only visible when you click the corresponding button on the Standard toolbar.

Status bar
Indicates the progress of loading a Web page, as well as other messages about selected actions

Navigating Basics

As you browse the Web or your local hard disk, you may want to retrace your steps and return to a Web page, document, or hard disk you've recently visited. You can move backward or forward one location at a time, or you can jump directly to any location from the Back list or Forward list, which shows locations you've previously visited in this session.

After you start to load a Web page, you can stop if the page opens too slowly or if you decide not to access it. If a Web page loads incorrectly or you want to update the information it contains, you can reload, or *refresh*, the page.

If you get lost on the Web, you can start over with a single click of the Home button. You can also resize your toolbars so you can see more of the Web address or Links bar.

Move Back or Forward

◆ To move back or forward one Web page or document at a time, click the Back button or Forward button on the Standard toolbar.

◆ To move back or forward to a specific Web page or document, click the Back or Forward drop-down arrow on the Standard toolbar, and then select the Web page or document you want to visit.

Back button
Forward button

Back button drop-down arrow

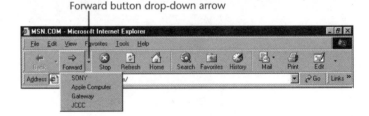

Forward button drop-down arrow

Stop an Unwanted Load

1 Click the Stop button on the Standard toolbar.

TIP

Change your home page.
Click the Tools menu, and then click Internet Options. Click the General tab. In the Address box, type the URL of the Web page you want for your home page.

TIP

Keyboard shortcuts. *Here are the keyboard shortcuts for navigating a Web page:*
Back   *Alt+left arrow*
Front   *Alt+right arrow*
Stop   *Esc*
Refresh   *F5*

TIP

Do I click here or not?
You'll know that you can click something because the mouse pointer changes from an arrow to a hand with a pointed finger whenever you hover over a clickable link.

TIP

Tab from link to link. *While viewing a Web page, you can move from link to link quickly by pressing Tab.*

Refresh a Web Page, Document, or Drive

1. Click the Refresh button on the Standard toolbar.

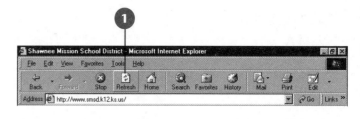

Go Home and Start Over

1. Click the Home button on the Standard toolbar.

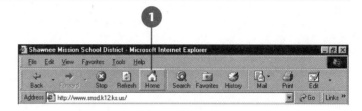

Resize the Links Bar

1. Position the mouse pointer over the handle on the far left of the Links bar.

2. Drag the handle to the left to reveal more of the links.

3. Click the double angle-bracket button at the far right to see the rest of the links.

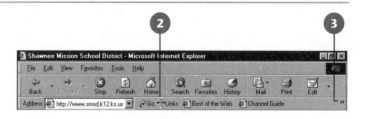

Make Room for All the Toolbars

1. Position the mouse pointer over the lowest toolbar.

2. Drag the toolbar downward to make room for both the Address and Links bars.

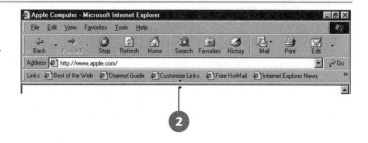

Browsing the Web

With Internet Explorer, you can browse sites on the Web with ease by entering a Web address or by clicking a link. Each method is better at different times. For example, you might type an address in the Address bar to start your session. Then you might click a link on that Web page to access a new site. With Internet Explorer, you can find Internet addresses faster with *AutoComplete*. When you type an Internet address in the Address bar, Internet Explorer tries to find a recently visited page that matches what you've typed so far. If Internet Explorer finds a match, it automatically fills in the rest of the address. You can also use AutoComplete to fill out forms on the Web, including single-line edits, and user names and passwords.

View a Web Page

Use any of the following methods to display a Web page.

◆ In the Address bar, type the Web page address, and click Go or press Enter.

◆ Click the Address bar drop-down arrow, and select a Web page address you've opened in the current session.

◆ Click the File menu, click Open, type the Web page address, and then click OK.

To open a folder located on a Web server, click to select the Open As Web Folder check box.

◆ Click any link, such as a 3-D image, a picture, or colored, underlined text on a Web page.

Address bar   Address bar drop-down arrow   A Web page link

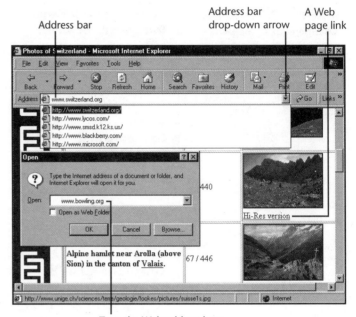

Type the Web address here.

Enter an Address Using AutoComplete

1 Begin to type an address that you have recently entered.

AutoComplete remembers previously entered addresses and tries to complete the address for you. The suggested match is highlighted.

If you want, continue to type until the address you want appears in the Address list.

2 Click the correct address in the Address list.

Turn Off AutoComplete Options

1 Click the Tools menu, and then click Internet Options.

2 Click the Content tab.

3 Click AutoComplete.

4 Click to clear the check boxes with the Auto-Complete options you want to turn off.

5 Click OK.

6 Click OK.

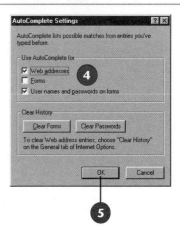

Browsing Your Local Hard Disk

Internet Explorer isn't only for viewing Web pages. You can also use it to browse folders on your local hard disk and run programs in the same way that you browse Web pages on the Internet—from the Address bar. You'll see an Address bar and the Links bar when you browse folders because Windows Explorer and Internet Explorer share many of the same functions. Because of this shared functionality, you have the option of changing the way your folders are displayed. You can have your folders and your computer act like the Web or work in the classic Windows mode.

TIP

Mind your slashes. *To open a file on your computer, type "\folder\filename." To open a Web page, type "/Web site." Internet Explorer knows the difference between \ and /.*

Browse Folders and Open Files from the Address Bar

1. Type the hard drive, folder, or file in the Address bar you want to open. For example, "C:" or "C:\My Documents\"

2. Click Go on the Address bar or press Enter.

   The menus and toolbar change to the ones used in Windows Explorer.

3. If you want, click the Views button drop-down arrow on the Standard toolbar, and then select the view option you want to use.

4. Double-click any icon to open that drive, folder, or program.

5. Click the Go menu, and then click Home Page to return to Internet Explorer.

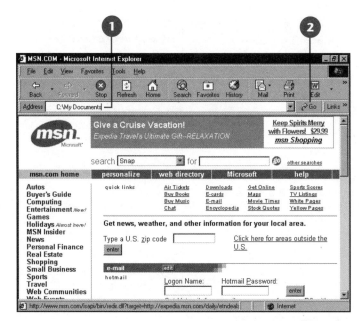

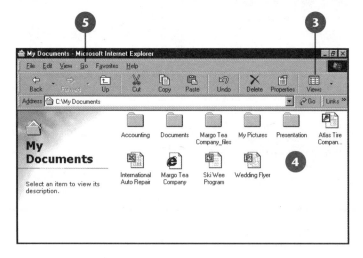

Editing an Office Web Page

You can edit an Office Web page—a Web page saved in an Office program—with the help of Internet Explorer. With an Office Web page displayed in the Internet Explorer window, you can launch the Office program that was used to create the Web page. This makes editing Web pages seamless and easy.

TIP

Edit an Office Web page in another program. *If the availability to edit an Office Web page in more than one program exists, a drop-down arrow appears next to the Edit button. When you click the Edit drop-down arrow, a list of programs appears from which you can edit the Office Web page.*

Edit an Office Web Page

1 Open the Office Web page you want to edit.

2 Click the Edit button on the Standard toolbar.

The toolbar button icon indicates the Office program associated with the Web page.

3 Begin editing the Web page in the Office program as usual.

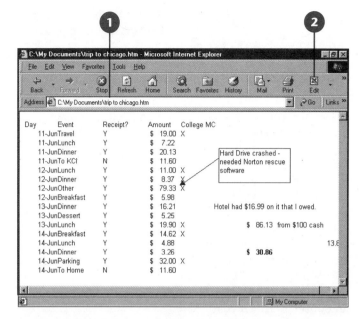

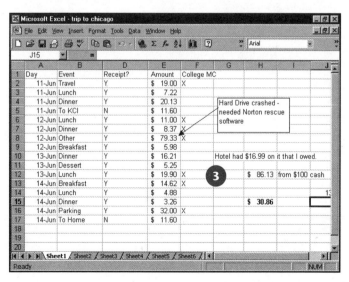

Viewing and Maintaining a History List

Sometimes you run across a great Web site and simply forget to add it to your Favorites list. With Internet Explorer there's no need to try to remember all the sites you've visited. The History feature keeps track of where you've been for days, weeks, or even months at a time. Because the History list can grow to occupy a large amount of space on your hard disk, it's important that you control the length of time visited Web sites are retained in the list. Internet Explorer will delete the History list periodically based on the settings you specify.

TIP

Clear the History List. *Click the Tools menu, click Internet Options, and then click the General tab. Click Clear History, click Yes, and then click OK.*

View a Web Site from the History List

1. Click the History button on the Standard toolbar.

2. Click a week or day to expand or compress the list of Web sites visited.

3. Click the folder for the Web site you want to view, and then click a page within the Web site.

4. When you're done, click the Close button.

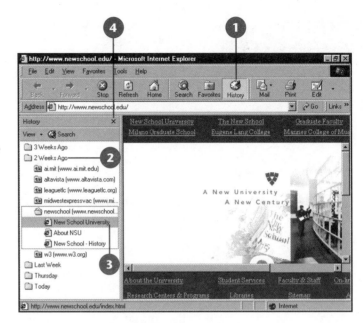

Change the History List View

1. Click the History button on the Standard toolbar.

2. Click the View button, and then click the view option you want.

3. When you're done, click the Close button.

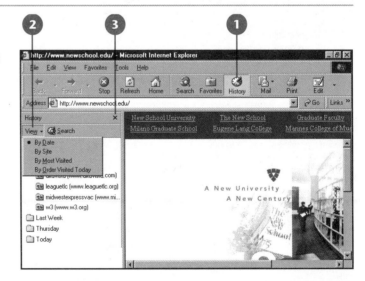

Understanding Search Sites, Favorites, and Channels

Search engines, such as AltaVista, AOL NetFind, and Lycos, gather their information by using "robots," or special programs, to collect words from Web pages. These words are then stored and indexed in the search engine's databases. The goal of any good search engine is to seek out and find as many Web pages on the Internet as possible and to create a quick reference to their locations. When you specify a word or phrase for a search engine to locate on the Internet, the search engine locates the word or phrase along with the corresponding Web address on which the word appears in the database. The more general your request is, the longer the list of results; the more specific your request, the fewer the number of Web sites in the results.

Internet directories, such as Yahoo, differ from search engines in that a person actually reviews every link placed in the directories' databases. And that person decides under which category, be it sports, news, weather, and so forth, a site should be cataloged. This level of editorial review guarantees a much smaller list of Web sites will be stored (compared to a search engine), but the list will have a much higher guarantee of quality. Only those sites that have been tested are listed in the database—not by the words that appear on the Web page, but by the category under which it falls.

When you search a directory of Web sites, you'll get far fewer choices than if you used a search engine, but those choices will be more in tune with your search request, particularly if you are looking for sites that fall under broad categories. Because Internet directories don't index most sites on the Web, they are not the place to go to locate hard-to-find information such as the name of a particular person. Search engines are a better choice for hard-to-find information because they have indexed words and phrases from millions of Web pages.

Whether searching the Web or just browsing it, you are likely to find a number of sites that you want to return to. You can easily add these pages to your Favorites folder. *Favorites* are links to your favorite Web sites, which you can immediately access at any time from the Favorites menu.

In addition to visiting Web pages for information, you can have the facts come to you through the use of channels. A *channel* is a Web site that delivers information to your computer—sometimes without the need of a browser. When you add a channel to your list of favorites, the content of that site—sports scores, financial information, movie reviews, and so on—can come directly to your computer. Internet Explorer follows the channel's schedule to automatically update the information. In addition to the channel's Web page, the data can be viewed as part of your desktop or in the form of a screen saver. Adding channels isn't the only way to automatically get up-to-date information. You can also have Internet Explorer periodically check some (or all) of your favorites to see if the Web pages have new information. You can then view the Web page offline and even be notified via e-mail when the Web page has changed.

Searching for Information on the Internet

The Web can be overwhelming; there is a great deal of information to plow through. Internet Explorer makes it easy for you to quickly access the most popular search engines and Internet directories with the click of a button. You can also customize your search settings so you work with only the search providers that you prefer. For quick searches, you can use *AutoSearch* to locate the information you want. You can enter a search request directly into Internet Explorer's Address bar. Simply type your keywords into the Address bar and press Enter.

Search the Internet Using the Search Button

1 Click the Search button on the Standard toolbar. Internet Explorer chooses a search engine at random.

2 Click the search category option button you want.

3 Type the information you want to use for the search.

4 Click the Search, Find, or Seek button. (Each search provider labels its search button differently.)

5 If a Security Alert message box appears, click Yes.

6 Click the link for the Web site you want to view.

7 If you don't find the Web site you want, click the Next button to perform the same search with another search engine.

8 To perform a new search, click the New button.

9 Click the Close button or click the Search button on the Standard toolbar to view the entire Web page.

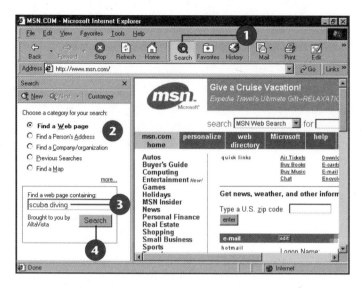

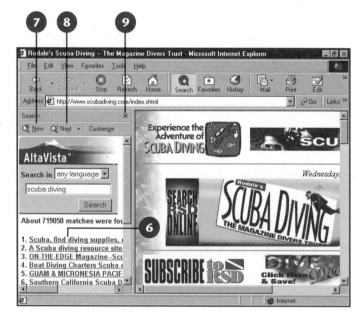

Choose a default search provider. *Click the Search button on the Standard toolbar, click the Customize button, scroll to the bottom of the page, click the Choose A Default Provider link, and then click the link for the search provider you want to use.*

Get ScreenTips when you search. *To get a description of a Web site returned by a search without clicking its link, move the pointer over the link in the Choose Search pane and hold it there. A ScreenTip appears, listing the Internet address, URL, and other relevant information about the Web page—if the search provider supports this feature.*

Other AutoSearch options. *You can also type the word "go" or* **find** *or just a question mark before your search request. For example, typing* **? Colorado hiking** *is the same as typing* **Colorado hiking**.

Customize Your Search Options

1. Click the Search button on the Standard toolbar.

2. Click the Customize button.

3. In the right pane, click the check box to select or deselect search providers.

4. Scroll down and select search providers in each search category.

5. When you're done, click Update.

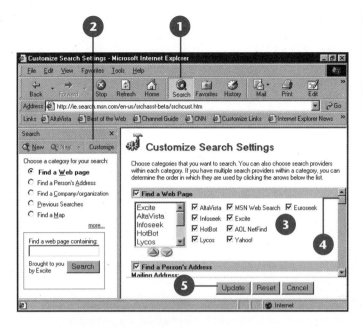

Use AutoSearch to Locate information

1. In the Address bar, type the keywords you want to use for the search. For example, type **scuba diving**.

2. Press Enter or click Go.

   Internet Explorer randomly selects a search provider and submits your request. The results are displayed in the main browser window.

3. Click the link for the Web site you want to view.

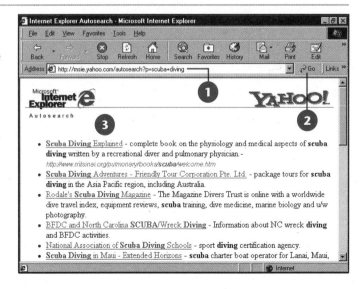

Creating and Organizing Your Favorites List

How about creating a permanent link to your favorite Web site? With a list of favorites you can quickly read top news headlines, check current weather conditions, or track stock prices. As your list of favorites grows, you can organize them into different folders. For example, if your hobby is fishing, you may have a Favorites folder named Fly Fishing Locations and another named, Fly Fishing Equipment. You can also find out the number of times you visited a favorite and the date it was last visited.

Create a Favorites List

1. Open the Web site you want to add to your Favorites list.

2. Click the Favorites menu, and then click Add To Favorites.

3. Type the name for the site, or use the default name supplied.

4. If you want, click Create In to add the site to a folder within the Favorites folder.

5. Click OK.

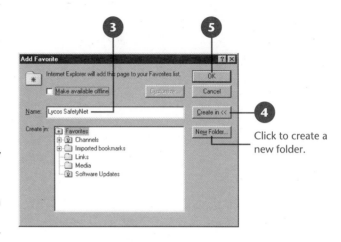

Click to create a new folder.

View Your Favorites List in the Explorer Bar

1. Click the Favorites button on the Standard toolbar.

2. If necessary, click the folder with the favorite you want to view.

   The contents of the folder are displayed. Click the folder again to hide the contents.

3. Click the favorite you want to view.

   Your favorite is displayed in the right pane.

4. When you're done, click the Close button.

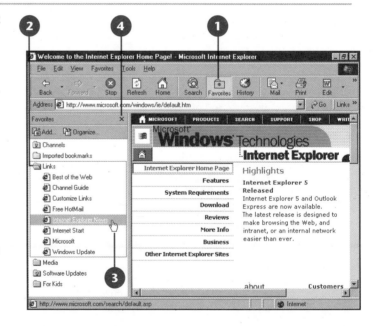

Create a Folder in Your Favorites List

1. Click the Favorites menu, and then click Organize Favorites.

2. Click Create Folder.

3. Type the name of the folder, and then press Enter.

4. When you're done, click Close.

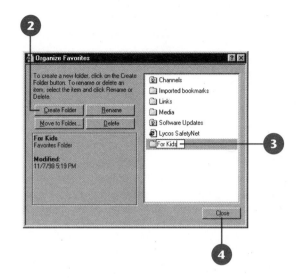

Move a Favorite to a Folder

1. Click the Favorites menu, and then click Organize Favorites.

2. Select the favorite you want to move into the new folder.

3. Click Move To Folder.

4. Click the folder where you want to move the favorite.

5. Click OK.

6. When you're done, click Close.

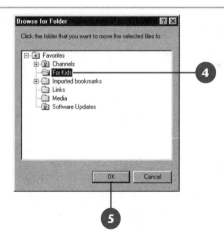

Viewing Your Favorites Offline

When you add a Web site to your list of favorites, you have the option of making that Web site available for viewing offline. Internet Explorer will store a copy of the site on your hard disk and you can view the contents anytime—not just when you are connected to the Internet. Offline viewing is much faster because the Web pages are being loaded from your hard disk instead of across your telephone line or company network. When you *synchronize* your offline pages, Internet Explorer visits each one and brings the most current version of the page back to your hard disk. You can also schedule automatic synchronization (every night, for example) so that each morning you can read your favorite Web sites offline at top speed.

Set Up a Web Site for Offline Viewing

1 Open the Web site you want to add.

2 Click the Favorites menu, and then click Add To Favorites.

3 Click to select the Make Available Offline check box.

4 Click Customize.

5 Click Next to configure your page for offline viewing.

6 Click the Yes option button to allow viewing of the entire Web site, or click the No option button to restrict your offline viewing to the single page. Click Next to continue.

7 Choose the synchronization schedule option you want, and then click Next to continue. If a Web site provides a schedule you may want to choose this option so you receive the latest information.

8 If the Web site requires user authentication, enter your user name and password. Click Finish.

9 Choose the folder, and then click OK.

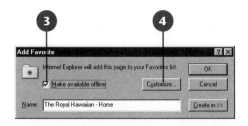

Set up an existing favorite for offline viewing. *Click the Favorites menu, and then click Organize Favorites. Click the name of a favorite you want to view offline, and then click the Make Available Offline check box. To set up your own schedule, click the Properties button, and then click the Schedule tab. Click the Add button to define and name a synchronization schedule. Click the Edit button to change the schedule settings.*

Not every link is available offline. *When Internet Explorer synchronizes a Web page, it can't gather every link on every Web page (eventually you would run out of hard disk space). You can tell that a link will require an online connection because the mouse pointer changes to a circle with a line through it. You can still click those links, but you will have to choose to go online (reconnect to the Internet) to see the content.*

Free Computer Training

Synchronize Your Favorites

1. Click the Tools menu, and then click Synchronize.

2. Select the Web site(s) you want to synchronize.

3. If you want, click Properties to change the availability of the Web document, the schedule of the synchronization, or the amount to download.

4. Click Synchronize.

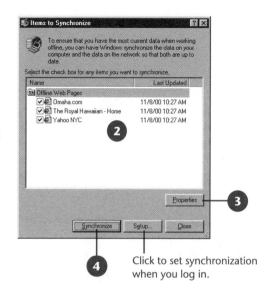

Click to set synchronization when you log in.

Work Offline

1. Click the File menu, and then click Work Offline.

2. Click the Favorites menu, and then click one of your favorites that has been synchronized.

3. Browse the site at high speed from your hard disk.

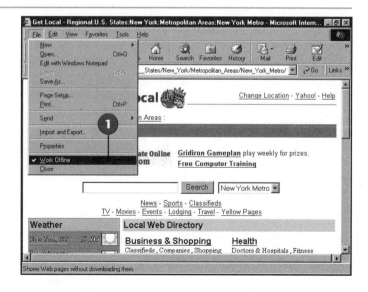

Adding a Channel

The first time you visit a channel from the Favorites menu, you will see the channel's *preview page*—a kind of ad for the channel's content. If the channel looks interesting, you can add the active version to Internet Explorer so that your next visit will reveal the channel's content. You can then have Internet Explorer update this active content whenever new information becomes available from the channel provider. There are hundreds of channel partners ready to deliver content to your computer, including MSNBC, Disney, and CBS SportsLine, to name a few. More are added every day.

> **TIP**
>
> **Add a channel quickly.**
> *Click the Favorites button on the Standard toolbar, and then click the Channels folder on the left pane. Right-click the channel you want to add, and then click Make Available Offline on the shortcut menu.*

View and Add a Channel to Your Favorites List

1 Click the Favorites button on the Standard toolbar.

2 Click the Channels folder in the left pane, click a channel topic, and then click the channel you want to add.

The channel's preview page appears in the right pane.

3 Click the Add Active Channel button. A Channel Refresh message box may appear, indicating that the channel is being synchronized. Click Next to continue.

4 Click the Yes option button to link to other pages when offline, or click the No option button to see just the first page. Click Next to continue.

5 Choose the synchronization schedule option you want.

6 Click Finish.

If a Channel Screen Saver message box appears, click Yes to use the channel on your desktop, or click No to close the message box.

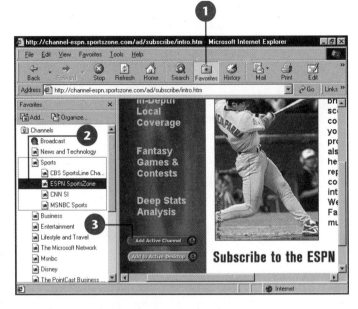

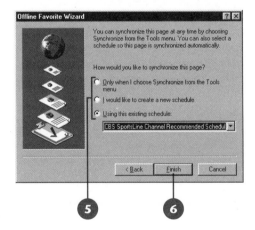

Creating Web Pages with Office 2000 Programs

World Wide Web technology is now available for all your Microsoft Office 2000 programs. For better productivity and faster location of information, add hyperlinks (graphic objects or text you click to jump to other Office documents and intranet or Internet pages) to your Office documents. Want to create your own Web page without spending any time learning the arcane HTML coding system used to format Web pages? The Web Page Wizard walks you through the process one step at a time. Office even provides several templates to start you off. In addition, you can save any document as a Web page just as you would save an Office document to your hard disk. Not sure how your document's layout will look as a Web page? Preview it in Office or in your browser.

Online Collaboration

Sharing information and working with others just got easier. Without ever leaving Office you can host or attend an online meeting, participate in a Web discussion about any document, send your document to others as an e-mail message, route a document to coworkers, and even download files from an FTP site on the Internet. Office makes working with people around the world as convenient as if they were in the same room.

Designing Web Pages

Web pages are multimedia documents that contain links to other documents on the Internet, an intranet, a local network, or a hard disk. These *links*—also called *hyperlinks*, *hypertext*, or *hypermedia*—are highlighted text or graphics that you click to follow a pathway from one Web page to another. Linked Web pages, often called a *Web site*, are generally related by topic.

Web pages are based on *Hypertext Markup Language* (HTML)—a simple coding system used to format Web pages. A browser program, such as Microsoft Internet Explorer, interprets these special codes to determine how a certain Web page should be displayed. Different codes mark the size, color, style, and placement of text and graphics as well as which words and graphics should be marked as hyperlinks and to what files they link.

As the World Wide Web becomes a household word and many businesses create intranet and Internet Web sites—both of which use HTML documents—the ability to create, read, open, and save HTML documents directly from Office becomes an important time-saver.

HTML and Office 2000

Office 2000 uses HTML as a *companion file format*. That means that Word, Excel, and Publisher all can save and read HTML documents without any compatibility problems. And Office recognizes the .html filename extension as accurately as it does those for its own programs (.doc, .xls, and .pub). In other words, you can use the familiar Office tools and features you use to create printed documents to create and share Web documents. Anyone with a browser can view your Office Web documents.

Converting Documents to Web Pages

In addition to creating Web pages from scratch in Office programs, you can also save any existing document as a Web page to your hard disk, intranet, or Web server. These HTML documents preserve such features as styles, revision marks, PivotTables, linked and embedded objects, and so forth. When the layout or an item in your document can't be converted to HTML in exactly the same way, a dialog box explains what items will be changed and how.

Each Office file saved as HTML creates a handful of individual files. For example, each graphic, worksheet, or slide in an Office document becomes its own file. To make it easy to manage these multiple files, Office creates a folder with the same name, and in the same location, as the original HTML file for the document. Any Office document saved as a Web page consists of an HTML file and a folder that stores supporting files, such as a file for each graphic, worksheet, slide, and so on.

Opening Web Pages

After saving an Office document as a Web page, you can open the Web page, an HTML file, in Office. This allows you to quickly and easily switch from HTML to the standard program format and back again without losing any formatting or functionality. For example, if you create a formatted chart in an Excel worksheet, save the workbook file as a Web page, and then reopen the Web page in Excel, the chart will look the same as the original chart in Excel. Office preserves the original formatting and functionality of the file.

TIP

Create a blank Web page in Word. *In Web Page view, the New button on the Standard toolbar changes to the New Web Page button. Click it to open a new HTML document quickly. Enter text, graphics, and frames as needed.*

Open an Office Web Page

1. Click the Open button on the Standard toolbar.

2. Click the Files Of Type drop-down arrow, and then click Web Pages.

3. Click one of the icons on the Places bar for access to often used folders.

4. If necessary, click the Look In drop-down arrow, and select the folder where the file is located.

5. Click the name of the file.

6. Click Open.

To open an Office Web page in your default Web browser, click the Open button drop-down arrow, and then click Open In Browser.

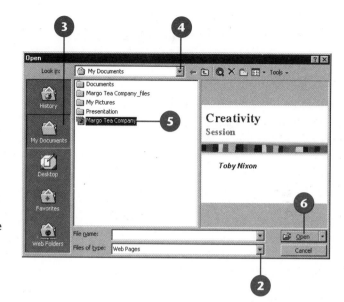

14

Creating Web Pages the Easy Way

With the Web Page Wizard, you don't need to learn HTML codes to create your own Web pages. The wizard walks you through each step of creating a visually appealing multipage site. First, you name your site and choose a storage location. Next, you decide if you want to place navigational links in a frame and where to display the frame. Add as many pages as you want that are blank, based on predesigned layout templates or existing files. Reorganize the sequence of the pages (visible in the order of the navigational links). Select a visual *theme,* or predesigned format, to give your site a professional and consistent look for the background, text, bullets, and so on. Finally, replace the placeholders with your own text and graphics.

Create a Web Page with a Wizard in Word

1. Click the Start button, and then click New Office Document, or click the File menu in Word, and then click New.

2. Click the Web Pages tab, and then double-click Web Page Wizard.

3. Click Next to continue.

4. Enter the title of your site, enter the location of your site, and then click Next.

5. Select the location of your site's navigational links. Click Next to continue.

6. Click one of the following buttons to set up the site structure.

   ◆ Add New Blank Page inserts an empty page.

   ◆ Add Template Page displays the Web Page Templates dialog box. Click a template, preview a sample, and then click OK.

   ◆ Add Existing File displays the Open dialog box. Double-click any file you want to include.

7. Click Next to continue.

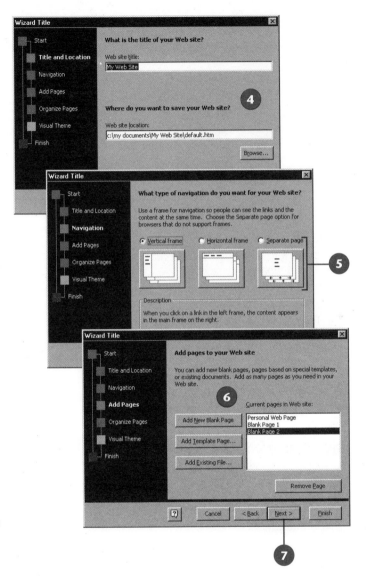

SEE ALSO

See "Creating a Web Site" on page 206 for information on creating Web pages in Publisher.

TIP

Depend on Office themes and design templates.
Word use themes that coordinate with the FrontPage Web site creation and management tool; Publisher use design templates that are consistent with the themes, and Outlook uses stationery to help you create a consistent-looking Web site.

TIP

What is placeholder text?
Office templates often open with text or graphics already inserted in the document. This existing text is called a placeholder. *To replace the placeholder, select the text and type new text, or select the graphic and insert a new image.*

8 Click the Move Up or Move Down button to change the order of the links. Click Next to continue.

9 To add a theme to your site, click the Add A Visual Theme option button, click Browse Themes, click the theme you want, and then click OK. Click Next to continue.

10 Click Finish.

11 Select the placeholder text, and enter your personalized text.

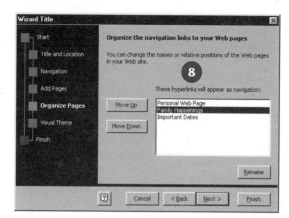

Create a Web Page from a Template in Word

1 In Word, click the File menu, and then click New.

2 Click the Web Pages tab.

3 Click a Web page template icon.

4 Click OK to create the selected Web page.

5 Select the placeholder text and graphics and add your own.

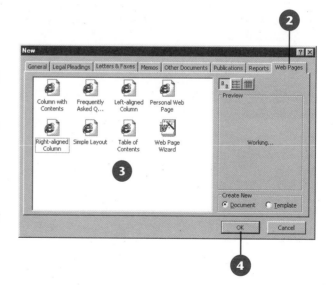

Inserting Hyperlinks

When you reference information included earlier in a document, you traditionally had to duplicate material or add a footnote. Now you can create a *hyperlink*—a graphic object or colored, underlined text that you click to move (or *jump*) to a new location (or *destination*). The destination can be in the same document, another file on your computer or network, or a Web page on your intranet or the Internet.

Insert a Hyperlink within a Document

1. Click where you want to insert the hyperlink, or select the text or object you want to use as the hyperlink.

2. Click the Insert Hyperlink button on the Standard toolbar.

3. Click Place In This Document.

4. Click a destination in the document.

   The destination can be a Word heading or bookmark; or an Excel cell reference or range name.

5. Type the text you want to appear as the hyperlink.

6. Click ScreenTip.

7. Type the text you want to appear when someone points to the hyperlink.

8. Click OK.

9. Click OK.

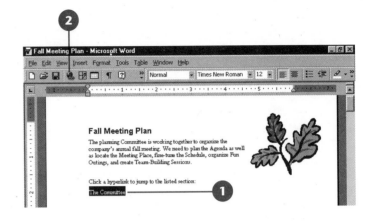

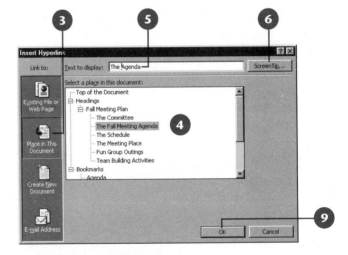

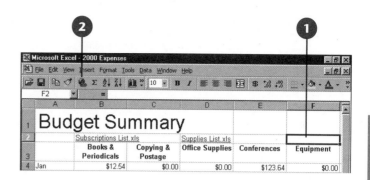

TIP

Create hyperlinks quickly.
Copy the selected text, graphic, range, or database object you want the hyperlink to jump to. Right-click where you want to insert the hyperlink, and then click Paste As Hyperlink.

TIP

Create a hyperlink to send e-mail. *Click where you want to insert the hyperlink, click the Insert Hyperlink button on the Standard toolbar, click E-Mail Address, enter the recipient's e-mail address, enter a subject, enter the hyperlink display text, and then click OK. An e-mail trigger is a great way for people to request information, offer feedback, or order quickly.*

SEE ALSO

See "Creating Bookmarks" on page 88 for information on using bookmarks.

Insert a Hyperlink Between Documents

1. Click where you want to insert the hyperlink, or select the text or object you want to use as the hyperlink.

2. Click the Insert Hyperlink button on the Standard toolbar.

3. Click Existing File Or Web Page.

4. Enter the name and path of the destination file or Web page.

   ◆ Or click the File, Web Page, or Bookmark button; select the file, Web page, or bookmark; and then click OK.

5. Type the text you want to appear as the hyperlink.

6. Click ScreenTip.

7. Type the text you want to appear when someone points to the hyperlink.

8. Click OK.

9. Click OK.

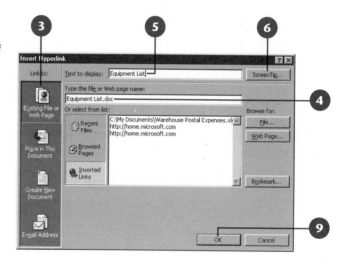

14

Using and Removing Hyperlinks

Hyperlinks connect you to information in other documents. Rather than duplicating the important information stored in other documents, you can create hyperlinks to the relevant material. When you click a hyperlink for the first time (during a session), the color of the hyperlink changes, indicating that you have accessed the hyperlink. If a link becomes outdated or unnecessary, you can easily revise or remove it.

SEE ALSO

See "Navigating Basics" on page 240 for information on moving between hyperlinked documents.

TIP

Display the Web toolbar.
Click the View menu, point to Toolbars, and then click Web.

Use a Hyperlink

1 Position the mouse pointer (which changes to a hand pointer) over any hyperlink.

2 Click the hyperlink.

Depending on the type of hyperlink, the screen

◆ Jumps to a new location within the same document.

◆ Jumps to a location on an intranet or Internet Web site.

◆ Opens a new file and the program in which it was created.

◆ Opens Outlook and displays a new e-mail message.

3 Navigate between open hyperlinked documents with the Web toolbar.

◆ Click the Back or Forward button to move between documents.

◆ Click the Start Page button to go to your home page.

◆ Click the Search The Web button to go to a search page.

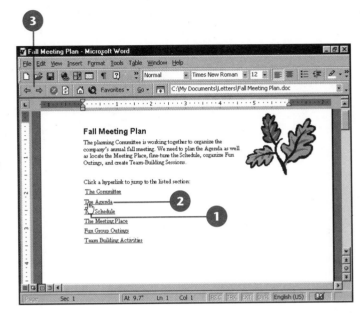

Web toolbar   Start Page button

Back and Forward buttons   Search The Web button

Edit a Hyperlink

1. Right-click the hyperlink you want to edit, point to Hyperlink, and then click Edit Hyperlink.

2. If you want, change the display text.

3. If you want, click ScreenTip, edit the custom text, and then click OK.

4. If necessary, change the destination.

5. Click OK.

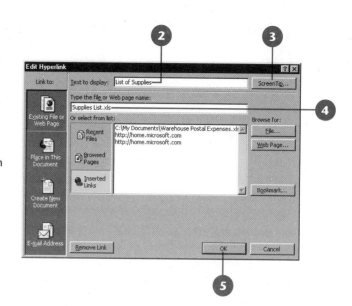

Remove a Hyperlink

1. Right-click the hyperlink you want to remove.

2. Point to Hyperlink.

3. Click Remove Hyperlink.

4. If necessary, delete the text or object.

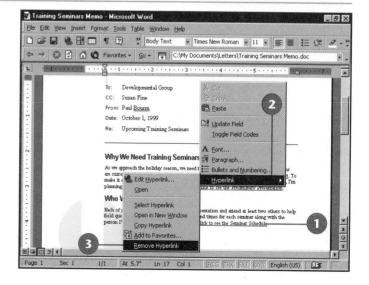

Enhancing Web Pages

A basic Web page usually includes text, graphics, and hyperlinks. You can change the look of your Web site by selecting a *theme*—a predesigned visual layout that changes text formatting (such as font type, size, format, and color), as well as bullets, backgrounds, colors, and horizontal lines to create a specific mood. Each theme has two color variations: default and vivid. Some themes include animations.

You can make your Web site easier to navigate by adding *frames*—separate panes that contain unique content and scroll independently. For example, you might place navigation links in one frame and a home page link in another frame.

Use Themes to Add a Color Scheme in Word

1. Open the Word document to which you want to add a theme.

2. Click the Format menu, and then click Theme.

3. Click a theme to view a sample.

4. Click to select the Vivid Colors check box to view a theme color variation.

5. Click OK.

Add or Remove Frames in Word

1. Open the Word document to which you want to add or remove a frame.

2. Right-click any toolbar, and then click Frames to display the Frames toolbar.

3. Click the appropriate button to add or remove a frame.

Table of contents frame

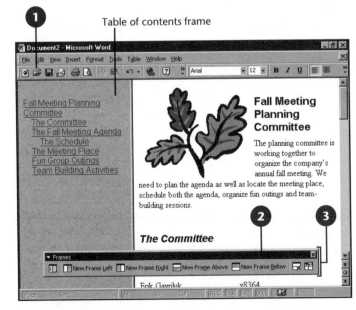

Previewing Web Pages

After you create a Web page, you should preview it in a Web browser, such as Microsoft Internet Explorer, or in the Office program to make sure others see your Web page the same way you do. *Web Page Preview* displays the open file in your default browser even if you haven't saved it yet. *Web Layout view* shows you how a document will be displayed on the Web. If the document includes formatting or layouts that cannot be achieved in HTML, Word switches to an HTML layout that closely matches the original look.

TIP

High-fidelity display of documents. *Office takes advantage of Internet Explorer support for Web technologies such as HTML 4.0 and Cascading Style Sheets to bring the familiar Office look and feel to HTML documents. For example, underlining and tables in HTML format appear nearly identical to the Office document format.*

Preview a Web Page in a Browser

1 In an Office program, open the Web page you want to preview.

2 Click the File menu, and then click Web Page Preview.

Your default Web browser starts and displays the Web page.

3 Scroll to view the entire page, click hyperlinks to test them, and so forth.

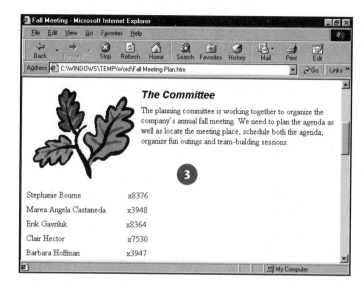

Preview a Web Page in Word

1 Open the Word document you want to preview.

2 Click the Web Layout View button.

The document appears just as it would on the Web.

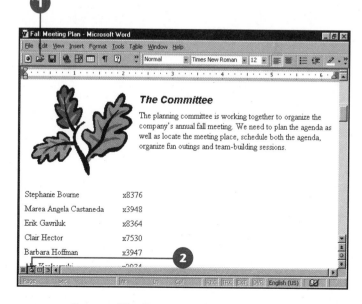

14

Saving Documents as Web Pages

No matter what Office program you are working in, you can save your document as a Web page. Then others can use a browser to view and even edit your document over the Internet or an intranet. You can continue to open and work with the file from its original Office program. Web pages use *Hypertext Markup Language* (HTML)—a simple coding system that specifies the formats a browser uses to display the document. Any Office document saved as a Web page consists of an HTML file and a folder that stores supporting files, such as a file for each graphic, worksheet, slide, and so on. Office automatically selects the appropriate graphic format for you based on the image's content.

Save an Office Document as a Web Page

1. Open the document you want to save as a Web page.

2. Click the File menu, and then click Save As Web Page.

3. Select the drive and folder in which to store the file.

4. Type a name for the file.

5. Click Save.

The Web page is saved in the selected folder, and the supporting graphics and related files are saved in another folder with the name of the Web page.

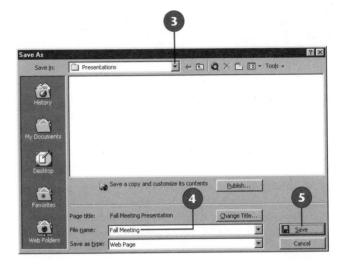

GRAPHIC FORMATS ON THE WEB	
Format	**Description**
GIF	*Graphics Interchange Format* (GIF) is a form of compression for line drawings or other artwork. Office converts to GIF such images as logos, graphs, line drawings, and specific colored objects.
JPEG	*Joint Photograhic Experts Group* (JPEG) is a high-quality form of compression for continuous tone images, such as photographs. Office converts to JPEG such images as photographs or other images that have many shades of colors.

Change a Web page's title.
The title *is text that appears in the title bar of the browser when that page is loaded. To change the title of a page, click Change Title in the Save As dialog box, type a new title, and then click OK.*

Similar functionality. *HTML documents preserve many Office functions, such as styles, PivotTable dynamic views, tables, revision marks, and objects. Be aware that some formatting, such as alignment, isn't available in HTML and might be displayed differently.*

See "Editing an Office Web Page" on page 245 for information on editing Office Web pages on your intranet.

Save an Excel Worksheet as an Interactive Web Page

1. Open the workbook you want to save as a Web page.

2. Click the File menu, and then click Save As Web Page.

3. Select the drive and folder in which to store the file.

4. Select an option button to save the entire workbook or the selection.

5. Click to select the Add Interactivity check box if you want others to be able to edit the file.

6. Type a name for the file.

7. Click Save.

   The Web page is saved in the selected folder, and the supporting graphics and related files are saved in another folder with the name of the Web page.

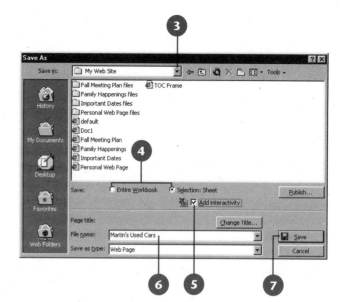

Publishing Web Pages

At times, you'll want to publish a copy of your current Office document in HTML format directly to a *Web server* (a computer on the Internet or intranet that stores Web pages) so others can view and manipulate your data. Publishing to a Web server is as simple as saving a file. With the *Office Web Components*, you can elect to let anyone using Internet Explorer 4.01 or later interact with your data from Excel. Any data published to a Web page can be returned to its Office program for additional analysis and tracking.

TIP

What happens when you publish a Web page? *When you publish a Web page, you move the Web page and graphic images to a Web server.*

SEE ALSO

See "Saving Documents as Web Pages" on page 266 for information on publishing from Word or Publisher.

Publish an Excel Worksheet Item as a Web Page

① Open the Excel workbook with the data or chart you want to publish.

② Click the File menu, and then click Save As Web Page.

③ Click Publish.

④ Select the items you want to include in the Web page.

⑤ Click to select the Add Interactivity With check box, click the drop-down arrow, and then select Spreadsheet Functionality.

⑥ Click Change, type a title for the Web page, and then click OK.

⑦ Type the folder and filename for the published Web page.

⑧ If you want, click to select the Open Published Web Page In Browser check box to preview the page in a browser.

⑨ Click Publish.

⑩ Start a Web browser and open the Web page.

⑪ Edit the data as needed.

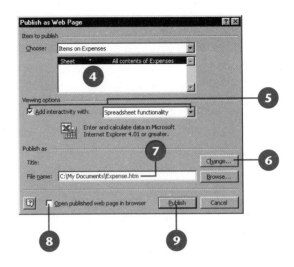

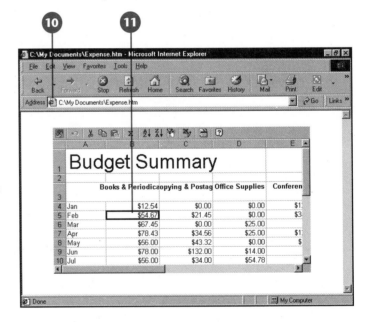

TIP

What are the Office Web components? *The* Spreadsheet component *provides basic spreadsheet functionality so users can enter data, create formulas, recalculate, sort, filter, and add basic formatting. The* Chart component *provides automatic updates to charts as the underlying data changes. The* PivotTable component *is created either in Excel or and provides efficient analysis of data by enabling users to browse, sort, filter, group, and total report data. A viewer can also modify the PivotTable by dragging different fields to and from the table.*

TIP

Manage your Web files. *You can add, move, or delete files stored on a Web server from the Windows Explorer just as you would with a file server.*

SEE ALSO

See "Analyzing Data Using a PivotTable" on page 150 for information about using PivotTables.

Publish an Excel Worksheet PivotTable as a Web Page

1. Open the Excel workbook with the data you want to publish as a PivotTable.

2. Click the File menu, and then click Save As Web Page.

3. Click Publish.

4. Select the items you want to include in the Web page.

5. Click to select the Add Interactivity With check box, click the drop-down arrow, and then select PivotTable Functionality.

6. Click Change, type a title for the Web page, and then click OK.

7. Type the folder and filename for the published Web page.

8. If you want, click to select the Open Published Web Page In Browser check box to preview the page in a browser.

9. Click Publish.

10. Start a Web browser and open the Web page.

11. Edit the PivotTable as needed.

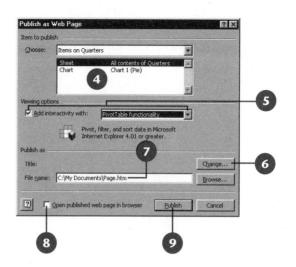

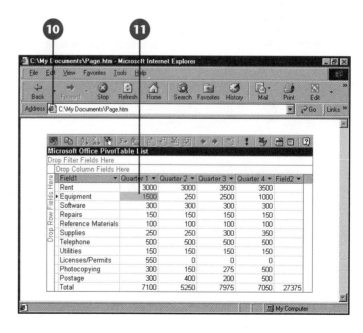

14

Holding an Online Meeting

What's the most convenient way to meet with a sales staff based around the world? *NetMeeting*—a conferencing program for meeting and collaborating over the Internet or a corporate intranet. Participants share and exchange information as if they were in one room. The *host* starts the meeting and controls access to the document. When the host allows editing, participants can work on the document one at a time. Otherwise, they cannot make changes, but they can see any changes the host makes. All participants can talk to each other, video conference, share programs, and collaborate on documents, send files, exchange messages in Chat, transfer files, and draw on the Whiteboard.

Schedule a Meeting

1. Click the Tools menu, point to Online Collaboration, and then click Schedule Meeting.

2. Enter participants' names or e-mail addresses, a subject, and the meeting location.

3. Click Browse, and then double-click a document you want to send.

4. Select a start and end date and time.

5. Type a message.

6. Click the Send button.

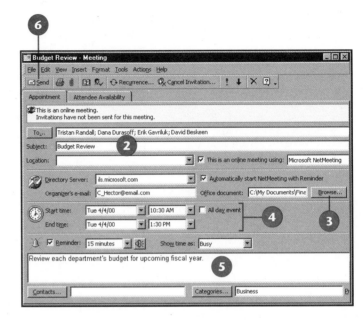

Hold a Meeting

1. Open the document you want to share.

2. Click the Tools menu, point to Online Collaboration, and then click Meet Now.

3. If this is your first meeting, enter your personal information, select a server, and then click OK.

4. Select participants for the meeting, and then click Call.

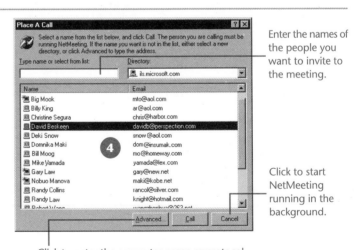

Enter the names of the people you want to invite to the meeting.

Click to start NetMeeting running in the background.

Click to enter the computer name or protocol address of the person you want to invite.

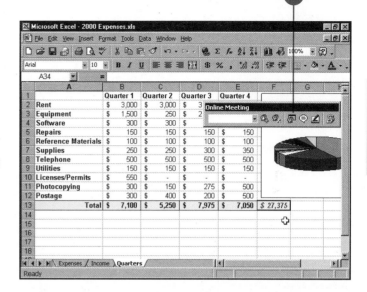

TIP

Receive an online meeting call. *You must have NetMeeting running on your computer to receive an online meeting call.*

TIP

Start NetMeeting from the Start menu. *If you don't have an Office program open, click the Start button, point to Programs, and then click NetMeeting.*

TIP

Join an online meeting. *If you receive an online meeting call, click Accept in the Join Meeting dialog box. If you receive an Outlook reminder for the meeting, click Start This NetMeeting (host), or Join This NetMeeting (participant). To receive an Outlook reminder to join a meeting, you need to have accepted the meeting from an e-mail message.*

SEE ALSO

See "Scheduling an Event and Appointment" on page 172 and "Planning a Meeting" on page 174 for more information on using Outlook to schedule online meetings, set up reminders, and join a meeting.

Collaborate in an Online Meeting

1. As the host, click the Allow Others To Edit button on the Online Meeting toolbar.

2. When collaboration is turned on, click anywhere in the document to gain control. If you are a participant, double-click anywhere in the document to gain control.

3. Click the Allow Others To Edit button again to turn off collaboration, or press Esc if you don't have control of the document.

Participate in an Online Meeting

◆ Use the buttons on the Online Meeting toolbar to participate in an online meeting.

ONLINE MEETING TOOLBAR	
Button	**Description**
	Allows the host to invite additional participants to the online meeting
	Allows the host to remove a participant from the online meeting
	Allows participants to edit and control the presentation during the online meeting
	Allows participants to send messages in a Chat session during the online meeting
	Allows participants to draw or type on the Whiteboard during the online meeting
	Allows the host to end the online meeting for the entire group, or a participant to disconnect

Having a Web Discussion

Need feedback on a document? Try a *Web discussion,* where multiple participants discuss an Office document over the Internet, an intranet, or a network by adding comments in the Discussion pane at the bottom of the document. Participants can also comment directly in the document. Either way, the Discussions toolbar provides all the commands you need to insert new comments, navigate, edit and reply to comments, and even hide or display the Discussion pane.

TIP

Where do discussions appear? *Discussions are anchored at the end of a paragraph in Word or to the current sheet in Excel.*

SEE ALSO

See "Understanding Office Server Extensions" on page 274 for information on setting up a server for a Web discussion.

Select a Web Discussion Server

1 Open the presentation for which you want to have a discussion.

2 Click the Tools menu, point to Online Collaboration, and then click Web Discussions.

If you are selecting a discussion server for the first time, skip to step 5.

3 On the Discussions toolbar, click the Discussions button, and then click Discussion Options.

4 Click Add.

5 Type the name of a discussion server provided by your administrator.

The discussion server needs to have Office Server Extensions to hold a Web discussion.

6 If your administrator has set up security by using the Secure Sockets Layer (SSL) message protocol, click to select the Secure Connection Required (SSL) check box.

7 Type the name you want to use for the server.

8 Click OK.

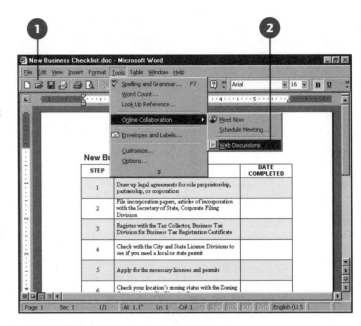

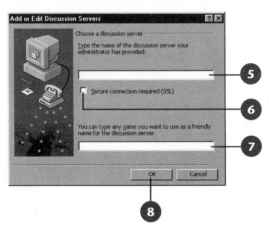

Start and Close a Web Discussion

1 Open the presentation for which you want to start a discussion.

2 Click the Tools menu, point to Online Collaboration, and then click Web Discussions.

3 Click the Insert About The Presentation button on the Discussions toolbar.

4 Type the subject of the discussion.

5 Type your comments.

6 Click OK.

7 Click the Close button on the Discussions toolbar.

Reply to a Web Discussion Remark

1 Open the presentation that contains the discussion you want to join.

2 Click the Tools menu, point to Online Collaboration, and then click Web Discussions.

3 Click the Show A Menu Of Actions button, and then click Reply.

4 Type your reply, and then click OK.

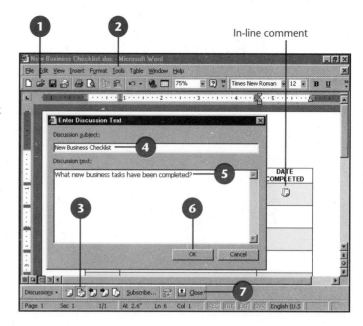

In-line comment

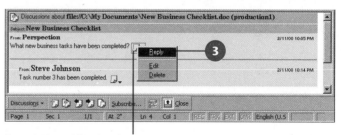

Show A Menu Of Actions button

Understanding Office Server Extensions

Microsoft Office 2000 uses *Office Server Extensions* to provide a bridge between current Web technologies and the functionality needed to make the Web a friendly place to work with people and information. Office Server Extensions are a set of features that makes it easy to work with Office files and collaborate on the Web. Office Server Extensions allow you to publish and view Web documents directly from a Web server—a computer on the Internet that stores Web pages—with Office programs or Internet Explorer; to perform Web discussions and exchange information on documents located on the Web server; and to receive notification when a document on a Web server has been changed, which is known as *Web Subscription* and *Web Notification*.

Office Server Extensions are a superset of Microsoft FrontPage Extensions and other technologies that reside on an Windows NT–based Web servers to provide additional publishing, collaboration, and document management capabilities. Office Server Extensions do not replace existing Web server technologies. Rather, the extensions in Office 2000 are designed to enhance your experience with Office in a Web-based environment.

Office Server Extensions are included with Office 2000 Premium. To set up your computer with Office Server Extensions, you need a computer with Windows NT Workstation 4.0 or later running Personal Web Server 4.0 or later, or Windows NT Server 4.0 or later running Internet Information Server 4.0 or later. With the Server Extensions Configuration Wizard, you can set up and configure an existing Web server to use the Office Server Extensions.

Web File Management

Office Server Extensions make publishing and sharing documents on Web servers as easy as working with documents on file servers. Office 2000 enables you to create folders, view properties, and perform file drag-and-drop operations on Web servers just as you would on normal file servers. You can also perform these same Web server file operations directly from the Windows Explorer. In Internet Explorer, Office Server Extensions enable on-the-fly display of Web directory listings, files, and HTML views of Web folders.

Web Discussions

With the Office Server Extensions installed on a Web server, you can have online discussions in Web page (HTML) files and Office 2000 documents. A *Web discussion* is an online, interactive conversation that takes place within the Web page or Office document (also called *in-line*) or that occurs as a general discussion about the Web page or Office document, which is stored in the discussion pane at the bottom of the page. A Web discussion can occur only through Internet Explorer or an Office program. Using the Discussions toolbar, users can insert new comments, edit and reply to existing comments, subscribe to a particular document, and view or hide the Discussion pane.

Sending Documents by E-Mail

The quickest way to send someone a copy of a document is to send them an electronic copy by e-mail. Without having to open your e-mail program and attach the file, you can send any Office document to others from within that program. The E-Mail button inserts a standard message header at the top of the open file so you can send it as an e-mail message.

TIP

Close an e-mail message without sending it. *If you decide not to send the message, just click the E-Mail button on the Standard toolbar to hide the message header.*

Send a Document in an E-Mail Message

1. Open the worksheet you want to send.

2. Click the File menu, point to Send To, and then click Mail Recipient.

3. Click the To or Cc button. Select the contacts to whom you want the message sent, and then click OK.

4. Click the Send This Sheet button.

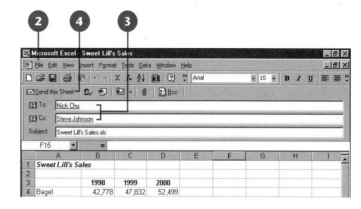

Send a Document as an E-Mail Attachment

1. Open the workbook you want to send.

2. Click the File menu, point to Send To, and then click Mail Recipient (As Attachment). Your default e-mail program opens, displaying a new e-mail message window.

3. Click the To or Cc button. Select the contacts to whom you want the message sent, and then click OK.

4. If you want, type a related message.

5. Click the Send button.

Icons representing attached documents appear here.

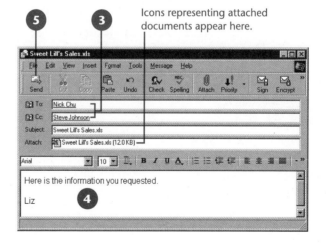

Getting Documents from the Internet

File Transfer Protocol (FTP) is an inexpensive and efficient way to transfer files between your computer and other computers on the Internet. You can *download*, or receive from another computer, any kind of file, including text, graphics, sound, and video files. To download a file, you need to access an FTP site. Whenever you do, you need an ID and password to identify who you are. Anonymous FTP sites are open to anyone; they usually use *anonymous* as an ID and your full e-mail address as the password. You can also save the FTP site address to revisit the site later.

Access an FTP Site

1. Click the Open button on the Standard toolbar.

2. Click the Look In drop-down arrow, and then click the FTP site you want to log in to.

3. Select a Log On As option.

4. Enter a password (your e-mail address or personal password).

5. Click OK.

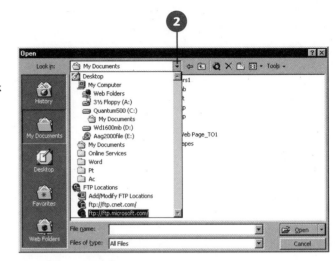

Add or Modify FTP Locations

1. Click the Open button on the Standard toolbar.

2. Click the Look In drop-down arrow, and then click Add/Modify FTP Locations.

3. Type the complete address for an FTP site.

4. Type your e-mail address as the password.

5. Click Add.

6. Click OK.

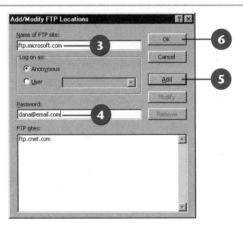

Sharing Information Between Office 2000 Programs

Microsoft Office 2000 has the power and flexibility to share information between programs. This means you can create, store, and manage information in the program that works best for that type of information, yet move that same information to another program for a specific purpose or presentation.

Share with Ease

Consider an example. Sarah coordinates her local school district's soccer teams. She sends out monthly newsletters that list the scheduled dates and times for practices and games as well as a brief roundup of scores and highlights from the previous month's games. In Microsoft Excel, she creates a list of team members and all their relevant information—names, addresses, phone numbers, emergency numbers, and team positions. She also tracks the year-to-date expenses and plans the tentative schedules between teams. Every month, Sarah writes the newsletter in Microsoft Word, imports the upcoming schedule from Excel, and then merges the newsletter with the Excel worksheet to create the mailing. This is just one scenario. As you work with Office programs, you'll find many ways to share information between them.

Sharing Information Between Programs

Office 2000 can convert data or text from one format to another using a technology known as *object linking and embedding (OLE)*. OLE allows you to move text or data between programs in much the same way as you move them within a program. The familiar cut and paste or drag and drop methods work between programs and documents just as they do within a document. In addition, all Office programs have special ways to move information from one program to another, including importing, exporting, embedding, linking, and hyperlinking.

Importing and Exporting

Importing and exporting information are two sides of the same coin. *Importing* copies a file created with the same or another program into your open file. The information becomes part of your open file, just as if you created it in that format, although formatting and program-specific information such as formulas can be lost. *Exporting* converts a copy of your open file into the file type of another program. In other words, importing brings information into your open document, while exporting moves information from your open document into another program file.

Embedding

Embedding inserts a copy of a file created in one program into a file created in another program. Unlike imported files, you can edit the information in embedded files with the same commands and toolbar buttons used to create the original file. The original file is called the *source file*, while the file in which it is embedded is called the *destination file*. Any changes you make to an embedded object appear only in the destination file; the source file remains unchanged.

Linking

Linking displays information from one file (the source file) in a file created in another program (the destination file). You can view and edit the linked object from either the source file or the destination file. The changes are stored in the source file but also appear in the destination file. As you work, Office updates the linked object to ensure you always have the most current information. Office keeps track of all the drive, folder, and filename information for a source file. However, if you move or rename the source file, the link between files will break.

Once the link is broken, the information in the destination file becomes embedded rather than linked. In other words, changes to one copy of the file will no longer affect the other.

TERM	DEFINITION
Source program	The program that created the original object
Source file	The file that contains the original object
Destination program	The program that created the document into which you are inserting the object
Destination file	The file into which you are inserting the object

Hyperlinking

The newest way to share information between programs is hyperlinks—a term borrowed from World Wide Web technology. A *hyperlink* is an object (either colored, underlined text or a graphic) that you click to jump to a different location in the same document or a different document. (See "Creating Web Pages with Office 2000 Programs" on page 225 for more information about creating and navigating hyperlinks in Office 2000 documents.)

Deciding Which Method to Use

With all theses different methods for sharing information between programs to choose from, sometimes it is hard to decide which method to use. To decide which method is best for your situation, answer the following questions.

1 Do you want the contents of another file displayed in the open document?

◆ **No**. Create a hyperlink. See "Inserting Hyperlinks" on page 260.

◆ **Yes**. Go to question 2.

2 Do you want to edit the content of the file from within the open document?

◆ **No**. Embed the file as a picture. See "Embedding and Linking Information" on page 282.

◆ **Yes**. Go to question 3.

3 Is the source program (the program used to create the file) available on your computer?

◆ **No**. Import the file. See "Importing and Exporting Files" on page 280.

◆ **Yes**. Go to question 4.

4 Do you want to use the source program commands to edit the file?

◆ **No**. Import the file. See "Importing and Exporting Files" on page 280.

◆ **Yes**. Go to question 5.

5 Do you want changes you make to the file to appear in the source file (the original copy of the file)?

◆ **No**. Embed the file. See "Embedding and Linking Information" on page 282.

◆ **Yes**. Link the file. See "Embedding and Linking Information" on page 282.

15

Importing and Exporting Files

When you *import* data, you insert a copy of a file (from the same or another program) into an open document. When you *export* data, you save an open document in a new format so that it can be opened in an entirely different program. For example, you might import an Excel worksheet into a Word document to create a one-page report with text and a table. Or you might want to export part of an Excel worksheet to use in another program.

Import part of a file into Word. *You can insert into a Word document a bookmarked section of a Word document or a specific range in an Excel worksheet. Click the Range button in the Insert File dialog box, enter a bookmark name or range, and then click OK.*

Import a File

1. Click where you want to insert the imported file.

2. Do one of the following.

   ◆ In Word, click the Insert menu, and then click File.

   ◆ In Excel, click the Data menu, point to Get External Data, and then click Import Text File.

   ◆ In Publisher, click in the text frame, click the Insert menu, and then click Text File.

3. Click the Files Of Type drop-down arrow, and then select All Files.

4. Click the Look In drop-down arrow, and then select the drive and folder of the file you want to import.

5. Double-click the name of the file you want to import.

6. Edit the imported information with the open program's commands.

Export a File to Another Program

1. Click the File menu, and then click Save As.

2. If necessary, click the Save In drop-down arrow, and then select the drive and folder where you want to save the file.

3. Click the Save As Type drop-down arrow, and then select the type of file you want.

4. If necessary, type a new name for the file.

5. Click Save.

6. Edit the file from within the new program.

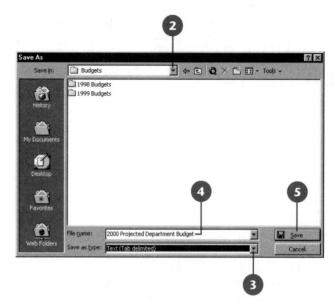

15

Embedding and Linking Information

Embedding inserts a copy of one document into another. Once data is embedded, you can edit it in the program in which it was created (the *source program*). *Linking* displays information stored in one document (the *source file*) into another (the *destination file*). You can edit the linked object from either file, although changes are stored in the source file. For example, you might link an Excel chart to a Publisher document and a Word document so you can update the chart from any of the files.

Embed an Existing Object

1. Click where you want to embed the object.

2. Click the Insert menu, and then click Object.

3. Click the Create From File tab or option button.

4. Click Browse and then double-click the file with the object you want to embed.

5. Click OK.

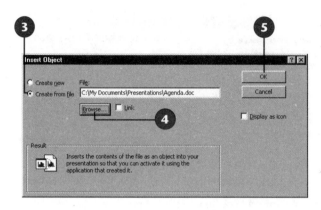

Embed a New Object

1. Click where you want to embed the object.

2. Click the Insert menu, and then click Object.

3. Click the Create New tab or option button.

4. Double-click the type of object you want to create.

5. Enter information in the new object using the source program's commands.

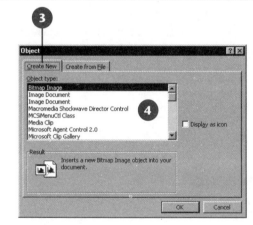

Link an Object Between Programs

1. Click where you want to link the object.

2. Click the Insert menu, and then click Object.

3. Click the Create From File tab or option button.

4. Click Browse, and then double-click the object you want to link.

5. Click to select the Link To File check box.

6. Click OK.

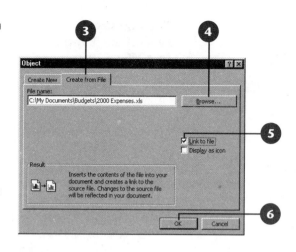

Edit an Embedded or Linked File

1. Double-click the linked or embedded object you want to edit to display the source program's menus and toolbars.

2. Edit the object as usual using the source program's commands.

3. When you're done, click outside the object to return to the destination program.

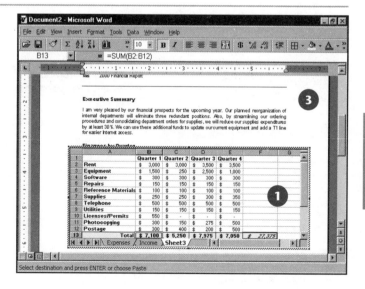

15

Creating a Word Document with Excel Data

A common pairing of Office programs combines Word and Excel. As you write a sales report, explain a budget, or create a memo showing distribution of sales, you often want to add existing spreadsheet data and charts to your text. Instead of re-creating the Excel data in Word, you can insert all or part of the data or chart into your Word document.

SEE ALSO

See "Naming Cells and Ranges" on page 119 for information on naming a range in Excel.

TIP

Name a range before pairing. *If you plan to insert part of an Excel worksheet in a Word document, name the range. This is easier to recall than the specific cell references.*

Copy an Excel Worksheet Range to a Word Document

1 Click in the Word document where you want to copy the Excel range.

2 Click the Insert menu, and then click File.

3 Click the Files Of Type drop-down arrow, and then select All Files.

4 Click the Look In drop-down arrow, and then select the drive and folder that contains the workbook you want to copy.

5 Double-click the filename of the workbook you want to copy.

6 Click the Open Document In Workbook drop-down arrow, and then select the worksheet you want.

7 Click the Name Or Cell Range drop-down arrow, and select the range or range name you want to copy.

8 Click OK.

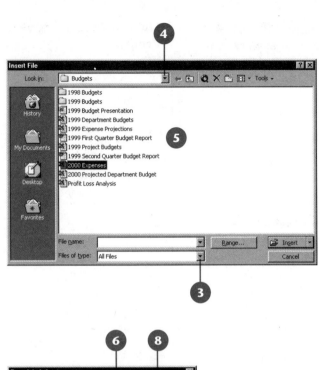

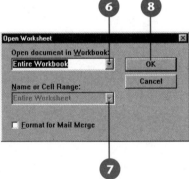

Import Excel data as a picture. *To save disk space, you can insert Excel data as a picture. Data inserted this way becomes a table that you cannot edit. Select the data you want to import, press the Shift key as you click the Edit menu, and then click Copy Picture. In the Copy Picture dialog box, click OK. Click in the Word document where you want to insert the picture, and then click the Paste button on the Standard toolbar. Drag the picture to a new location, or drag its resize handles to enlarge or shrink it.*

Create a new Excel worksheet directly in a Word document. *Place the insertion point where you want the worksheet, click the Insert Microsoft Excel Worksheet button on the Standard toolbar, drag to select the number of rows and columns you want, enter data and format the worksheet as needed, and then click outside the worksheet to return to the Word window. When you save the file, the worksheet becomes embedded in the Word document. Double-click the worksheet to edit it with Excel commands.*

Embed an Excel Chart in Word

1. Open the Excel worksheet where the chart you want to use appears.

2. Click to select the Excel chart you want to embed.

3. Click the Copy button on the Standard toolbar.

4. Click the Word document where you want to embed the chart.

5. Click the Paste button on the Standard toolbar.

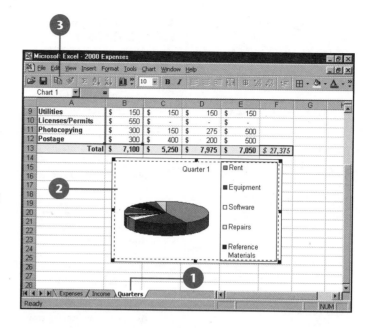

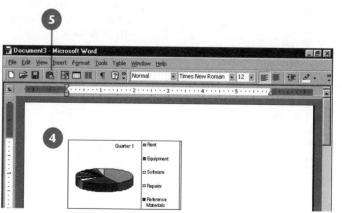

15

Copying a Web Table to an Excel Worksheet

You can copy tabular information on a Web page and paste or drag the information into an Excel worksheet. It's an easy way to transfer and manipulate Web-based table data using Excel. Excel simplifies access to table data by making it available to anyone with a Web browser.

TIP

Use Copy and Paste to transfer table data to Excel. *In your browser, select the table data you want, click the Edit menu, click Copy, switch to Excel, click the cell where you want to place the table data, and then click the Paste button on the Standard toolbar.*

Copy a Web Table to a Worksheet

1. Open your Web browser.

2. In the Address bar, type the location of the Web page with the table data you want to copy, and then press Enter.

3. Select the table data in the Web page you want to copy.

4. Open the Excel worksheet where you want to paste the table data.

5. Right-click the taskbar, and then click Tile Vertically.

6. Drag the table data from the Web browser window to the location on the worksheet where you want the table data.

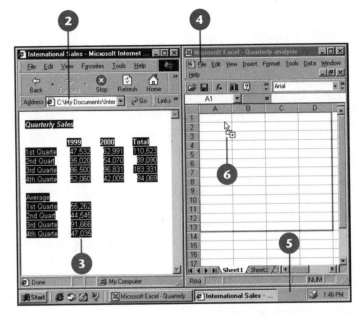

Using Small Business Tools

Working efficiently is the goal of Microsoft Office 2000 Small Business. To help you achieve that goal, several analytical programs called the *Small Business Tools* are included with Office 2000.

Using Powerful Analytical Tools

The Small Business Tools include the Small Business Customer Manager, the Business Planner, the Direct Mail Manager, and the Small Business Financial Manager. With Small Business Customer Manager, you'll be able to develop a customer and sales database using existing data from popular accounting programs and Outlook contacts. You can track customer activity, generate a variety of reports, and automate frequently created documents. The Business Planner makes it possible to write a professional-looking business plan and provides a variety of Office templates designed with the small business in mind. You can use the Direct Mail Manager with Word and Publisher to create direct mailings, verify and sort an address list, and prepare your mailing to take advantage of U.S. Postal Service discounts. The Small Business Financial Manager uses Excel to compare financing options, create standard financial reports and attractive charts, and create growth projections and what-if scenarios.

Starting Small Business Tools

Before you can use any of the Microsoft Small Business Tools, you need to start them. You can start any of the Small Business Tools using the Start menu on the taskbar. When each tool starts, it displays a Welcome screen that gives you a description of its functions. You quit a tool using the File menu, as you would any Office 2000 program.

TRY THIS

Locate each Small Business Tool. *Once you have located each tool on the Start menu, open and quit each one.*

TIP

File menus contain different options. *Although the File menu of each tool may contain different commands, the last command is always Exit.*

Start a Small Business Tool from the Start Menu

1. Click the Start button on the taskbar.

2. Point to Programs.

   If you see the Microsoft Small Business Tools folder on the Programs menu, point to it and then proceed to step 3.

3. Click a Small Business Tool.

   ◆ Microsoft Business Planner to create business and marketing plans

   ◆ Microsoft Direct Mail Manager to produce direct mailings

   ◆ Microsoft Small Business Customer Manager to manage and analyze customer data

   ◆ Microsoft Small Business Financial Manager to analyze financial data

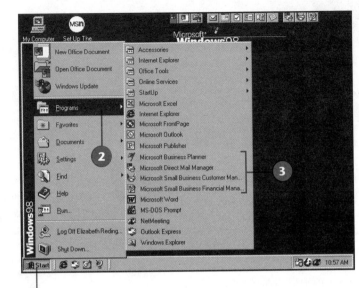

Creating a Customer Database

Existing information from a database, accounting software, or Outlook contacts can easily be imported into the Microsoft Small Business Customer Manager. Using existing data means less work and more efficiency: you can track, analyze, and communicate with customers and coworkers. The importing process brings the existing data into the Small Business Customer Manager in an easy-to-understand format that you can then manipulate.

Create a New Database

1. Start the Microsoft Small Business Customer Manager.

2. Click the New Wizard Database option button, and then click OK.

3. Follow the Database Wizard to enter user information, select accounting and Outlook data, enter contact ownership, select activity tracking, enter a database name, select import data, and then click Finish.

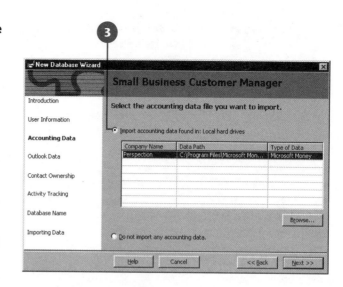

Open an Existing Database

1. Start the Microsoft Small Business Customer Manager.

2. Click the Open An Existing Database option button.

3. Select a database. If necessary, use the Browse button to locate the file.

4. Click OK.

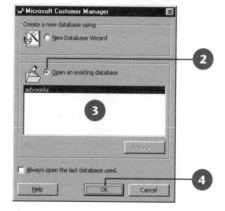

16

Displaying a View

Data can be of little or no use if its organization is incompatible with your needs. A Small Business Customer Manager view is a format you can use to see your data in a way that suits your needs. You might have an alphabetical list of customers, but you need to see that list sorted by sales volume or profitability. Applying a view makes it easy to see the information in the form you need. The Small Business Customer Manager comes with a large selection of predesigned views and *Hot Views* (views most often used). Once a view or Hot View is applied, you can use a filter to narrow your list.

Display a View or Hot View

1. Start the Small Business Customer Manager, and then open a database.

2. Click the View menu, and then point to Go.

3. Point to a View submenu, and then click the view you want to apply.

Click to select a Hot View.

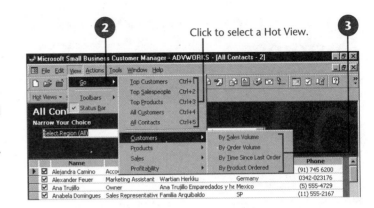

Apply a Filter

1. Start the Small Business Customer Manager, and then open a database.

2. Click the Narrow Your Choice drop-down arrow.

3. Click the choices you want.

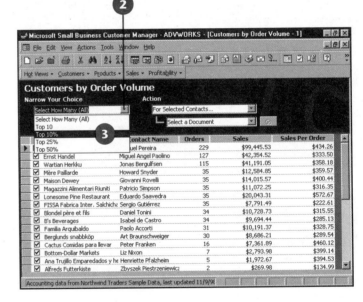

Automating a Task

It's easy to complete repetitive tasks in the Microsoft Small Business Customer Manager using automated Word and Publisher templates. Once you've applied a view to data in the Customer Manager, you can send a letter or mail message to the resulting list of names with the click of a mouse button. Using automated tasks, you can use mail merge capabilities to combine the results of a view with existing Word or Publisher documents.

TRY THIS

Send e-mail quickly. *Send e-mail to those on the list that results when you apply a view to Customer Manager data.*

TIP

Customer Manager contains over 20 templates. *You can customize each of the Word and Publisher templates.*

Automate a Task

1. Start the Small Business Customer Manager, open a database, and then apply a view, if necessary.

2. Click the top Action drop-down arrow, and then select the records that will be affected.

3. Click the bottom Action drop-down arrow, and then select the type of document you create.

4. Click Go, select a template, and then click OK.

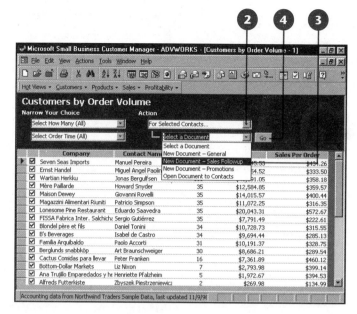

Access a Template

1. Click the Template button on the toolbar.

2. Click one of the Customer Manager template tabs.

3. Click the type of template document you want to create.

4. Click OK.

5. Follow the instructions in the automated template.

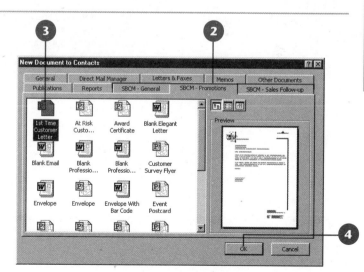

16

Tracking Customer Activity

Actions performed on records in the Microsoft Small Business Customer Manager are automatically tracked so you will always have a record of letters sent and appointments made. For example, you can use the Activity Tracker to check a contact's record to find out the last time a mailing was sent out or to determine the last appointment you had with a client.

TIP

Track Customer Manager or Outlook events. *Click the Tools menu, click Options, click the General tab, click to select either the Customer Manager Events or Outlook Events check box, and then click OK.*

SEE ALSO

See "Scheduling an Event and Appointment" on page 172 for information on creating appointments with Outlook.

View Contact Activity

1. Start the Small Business Customer Manager, open a database, click the Tools menu, point to Activity Tracker, and then click Show.

2. If necessary, click the Company drop-down list, and then make a selection.

3. If necessary, click the Contacts drop-down list, and then make a selection.

4. Click Close.

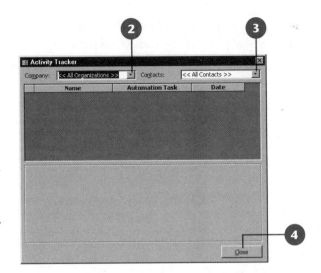

View Contact Information

1. In the Small Business Customer Manager, double-click the company or contact name you want to view.

2. Click the tab to display the information you want to view.

3. Click Close.

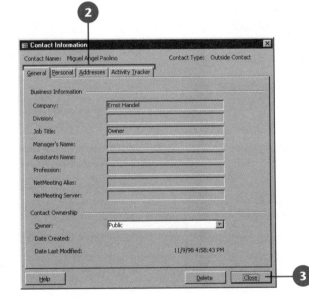

Tailoring the Business Planner

The Microsoft Business Planner will give you access to tools, information, and templates you can use to start, run, and grow your business. When you initially open the Business Planner, you complete an "interview" that tells the program about your business. The Personal Interviewer consists of three steps in which you use option buttons, text boxes, and drop-down lists to provide answers to specific questions about your business. After you complete the third step, the Business Planner opens.

TIP

Change information on your company. *To make changes to your business information, click the Go button on the toolbar, click Personal Interviewer, and then make the modifications.*

Complete the Personal Interview

1 Start the Microsoft Business Planner.

2 If the Personal Interviewer does not automatically open, click the Go button on the toolbar, and then click Personal Interviewer.

3 Complete the questions in each step, and then click the Step arrows on the toolbar.

4 If necessary, click the Exit button to end the Personal Interviewer session.

Click to open the Personal Interviewer.

Click to see previous interview steps.

Step arrows

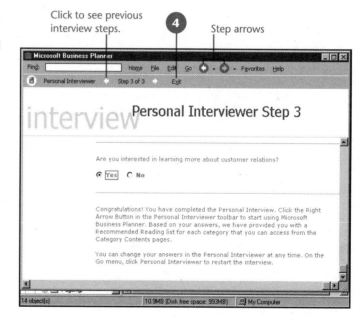

Browsing Business Resources

Each Microsoft Business Planner contains categories on planning, operations, legal, finance, and marketing, which you can open with the click of a button. Its Resource Center makes use of a variety of references—some utilizing the Internet—thereby ensuring that you receive the most up-to-date information. Online resources range from company profiles, phone directories, and business listings to ready-to-use Excel and Word templates for common business uses. You can also search Business Planner content using the Find box.

TIP

Drill down required. *Some topics require that you click several layers of information in order to reach the article you want. A fully expanded topic contains a minus sign.*

Browse a Business Topic

1 Start the Microsoft Business Planner, click a category, such as Planning, on the Business Planner home page.

2 Click the topic link you need to access the information you want to read.

Some topics require Internet access. If so, your Web browser will open.

3 If necessary, continue to click links until you have found what you are looking for.

Search for Content Quickly

1 Start the Microsoft Business Planner, click the Find box, and then type the keywords you want to search for.

2 Click the Search Keywords And Titles or Search All Text option button.

3 Click the entry you want.

4 Press Esc to close the Search window when you're done.

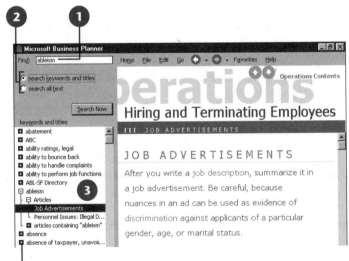

A plus sign indicates multiple levels of information.

Creating Business Plans

Having a business plan and marketing strategy can spell success for any business. Using the Business Plan Wizard's interviewing style makes it easy to complete a business plan. It also provides predesigned plans, which are divided into multiple sections, containing selected articles and interview questions for you to complete. When you're finished, you'll have a working outline for each section of your plan that can be completed later. The Marketing Wizard will help you develop a marketing strategy. You will also be able to evaluate the marketing methods that best suit your needs.

Create a Business Plan or Marketing Strategy

1. Start the Microsoft Business Planner, click the Business Plan Wizard or Marketing Wizard link on the Business Planner home page.

2. Click a link for one of the available sections.

3. Use the Next button to proceed through each screen in a section until business plan or marketing strategy is complete.

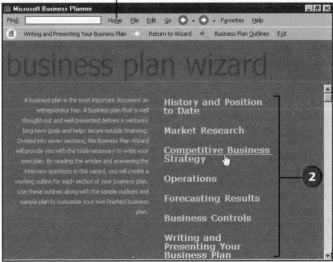

Click to return to the Business Planner home page.

16

Creating a Direct Mailing

You can develop targeted and cost-effective direct mailings using the Microsoft Direct Mail Manager. You create a mailing list in four steps: importing the data, verifying it for accuracy, printing the mailing, and saving it for future use. With your Internet connection, you can access prospect lists and then purchase and download them into Excel. Your mailing list addresses are automatically checked for duplication and accuracy, and they are verified against the U.S. Postal Service's ZIP+4 database.

TIP

Restarting a procedure.
You can resume a procedure or start over if you have to terminate it before it is completed.

Import and Verify Address Data

1 Start the Microsoft Direct Mail Manager. Click Next to continue.

2 Click the File option button, and then type the name of the file that contains your address list, or click Browse to locate the file. To use your Contacts folder, click the Outlook Folder option.

3 Click Next to continue.

4 Click Next to verify that the imported addresses are in the correct form.

5 Click the Yes, Import The Whole List option button, or click the No, Import Only This Part Of The List option button. Click Next to continue.

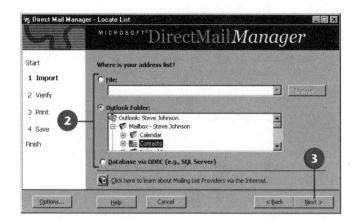

Displays total number of addresses imported

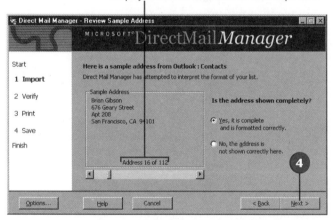

Install necessary programs. *Certain features within the Direct Mail Manager may require the use of Word, Publisher, or Excel.*

Create a mailing list. *Import a targeted mailing list from the Internet.*

Import the following file types. *The following file types can be imported into the Direct Mail Manager: Microsoft Access database, dBASE III or dBASE IV file, Microsoft Excel worksheet, Microsoft Word document, Paradox 5.x database, text file (delimited), and Microsoft Outlook Contacts file.*

Skip address verification. *In the Direct Mail Manager, click Options, click to clear the Run Address Verification check box, and then click OK.*

6 After your list is imported, click the Yes option button to import another list, or click the No option button if you have no other data to import.

7 Click Next to continue.

8 If necessary, click OK to acknowledge the Address Verification message that indicates if the address format is U.S. Postal Service–compliant.

9 Type missing information in the grid.

10 Use the scroll bars to see more data.

11 Click the Limit List To drop-down arrow, and then select All Addresses, Non-Verified Addresses, or Verified Addresses.

12 Click the Sort By drop-down arrow, and then select the address list field you want to sort by.

13 Type the name of the contact you want to find in the Find In Full Name box.

14 Click Next to continue.

To complete the Direct Mail Manager, go to "Printing and Saving a Direct Mailing" on page 298.

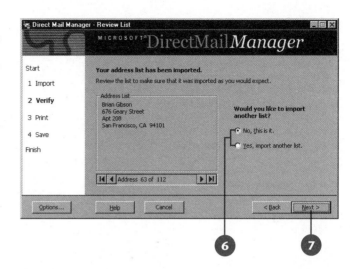

16

Printing and Saving a Direct Mailing

Once your mailing is created, you'll need to print it and prepare it for mailing. The Microsoft Direct Mail Manager verifies the accuracy of your list and sorts it according to the requirements of the U.S. Postal Service. This ability enables you to take advantage of bulk mailing discounts.

You can use Word or Publisher to print the mailing list using the easy-to-follow mail merge features in each program. Using the provided form letters makes this a simple process.

SEE ALSO

See "Creating a Direct Mailing" on page 296 for information how the Direct Mail Manager helps you create a direct mailing.

Print and Save a Mailing

1. Complete the Import and Verify sections of the Direct Mail Manager.

2. Click an option button to determine how the mailing will be sent.

   ◆ First-Class Mail uses no sorting and receives no discounts from the U.S. Postal Service.

   ◆ Standard Mail appears only if you have at least 200 pieces in your mailing (which receives bulk mail postal rate).

   ◆ Use A Mailing Service allows you to have an outside mailing service print and process your mailing.

   ◆ Do Not Print The Mailing Now saves the file and prints it later.

3. Click Next to continue.

4. Click Design to determine how envelopes will look.

5. Click Test to test print an envelope.

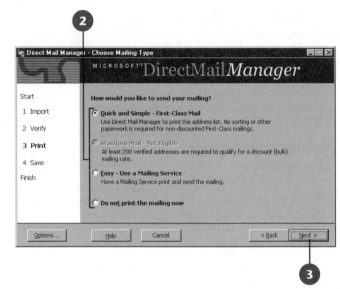

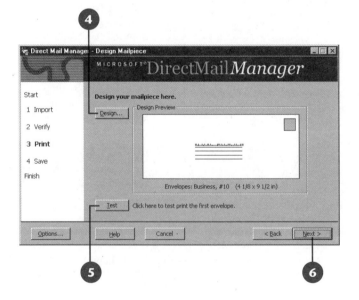

SEE ALSO

See "Creating a Form Letter" on page 106 and "Merging a Form Letter with Data" on page 108 for information on creating a form letter and merging the letter with data in Word.

SEE ALSO

See "Merging Information in a Publication" on page 212 for information on merging data in a Publisher document.

6 Click Next to continue.

7 Click an option button to determine how the direct mailing file will be saved.

8 Click Next to continue.

9 Click an option button to determine which program (Word or Publisher) will be used to create the form letter.

10 Click Next to continue.

11 Select or create the document in which to merge the data.

12 Click Next, and then click Finish.

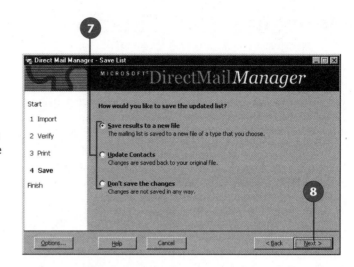

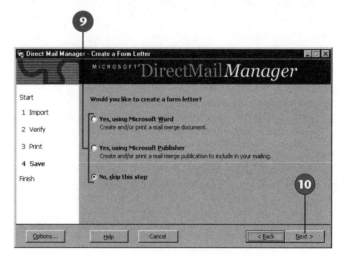

16

Managing Your Finances

The Microsoft Small Business Financial Manager helps you make better use of your existing accounting data. Working within Excel, which must be installed on your computer to use the Small Business Financial Manager, you can create financial reports and charts, analyze data, and develop "what-if" scenarios. For example, you can create a cash flow report to see whether you have a positive operating cash flow, a balance sheet and income statement to determine whether your business is becoming more or less profitable, a sales comparison chart to identify product sales and customer trends, and a buy vs. lease analysis report to determine the best way to acquire new equipment.

The first step in getting started with Small Business Financial Manager is to import your accounting data. The New Database Wizard steps you through the process of importing financial data from your accounting software files and saving the data as a Microsoft Access database. After you have imported your accounting data and created a financial database, you can begin using Small Business Financial Manager. Because the Financial Manager opens in Excel, all of Excel's analytical tools are at your disposal.

The Small Business Financial Manager uses wizards to step you through the process of creating reports, charts, and analyses with information you provide. To start a wizard, click Report, Chart, or Analyze on the startup screen, depending on the type of result you want to

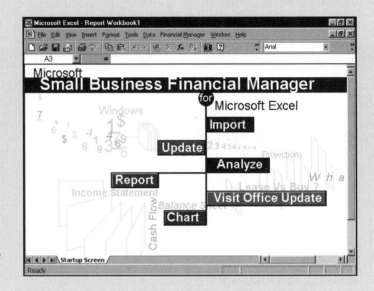

achieve. If you choose Analyze, Small Business Financial Manager provides a list of wizards including Business Comparison, Buy Vs. Lease, Create Projection, Projection Reports, and What-If Analysis.

You can get help at any time by clicking the Help menu, and then clicking Financial Manager Help Topics. If you need help while you are using a wizard, click the Help button located on most wizard screens. On many reports, charts, and worksheets, you can also click a Help button to get more information on working with the report, chart, or worksheet.

Importing Financial Data

With the Microsoft Small Business Financial Manager, you can take advantage of accounting data that you already have on your computer. You can use the Import feature to locate accounting data from specific programs. Once the data files are located, you can convert them for use in the Financial Manager.

> **TIP**
>
> **Enable macros in the Report Workbook.** *When the Small Business Financial Manager opens, you'll see a macro warning box. For complete functionality, you must click the Enable Macros button.*
>
> **TIP**
>
> **Install necessary programs.** *The Small Business Financial Manager will not work unless Excel is installed on your computer.*

Import Accounting Data in Financial Manager

1. Start the Microsoft Small Business Financial Manager, and then click Import.

2. Click Next on the Welcome screen.

3. Type your user name and password, and then retype your password to confirm it. Click Next to continue.

4. Click the Import Accounting Data Found In option button.

5. Click the entry for the company's accounting data you want to import.

6. Click Next to continue.

7. Click OK in the Financial Manager warning box.

8. Click Finish, and then type the user name and password you entered in step 3.

A database created during the import process is designed to be accessed only by the Small Business Financial Manager.

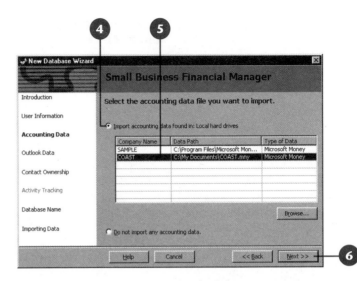

IMPORTABLE ACCOUNTING DATA		
Software	**Version**	**Vendor**
Money Personal & Business	99	Microsoft
M.Y.O.B	6.0	Best!Ware, Inc.
M.Y.O.B	7.x	Best!Ware, Inc.
Peachtree Office Accounting	1.1	Peachtree Software, Inc.
QuickBooks	6.0	Intuit, Inc.
Sage Line 50	4.1	Sage
TASBooks Accounting	3.1	TAS software

16

Producing Financial Reports and Charts

The Microsoft Small Business Financial Manager produces an impressive array of important reports and charts based on your data. You can create—and customize—reports, including an income statement, balance sheet, cash flow statement, sales analysis, and ratio report. These reports are necessary for you to make and keep your business healthy.

TRY THIS

Produce a balance sheet or income statement. *Use the Financial Manager's Report feature to create a balance sheet or income statement for your business.*

SEE ALSO

See "Creating a Chart" on page 140 and "Enhancing a Chart" on page 144 for information how to create and modify charts in Excel.

Create a Financial Report or Chart

1. Start the Microsoft Small Business Financial Manager, and then click Report or Chart.

2. Click the type of report or chart you want to create.

3. Click the Company Name drop-down arrow, and then select a company name. You can type a company name in the text box, if necessary.

4. Click Next to continue. (If the Database logon dialog box appears, enter your user name and password.)

5. Click the type of report you want to use, or click to select the check boxes in the Type Values To Show list to indicate what you want to chart.

6. Click Next to continue.

7. Click the end date for the report or chart option.

8. Click Finish.

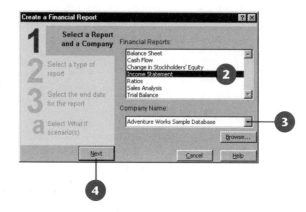

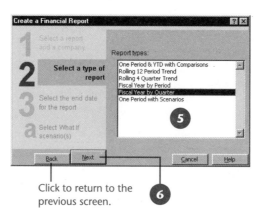

Click to return to the previous screen.

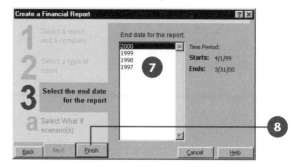

Performing a What-If Analysis

What-if scenarios are data schemes in which you can insert various numbers and see how these data changes affect a company's financial condition. The Microsoft Small Business Financial Manager includes the What-If Wizard, which you can use to select and set up business scenarios. The What-If Wizard creates an overview of your data that lets you analyze your company's financial situation in the following areas: profitability, accounts receivable, accounts payable, inventory, expenses, and buying versus leasing of equipment.

TIP

Benefits of what-if analysis. *Selecting the AP/AR/ Inventory module assists you in optimizing your cash position.*

Create and Save a What-If Analysis

1. Start the Small Business Financial Manager, and then click Analyze.

2. Click What-If Analysis. Click Next to continue.

3. Select a company. Click Next to continue.

4. Click the Begin Date drop-down arrow, and then select a date.

5. Click the End Date drop-down arrow, and then select a date.

6. Click Finish, select a location in which to save the file, and then click Save.

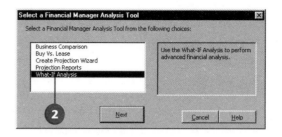

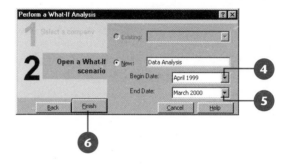

Manipulate a What-If Analysis

1. Open the What-If scenario you want to manipulate, and then click any analysis categories to fine-tune the analysis.

2. Click to create a query to generate a data-specific report.

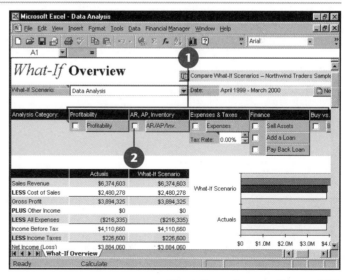

16

Creating a Comparative Analysis

A comparative analysis helps you see how your business is doing relative to the results of other similar businesses. While you might think your business is doing well, it can be helpful to compare your company's standing to those engaging in the same type of business. Using standardized data collected from all business types, you can compare your financial standing with businesses that have similar conditions and decision-making problems. To make sure your analysis is accurate, the Microsoft Small Business Financial Manager uses SIC (Standard Industrial Classification) codes to ensure a fair comparison.

Create a Comparative Analysis

1️⃣ Start the Microsoft Small Business Financial Manager, and then click Analyze.

2️⃣ Click Business Comparison. Click Next to continue.

3️⃣ Click the Select A Company For Report drop-down arrow, and then select a company name.

4️⃣ Click the Select A Date Range For Report drop-down arrow, and then select a date range.

5️⃣ Click Next to continue.

6️⃣ Click Send.

7️⃣ Click the industry classification that most closely matches your business.

8️⃣ Click Finish.

9️⃣ Click Change Wizard Choices to modify the settings.

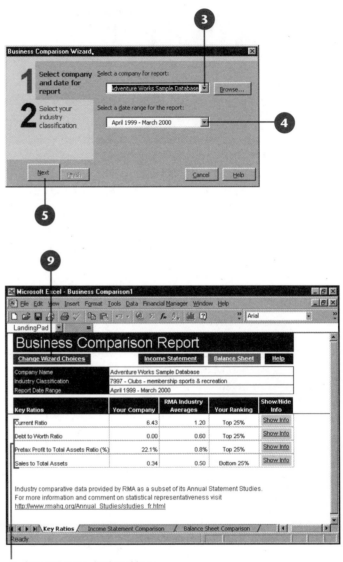

Analysis ratios are displayed here.

Index

SPECIAL CHARACTERS

A

Alt key, navigating Web pages, 241
AltaVista (search engine), 247
animating, text, 73
animations, on Web pages, adding, 264
annotations, adding to Excel charts, 144
antonyms, finding in Word, 68
AOL NetFind (search engine), 247
apostrophe ('), numeric label prefix (in Excel), 116
applications. *See* programs
appointments, 172
   canceling, 176
   changing into meetings, 177
   editing, 172
   interchanging with events, 173
   recording, 182
   requesting reminders, 173
   rescheduling, 176, 177
   scheduling, 172, 173, 176, 177
   viewing
      in the Calendar, 171, 178
      in Outlook Today, 159
archiving Outlook folders, 191
arithmetic operators, 124
   order of precedence, 125
arranging
   objects, 220
   windows, 16–17
arrowheads
   double down-pointing (⋎), menu symbol, 12
   double right-pointing (↔), toolbar symbol, 14
   right-pointing (▶), menu symbol, 12
arrows, drawing, 41
ascending order, sorting records in, 148
asterisk (*)

multiplication operator, 124
wildcard character, 9
attached files, saving, 170
auditing Excel worksheets, 145
AutoCalculate, calculating worksheet totals, 129
AutoComplete
   entering cell labels with, 117
   entering Web addresses, 242, 243
   finishing words with, 35
   turning off, 243
AutoCorrect
   adding/deleting entries to, 35
   correcting spelling while typing, 34, 67
   creating exceptions to, 35
   disabling, 35
   as multilingual, 33
   reversing changes made by, 34
   URL spelling correction, 243
AutoFill
   copying worksheet formulas, 125
   entering worksheet data, 129
AutoFilter, filtering Excel lists, 148
AutoFit, fitting text in frames, 223
AutoFormat, formatting worksheet cells, 135
automatic replies (e-mail), 167
automating
   tasks, 291
   work with macros, 50–51
AutoPreview, 178
AutoSave reminder (Publisher), turning off, 199
AutoSearch, finding information on the Web, 248–49, 249
AutoSum, calculating worksheet totals, 128
AutoText, creating/inserting, 93
AVERAGE function (Excel), 128
axis titles, in Excel charts, 144

B

Back list (Internet Explorer), jumping to locations from, 240
backslash (\), pathname character, 244
Backspace key, deleting characters/words, 36
balance sheets, creating, 302, 303
blank publications, creating, 202–3
boldface, applying (in Word), 72
bookmarks (in Word), creating/ going to, 88
borders
   adding to cells (in Excel), 139
   adding to pages (in Word), 94
   adding to paragraphs (in Word), 95
   adding to pictures, 45
   adding to tables (in Word), 94, 95, 104
   See also frames (for objects); text frames
Break dialog box (Word), inserting page/section breaks, 86
breaking links, 282
brochures, converting Web sites to, 207
Browse button (Word window), 57
Browse for Folder dialog box (Internet Explorer), 251
Browser pane (Internet Explorer window), 239
Browse toolbar (Word), 57
browsing
   local hard drives, 244–45
   the Web, 242–43
   Word documents, 57
Bullet and Numbering dialog box (Word), 83

bulleted lists
   creating, 34
      in Word, 82, 83
   restyling in Word, 83
   switching between numbered lists and, 83
bulleting text, 221
bullets, spacing/restyling, 83
business cards, creating/attaching to e-mail messages, 165
Business Comparison Report, 300, 305
Business Comparison Wizard, 305
Business Planner, 287
   browsing topics, 294
   creating business plans, 295
   searching for content, 294
   setting up, 293
business plans, creating, 295
Business Plan Wizard, 295
buttons
   column/row header buttons (in Excel), 121
   group buttons (Outlook window), 157
   option buttons (dialog boxes), 13
   view buttons, 54
   See also toolbar buttons; *and specific buttons*

calculating worksheet totals, 128, 129
Calendar (Outlook), 155, 171–78
   customizing, 178
   print options, 193
   saving, as a Web page, 171
   scheduling appointments/ events, 172, 173, 176, 177

e-mail messages, *continued*
  deleting, 168
  delivery options, 163
  filtering, 190, 191
  finding, 168
  flagging for follow up, 191
  flags, 166
  forwarding, 166, 167
  hyperlinks for sending, 261
  junk messages, 190, 191
  opening, 166
  organizing, 168–69, 190
  previewing, 166
  recording, 182
  replying to, 166, 167
  retrieving deleted, 169
  saving, without sending, 163
  saving as files, 169
  selecting multiple, 168
  sending, 162, 163, 291
  sending documents by, 275
  signatures, 165
  tracking, 163
e-mail service options (Outlook), 234
embedded objects
  changing linked objects to, 282
  charts as, 141
  editing, 282, 283
embedding
  Excel charts in Word documents, 285
  files, 278, 282, 283
    vs. importing/linking files, 279
em dash (—), entering, 34
Enter button (formula bar), entering worksheet data, 116
Enter key, entering worksheet data, 116

entering
  cell references into formulas, 124
  data
    into Excel lists, 147
    into Excel worksheets, 116–17, 129
    into Graph datasheets, 48
    into merge fields, 107
  em dashes, 34
  formulas into Excel worksheets, 124
  fractions, 34
  functions into Excel worksheets, 128
  labels into Excel worksheets, 116–17
  records into Excel lists, 147
  superscripts, 34
  text
    into Excel worksheets, 116–17
    into publications, 210
    into text frames, 220
    into Word documents, 56
    into Word tables, 99
  Web addresses, 242, 243
  See also inserting
envelopes
  addressing, 87
  designing and printing, 298
Envelopes and Labels dialog box (Word), 87
equal sign (=), formula prefix, 124
erasing the Office Clipboard, 29
events, 172
  canceling, 176
  editing, 172
  interchanging with appointments, 173
  recording, 182
  requesting reminders, 173
  rescheduling, 176, 177

scheduling, 172, 173, 176, 177
  viewing
    in the Calendar, 171, 178
    in Outlook Today, 159
Excel (Microsoft), 111–54
  calculations, 128
  data analysis tools, 133
  See also charts, in Excel; lists, in Excel; workbooks (in Excel); worksheets (in Excel)
Excel window, elements, 112, 116, 118
exiting Office programs, 26
expanded menu commands, 12
Explorer bar (Internet Explorer window), 239
  viewing the Favorites list, 250
exporting
  files, 278, 280, 281
  See also inserting
extensions (for filenames), 10

F

favorites, 247
  channels as, 254
  deleting, 251
  organizing, 250, 251
  renaming, 251
  synchronizing, 252, 253
  viewing offline, 252–53
  See also Favorites list
Favorites folder, 247
Favorites list
  adding channels, 254
  adding clips, 45
  adding Web pages, 251
  adding Web sites, 250, 252
  viewing, 250
faxes
  creating and sending, 19

recording, 182
field names
  in Excel lists, 146, 147
  for merge fields, 107
fields
  in Excel lists, 146
    index fields, 149
    names, 146, 147
    sort fields, 148
    sorting records on more than one, 149
  merge fields, 107, 108, 212–13
  in PivotTables/PivotCharts, 150, 152
filenames
  adding to footers, 91
  extensions, 10
  saving files with another name, 10
  searching with wildcards, 9
File Transfer Protocol. *See* FTP
files
  attaching to e-mail messages, 170, 275
  browsing local hard disk files, 244–45
  closing, 25, 26
  for commercial printing, 216
  copying, 9
  deleting, 9
  destination files, 278, 279, 282
  downloading from the Internet, 276
  embedding, 278, 282, 283
  exporting, 278, 280, 281
  finding, 9
  importing, 278, 280–81
  inserting into tasks, 181
  linking, 278–79, 282, 283
  moving, 9
  opening
    as copies, 8
    existing files, 8–9

FrontPage Express (Microsoft), 236
FTP (File Transfer Protocol), 276
FTP sites
    accessing/downloading files from, 276
    adding/modifying locations, 276
function keys. *See* F keys
functions (in Excel), 128
    calculating with, 128
    common, 128
    entering, 128

GIF format (Graphics Interchange Format), 266
grammar, correcting, 34
    in Word, 66–67
grammar options, setting, 67
Graph (Microsoft), 48
    See also charts, in Graph
graphic formats (on the Web), 266
graphic images
    adding to publications, 217
    Web formats, 266
    See also clips; pictures
graphic links, supporting (in Publisher), 215
graphic objects. *See* objects
Graphics Interchange Format (GIF), 266
graphs. *See* charts
gridlines, 140
    adding to Excel charts, 141
    major vs. minor, 141
    printing worksheets with, 131
Group (Outlook), 179, 187
group buttons (Outlook window), 157

grouping
    objects, 41, 234
    Outlook items, 187
groups (in Outlook). *See* Outlook groups
groups (of objects), identifying, 234

handles, selection handles, 38
hard disks (local), browsing in Internet Explorer, 244–45
header buttons (in Excel), 121
header rows (in Excel), 149
headers
    in Excel worksheets, adding and printing, 131
    in Word documents, 90
        aligning text in, 90, 91
        creating, 90–91
        setting margins for, 61
headings, browsing, 57
    in Word documents, 76
Help, 20–23
    getting information on particular topics, 21
    Office Assistant, 22–23
    ScreenTips, 20
Help pane, 21
Help window, using while working, 21
hiding
    columns/rows in Excel worksheets, 123
    the Discussion pane, 273
    Excel worksheets, 115
    the Office Assistant, 22
    rulers (in Word), 76
    ScreenTips, 15
    toolbars, 14
    wizards, 202
highlighting points, in Word, 73

History list (Internet Explorer)
    changing the view, 246
    clearing, 246
    viewing Web sites, 246
home pages, going to/changing, 241
hot spots, creating hyperlinks at, 207
HTML (HyperText Markup Language), 256, 266
    and Office programs, 256, 265, 268
HTML documents. *See* Web documents (HTML documents)
Hyperlink dialog box, 207
hyperlinking, 279
hyperlinks, 255, 256, 279
    absolute, 260
    clickable, 241
    editing, 263
    formatting, 263
    to hot spots, 207
    inserting, 34, 207, 260–61
    jumping to new locations with, 260, 262
    moving from link to link, 241
    offline availability, 253
    relative, 260
    removing, 263
    using, 262
HyperText Markup Language. *See* HTML
hyphenating words (in Word), 66, 97

iCalendar format, 175
images. *See* clip art; pictures
importing
    files, 278, 280–81

vs. embedding/linking files, 279
financial data, 301
PIM program information, 156
text styles (in Publisher), 225
See also inserting
Inbox (Outlook), 155, 166, 190
    displaying, 167
    organizing, 168–69, 190
income statements, creating, 302, 303
indenting
    text, 78
    Word tables, 103
indents, types, 78
index fields (in Excel), 149
information
    contact information, 160, 161
    sharing information between Office programs, 277–86
    viewing Journal information on timelines, 185
    See also Help
information viewer (Outlook window), 157
in-line comments (in Web discussions), 272
Insert Clip Art dialog box, 44
Insert File dialog box
    in Outlook, 170
    in Word, 280, 284
Insert Hyperlink dialog box, 260, 261
inserting
    cells (new) into worksheets, 120
    clip art, 44
    columns (new)
        into Word tables, 100
        into Excel worksheets, 121
    comments into Word documents, 37
    continued notices into publications, 223

Publisher (Microsoft), 197–234
  getting tips, 219
Publisher window, elements, 198
publishing Web pages, 268–69

question mark (?), wildcard
  character, 9
Quick Pages Wizard (Publisher),
  199
quick publications, creating, 199
quitting Office programs, 26
quotation marks. *See* smart quotes

range names (in Excel), using in
  formulas, 126
range reference character (:), 113
range references, 113
ranges (in Excel), 113
  calculating, 129
  copying into Word
    documents, 284
  entering (inserting), 129
  list ranges, 146
  named/naming, 119
  selecting, 113, 119
    for charting, 140
  using in formulas, 126
ratio reports, creating, 302
reading offline, 252–53
recoloring pictures, 228
recording
  contact activity, 183
  macros, 50, 51
  Outlook items, 182–83, 185
records (in Excel lists), 146
  entering, 147
  filtering, 133, 148
  sorting, 133, 148–49

rectangles, drawing, 41, 229
Redo button, 36
redoing actions, 36
refreshing (reloading) Web pages/
  documents, 240, 241
relative cell references (in Excel),
  127
renaming
  favorites, 251
  files, 9
  text styles (in Publisher), 225
repairing
  of hyperlinks, 263
  Office program problems, 52
Replace dialog boxes, 30, 31
replacing
  text, 31
    while typing, 34
    in Word, 64
  text formatting (in Word),
    64–65
rescheduling
  appointments/events, 176, 177
  meetings, 176
resizing
  Excel charts, 144
  the Links bar, 241
  objects, 39
  window panes (in Word), 59
  windows, 16, 17
  Word tables, 105
Resource Center (Business
  Planner), 294
Restore button (windows), 16
rotating objects, 41, 233
  removing rotation, 233
row numbers (in Excel), printing,
  131
row titles (in Excel), printing, 131
rows
  in Excel lists, sorting data in,
    149
  in Excel worksheets

adjusting heights, 122
  freezing/unfreezing, 123
  header rows, 149
  hiding/unhiding, 123
  inserting/deleting, 121
in publication tables, selecting,
  227
in Word tables
  adjusting heights, 101, 103
  deleting, 100, 101
  inserting, 100
  moving, 101
  selecting, 99
rulers (in Word)
  changing measurement
    units, 76
  displaying/hiding, 76
  indenting text, 78
rules. *See* criteria
Rules Wizard (Outlook), 191
running
  macros, 51
  programs, from Internet
    Explorer, 244

sales analyses, creating, 302
Save As command (File menu), vs.
  Save command, 10
Save As dialog box
  exporting files, 281
  saving files, 10–11
  saving Office documents as
    Web pages, 266, 267
  saving Word documents
    in multiple versions, 11
    as templates, 84
Save command (File menu), vs.
  Save As command, 10
save options, changing, 11
saving
  attached files, 170

the Calendar as a Web page,
  171
direct mailings, 299
e-mail messages
  as files, 169
  without sending, 163
files, 10–11
  all open files at once, 11
  with another name, 10
  as different types, 11
  for the first time, 10
  in new folders, 11
not saving merged files, 213
Office documents as Web
  pages, 256, 257, 266–67
Word documents
  in multiple versions, 11
  as templates, 84
  worksheets, as Web pages, 267
scaling objects, 39
scanners, inserting images
  from, 45
Schedule+ (Microsoft), opening
  calendars from, 171, 178
schedules
  viewing
    in the Calendar, 171, 178
    in Outlook Today, 159
  See also scheduling
scheduling
  appointments, 172, 173, 176,
    177
  events, 172, 173, 176, 177
  meetings, 174–75, 176, 177
  online meetings, 270
ScreenTips
  getting, 20
  hiding, 15
  for Web sites, 249
scroll arrows, 57
scroll boxes, 57
scrolling
  with the Intellimouse, 208
  Word documents, 57

Search button (Standard toolbar, Internet Explorer window), finding information on the Web, 248–49
search engines (Web), 247
    accessing, 248
    choosing a default provider, 249
searching. *See* finding
section breaks, inserting/deleting in Word, 86
sections
    of documents, 86
        creating columns in Word, 96
see-through selections (in Excel), 113
Select Attendees And Resources dialog box (Outlook), 177
selecting
    objects, 38
    table elements (in Word), 99
    text, 28, 63
    worksheet ranges, 113, 119
selection handles, 38
Select Names dialog box (Outlook), 162
sending
    documents by e-mail messages, 275
    e-mail messages, 162, 163, 291
    faxes, 19
    objects to the front/back of the stack/other objects, 232
Services dialog box (Outlook), 156
shading
    adding to paragraphs (in Word), 95
    adding to tables (in Word), 94, 95, 104
    adding to text frames, 221
shadows, adding to objects, 41
shapes, drawing, 40, 41, 228, 229

sheet tabs (of Excel worksheets), 112, 114
Shift key
    removing hyperlinks, 263
    selecting multiple e-mail messages, 168
    window commands, 17
shortcut keys. *See* Ctrl key; F keys; keyboard shortcuts; Shift key; Tab key
shortcut menus, 12
Show/Hide button (Standard toolbar), 37
signatures for e-mail messages, creating/inserting, 165
slash (/)
    division operator, 124
    Web address character, 244
Small Business Customer Manager, 287
    automating tasks, 291
    creating databases, 289
    displaying views, 290
    filtering databases, 290
    inserting Excel data into, 289
    tracking customer activity, 292
Small Business Financial Manager, 287, 300
    comparative analyses, 305
    importing accounting data, 301
    managing finances, 300
    producing financial reports or charts, 302
    what-if analyses, 300, 304
Small Business Tools, 287–305
    File menus of, 288
    starting, 288
smart quotes (curly quotes) ("")
    entering, 34
    replacing straight quotes with, 31
Snap feature, arranging objects, 220

Sort (Outlook), 179, 188
sort fields, 148
sorting
    mail merges, 213
    Outlook items, 157, 169, 188
        removing sorts, 188
    records, in Excel lists, 133, 148–49
source files, 278, 279, 282
source programs, 279, 282
special characters
    finding and replacing, 31
        in Word, 64
    inserting, 34, 93
    wildcard search characters, 9
    See also Special Characters section of this index
Spelling and Grammar dialog box (Word), 67
spelling, correcting
    in publications, 211
    undoing Autocorrect changes, 34
    while typing, 34, 66
    in Word documents, 66–67
spelling options, setting, 67
spin boxes, in dialog boxes, 13
splitting cells in Word tables, 102
Spreadsheet component (Office Web Components), 269
squares, drawing, 40
stack (of objects), sending objects to the front/back, 232
stacked fractions, entering, 34
Standard toolbar, 14
    in Office program windows, 54, 112, 157, 198, 239
    Show/Hide button, 37
starting
    NetMeeting, 271
    Office programs, 6–7
    Small Business Tools, 288
    Web discussions, 273
Start menu

opening existing files, 8
starting NetMeeting, 271
starting Office programs, 6
starting Small Business Tools, 288
stationery (for e-mail messages)
    creating, 164
    creating e-mail messages using, 164
status bars, in Office program windows, 54, 112, 157, 194, 198, 239
storing, macros, 51
Style Gallery (Word), 85
styles (in Word), 71, 79–81
    copying (applying), 79
    creating, 80, 81
    modifying, 81
submenu commands, 12
subscribing
    to newsgroups, 195
    to Web pages, 273
subtraction operator (–), 124
SUM function (Excel), 128
summarizing
    data, 133, 150–52
    Word documents, 88
superscripts, entering, 34
symbols. *See* special characters
synchronizing favorite Web pages, 252, 253
synonyms, finding in Word, 68

tab characters, displaying in Word, 77
Tab key
    indenting text, 78
    moving from link to link, 241
    navigating dialog boxes, 13
    navigating tables, 99
    navigating Web pages, 241

Robin Romer founded Pale Moon Productions in 1993 to help shed some light on the sometimes confusingly dark path to understanding software and technology. She specializes in writing and editing books about computer applications and technology, including the Microsoft Office suite, Netscape Navigator, PageMaker, the Internet, and Help Desks.

Marie Swanson has authored more than 30 books, including *Microsoft Access 97 At a Glance*, and Microsoft Word 6.0, Word 95, and Word 97 *Step by Step* books (Microsoft Press). With 17 years experience in corporate PC support and training environments, Marie and her company, WriteWorks, have written customized training materials and end-user documentation for internal accounting systems and image retrieval applications, as well as for major software packages.

Author's Acknowledgments

Thanks to my husband, Brian Romer, who made sure I ate, slept, and laughed during this project. Lisa Ruffulo at the Software Connection, thank you for always suggesting the perfect edits. Also, thank you to Steve Johnson, David Beskeen, and the rest of the At a Glance team for providing that extra support when I needed a helping hand. I enjoy working with such a great group of people.

Author's Acknowledgments

In addition to my assistants who provide valuable support, I would like to thank Lisa Ruffulo at the Software Connection and Jane Pedicini for their insightful editorial contributions. Of course, the greatest thanks must go to the people at Perspection, Inc., who provided me the opportunity to work on this project and who shepherded the entire process.

The manuscript for this book was prepared and submitted to Microsoft Press in electronic form. Text files were prepared using Microsoft Word 97 for Windows 95. Pages were composed in PageMaker for Windows, with text in Stone Sans and display type in Stone Serif. Composed pages were delivered to the printer as electronic files.

Cover Design
Tim Girvin Design

Graphic Layout
David Beskeen

Compositors
Gary Bellig
Tracy Teyler

Proofreader
Jane Pedicini

Indexer
Michael Brackney
Savage Indexing Service

Stay in the *running* for maximum *productivity.*

These are *the* answer books for business users of Microsoft® Office 2000. They are packed with everything from quick, clear instructions for new users to comprehensive answers for power users—the authoritative reference to keep by your computer and use every day. THE RUNNING SERIES—learning solutions made by Microsoft.

- RUNNING MICROSOFT EXCEL 2000
- RUNNING MICROSOFT OFFICE 2000 PREMIUM
- RUNNING MICROSOFT OFFICE 2000 PROFESSIONAL
- RUNNING MICROSOFT OFFICE 2000 SMALL BUSINESS
- RUNNING MICROSOFT WORD 2000
- RUNNING MICROSOFT POWERPOINT® 2000
- RUNNING MICROSOFT ACCESS 2000
- RUNNING MICROSOFT INTERNET EXPLORER 5
- RUNNING MICROSOFT FRONTPAGE® 2000
- RUNNING MICROSOFT OUTLOOK® 2000

Microsoft®

mspress.microsoft.com